THE HEART OF

THOREAU'S
JOURNALS

EDITED BY
ODELL SHEPARD

DOVER PUBLICATIONS, INC.
NEW YORK

Published in Canada by General Publishing Company, Ltd., 30 Lesmill Road, Don Mills, Toronto, Ontario.
Published in the United Kingdom by Constable and Company, Ltd., 10 Orange Street, London WC 2.

This Dover edition, first published in 1961, is a revised version of the work originally published by Houghton Mifflin Company in 1927.

International Standard Book Number: 0-486-20741-2

Library of Congress Catalog Card Number: 61-1256

Manufactured in the United States of America
Dover Publications, Inc.
180 Varick Street
New York, N. Y. 10014

CONTENTS

v

INTRODUCTION
TO DOVER EDITION

The most valuable articles of private property left by Henry Thoreau at his death in 1862 were thirty-nine notebooks containing his diaries or journals (he had usually referred to them in the singular) packed in a homemade box. On the death of his sister Sophia, they went to H. G. O. Blake of Worcester, who made from them the compilations called *Early Spring in Massachusetts, Summer, Winter,* and *Autumn.* These books, appearing at intervals between 1881 and 1892, extended Thoreau's reputation but unfortunately suggested that he had been in the main a field naturalist. Blake left the notebooks to a friend by whose permission all but the third of them, then missing, were carefully transcribed. In 1906 the Houghton Mifflin Company, of Boston, published in fourteen volumes an edition suggested by Bliss Perry and the product of expert and devoted toil by Bradford Torrey and Francis H. Allen. These editors emended the punctuation found in the manuscripts and made a few other equally justifiable alterations. In the present book of selections their text is followed exactly but the footnotes are newly written. Nothing is here excerpted from the so-called "Lost Journal" published by the Houghton Mifflin Company in 1958 under the title *Consciousness in Concord.*

Thoreau's journals, some two million words in length and the work of twenty-four years, are his most comprehensive and characteristic production. His fame is chiefly due to one great book, but *Walden* is a sprout of the journals. At them he worked more steadily than at any other thing. He feared at times that he was living only for them, and often it must have been clear to him that they comprised the most veracious biography his mind would ever have.

That belief is easily defended. For one thing, the journals were private discourse, no matter how often he may have hoped that this or that entry might find a place at last in some publishable context. As pure soliloquy, wholly composed of what he had said to himself and mostly about himself, they were unquestionably authentic. They told the intrinsic truth, undiscoverable without their guidance, about his innermost life. To be sure, they told it piecemeal, just as his thoughts had come to him with here a glimmer and there a gleam, but his feeling was that for that very reason they would be the more persuasive. Like the "patrins" of withered grass and leaves left behind by wandering Romanies to mark a trail, they would show the way his mind had gone step by step.

There was also the fact that most of his published writings were works of deliberate and often laborious contrivance—concoctions, really, or *rifacimenti* of matters drawn from the journals. As he would put it, they were products not of his genius but of his talent, and that often working against the grain. Ingeniously wrought they might be, but still they were cages for birds better left on the bough. On the other hand, the thoughts in his journals had sought him out, not he them, and he liked them no less because they had come in any order or in none. Problems of logical arrangement, continuity, structure, and the like had been indefinitely postponed while he wrote them down, his sole intent being to capture and fix each color and tint of the dolphin-hued moment before it died.

Thoreau's concern with the "moment"—that is, with the sudden illumination which enabled him to see the fleeting instant as everlasting—was perennial and obsessive. Thus we should take quite seriously his declaration, in *Walden*, that he had long sought "to improve the nick of the time . . . to stand on the meeting of two eternities, the past and future, which is precisely the present moment." There he implies the whole purpose and strategy of the journals, in which he constantly strives not only to overtake the instantaneous present but to ransack its very quick and marrow. Full success in that effort is unattainable, yet any good reader can find in the pages of this book many an approach to such immediacy. The entry for March 30, 1840, for example, seems to crumple space and time. It deserves to be read, as it was written, in an everlasting Now. It is "a moment's monument."

On the other hand, the writings that Thoreau prepared for the press are, for the most part, retrospective. Often they gain much from the mellowing effect of time, but not enough to compensate for the loss of spontaneity. The best things even in *Walden* are likely to remind us of the journals, often because they come from there.

"I do not know," Thoreau wrote in 1852, "but that thoughts written down thus in a journal might be printed in the same form with greater advantage than if the selected ones were brought together into separate essays. They are now allied to life, and are seen by the reader not to be far-fetched. . . . Perhaps I shall never find so good a setting for my thoughts as I shall have taken them out of. The crystal never sparkles more brightly than in the cavern."

When he wrote those words, Thoreau had before him a really complete though not quite final manuscript of *Walden*, a work in which he had done his best to convert private into public discourse. That effort had cost him a prolonged mental anguish which can be appreciated only by those who have studied the several drafts now owned by the Huntington Library in California. He would not have minded the effort if the result had been satisfactory, but it is a safe inference from the passage just quoted that he did not find it so. In comparison even with *Walden*, the disconnected jottings of the journals seemed to him in some ways more truly his own.

That was in 1852, but in the years that remained to him Thoreau tended more and more to use the journals as a catchall for memoranda which he thought might be useful in his projected but never finished history of Concord. The preparations for that work were prodigious, but the record of them makes dull reading. In this book of selections, 1,600 lines have been chosen from the first volume of the journals as published and only 250 lines from the last.

The habit of journalizing gave Thoreau much practice in the art of writing detached and laconic passages of the sort the French call *pensées*. Although he is often admirable in narrative and excellent in description, he is most at home, so to speak, in the brief gnomic sentences that pack much thought into little room. Few writers of English have equalled, and no one has excelled him, in this difficult art.

Journal writing was helpful to Thoreau in several other ways. It sharpened his observation and deepened his thought. By preserving the memory of his best hours—those that had "a certain individuality and separate existence, aye, personality"—it enabled him to survey long stretches of earlier experience and thus to estimate his development or decline. This habit, moreover, was a mainstay of his self-respect when other supports were rejected or withdrawn. He could watch a farmer at work in a field of grain with no twinge of conscience while thinking of how his own lonely sickle would swing at nightfall among the thoughts of the day. Because he too was keeping a book of accounts, always up-to-date, he was not unduly impressed by the ledgers of tradesmen on Concord's Mill Dam. When other energetic Yankees were going West in search of gold or adventure, he was more than content to sit in his attic or woodland hut recording his explorations of thought's wilderness and staking out his claims in the West of the Mind. It was the concentration enforced by this daily task that taught him to see the snug and smug little town of his lifelong residence as a sufficient epitome of the world, well furnished with creatures refreshingly wild and with others far gone in the dry rot of respectability. To a mind naturally expansive and all but vagrant, that task brought discipline, routine, and focus. Largely it was due to the journals that, instead of remaining what he once called "a parcel of vain strivings held by a chance bond together," Henry Thoreau achieved a unanimous personality, sharply defined, and marched through life with an unerring sense of direction and goal.

Thoreau's journals reveal one of the most spermatic and contagious minds we have produced on this continent. They bring back alive a man who, with all his extravagances, perversities, and fierce denunciations of much that America now stands for, is as quintessentially American as Abraham Lincoln. He comes, moreover, as great men are wont to do, in a time of great need. With a fit audience, though few, he is likely to win a more thoughtful reading now that the superficial critics have had their say, now that individuals are so obviously withering among us, now that men are quite obviously enslaved by machines, now that we have floundered about as far as we can in the bogs of stupidity, greed, and cowering compliance that he warned us against long ago.

This man's love of his country was none the less deep and devoted because he expressed it mostly in finding fault. His vision of what America might be, and indeed must be unless sinning greatly, made impossible any patience with what she actually was. He saw her not only from within but from above, and with an eye open to wide ranges of space and time. For Thoreau was first of all a man and then an American, so that his deeper thoughts might as well have come to him on the banks of the Ganges or the Tiber as beside the Musketaquid. For that reason we have all the more to learn from him. Better, perhaps, than any other mentor and prophet we have yet had, the man who read his Roman, Greek, and Hindu classics at Walden Pond can teach us how to coordinate whatsoever is new in our civilization with the wisdom of the ages.

ODELL SHEPARD

Waterford, Connecticut, 1960.

CHRONOLOGICAL TABLE

1817. Thoreau born, in Concord, July 12.

1818-23. At Chelmsford and Boston.

1823. Thoreau family returned to Concord.

1833. Entered Harvard College.

1834. Emerson settled in Concord.

1836. "Went to New York with Father, peddling."

1837. Graduated from Harvard College. Close acquaintance with Emerson began. First entry in Journal, October 22.

1838. Taught school in Concord. Read first lecture before the Concord Lyceum.

1839. Voyage on the Concord and Merrimack rivers with brother John.

1841. Emerson's *Essays. First Series*.

1841-43. At Emerson's home in Concord.

1842. Brother John died.

1843. On Staten Island as tutor.

1844. "Made pencils."

1845-47. At Walden Pond.

1846. Spent night in Concord Jail.

1847-48. At Emerson's home.

1849. *A Week on the Concord and Merrimack Rivers*.

1850. Visited Canada.

1854. *Walden*.

1859. Speech in defense of John Brown.

1861. Went to Minnesota for health.

1862. Died at Concord, May 6.

By all means use sometimes to be alone.
Salute thyself: see what thy soul doth wear.
Dare to look in thy chest; for 'tis thine own:
And tumble up and down what thou find'st there.
    Who cannot rest till he good fellows find,
    He breaks up house, turns out of doors his mind.

HERBERT, The Church Porch

Friends and companions, get you gone!
'Tis my desire to be alone;
Ne'er well, but when my thoughts and I
Do domineer in privacy.

BURTON, Anatomy of Melancholy

Two Paradises are in one,
To live in Paradise alone.

MARVELL, The Garden

The Heart of
THOREAU'S JOURNALS
1837—47

Many of the earlier entries in this chapter are transcriptions, no doubt much revised, from manuscripts now lost. Possibly the work of selection and revision was part of the "private business" carried on by Thoreau in his Walden hut. On that supposition we can more readily explain the fact that in passages dated as early as his twenty-third year, he comes before us with a prose style unmistakably his own and also with that set of ideas, opinions, sympathies, and antipathies which thereafter so strongly marked him as a unique individual. What we chiefly miss in them is the admirable factuality of his best writing. He has not yet fully learned to think in terms of things, to make the fact flower into a truth, to write in complete accord with his belief that all stuff of the senses is profoundly metaphorical.

Yet even in these first pages Thoreau shows again and again his power of packing huge significance into a few simple words. "We look to windward for fair weather" he says, in a sentence we do not soon come to the end of. It is drawn from the very core of the man. In the language of a meteorological observation it implies his whole theory and practice of heroism. When he wrote those seven words and saw that they were good, he had passed his apprenticeship.

During these years Thoreau taught school for a while, made pencils, surveyed wood lots, served as Secretary of the Concord Lyceum, helped to edit The Dial, *wrote a considerable amount of verse, travelled somewhat in New England, saw more than he liked of New York City, lived for some time in the Emerson household, lost his dearly loved brother John, spent 26 months at Walden Pond, and composed the greater part of* A Week on the Concord and Merrimack Rivers *and of* Walden. *Except for one never forgotten bereavement, these were happy years. By Thoreau's standards, they were successful. He learned to long for what he had, to discern the underlying and overarching marvel of things familiar, and thus to turn what others might think his deprivations into shining advantages. As one of the "nobly poor" he found that by one month of labor he could earn eleven months of leisure in which to strive for perfection as a writer, a thinker, and a man.*

Oct. 22, 1837

"What are you doing now?" he[1] asked. "Do you keep a journal?" So I make my first entry today.

To be alone I find it necessary to escape the present—I avoid myself. How could I be alone in the Roman emperor's chamber of mirrors? I seek a garret. The spiders must not be disturbed, nor the floor swept, nor the lumber arranged.

Oct. 29

A curious incident happened some four or six weeks ago which I think it worth the while to record. John[2] and I had been searching for Indian relics, and been successful enough to find two arrowheads and a pestle, when, of a Sunday evening, with our heads full of the past and its remains, we strolled to the mouth of Swamp Bridge Brook. As we neared the brow of the hill forming the bank of the river, inspired by my theme, I broke forth into an extravagant eulogy on those savage times, using most violent gesticulations by way of illustration. "There on Nawshawtuct,"[3] said I, "was their lodge, the rendezvous of the tribe, and yonder, on Clamshell Hill, their feasting ground. This was, no doubt, a favorite haunt; here on this brow was an eligible lookout post. How often have they stood on this very spot, at this very hour, when the sun was sinking behind yonder woods and gilding with his last rays the waters of the Musketaquid, and pondered the day's success and the morrow's prospects, or communed with the spirit of their fathers gone before them to the land of shades!

"Here," I exclaimed, "stood Tahatawan;[4] and there" (to complete the period) "is Tahatawan's arrowhead."

We instantly proceeded to sit down on the spot I had pointed to, and I, to carry out the joke, to lay bare an ordinary stone which my whim had selected, when lo! the first I laid hands on, the grubbing stone that was to be, proved a most perfect arrowhead, as sharp as if just from the hands of the Indian fabricator!!!

Nov. 3

If one would reflect, let him embark on some placid stream, and float with the current. He cannot resist the Muse. As we ascend the stream, plying the paddle with might and main, snatched and im-

1 [Ralph Waldo Emerson.]
2 [John Thoreau, elder brother of Henry.]
3 [A hill near the center of Concord.]
4 [An Indian chief who lived near Concord in its early years.]

petuous thoughts course through the brain. We dream of conflict, power, and grandeur. But turn the prow downstream, and rock, tree, kine, knoll, assuming new and varying positions, as wind and water shift the scene, favor the liquid lapse of thought, far-reaching and sublime, but ever calm and gently undulating.

Nov. 13

This shall be the test of innocence—if I can hear a taunt, and look out on this friendly moon, pacing the heavens in queen-like majesty, with the accustomed yearning.

Dec. 12

When we speak of a peculiarity in a man or a nation, we think to describe only one part, a mere mathematical point; but it is not so. It pervades all. Some parts may be further removed than others from this centre, but not a particle so remote as not to be either shined on or shaded by it.

Dec. 16

How indispensable to a correct study of Nature is a perception of her true meaning. The fact will one day flower out into a truth. The season[1] will mature and fructify what the understanding had cultivated. Mere accumulators of facts—collectors of materials for the master-workmen—are like those plants growing in dark forests, which "put forth only leaves instead of blossoms."

Dec. 19

Hell itself may be contained within the compass of a spark.

Dec. 31

As the least drop of wine tinges the whole goblet, so the least particle of truth colors our whole life. It is never isolated, or simply added as treasure to our stock. When any real progress is made, we unlearn and learn anew what we thought we knew before.

Jan. 16, 1838

The world is never the less beautiful though viewed through a chink or knot-hole.

[1] [Thoreau may have written "reason" to balance "understanding."]

Jan. 21

Every leaf and twig was this morning covered with a sparkling ice
armor; even the grasses in exposed fields were hung with innumerable
diamond pendants, which jingled merrily when brushed by the foot
of the traveller. It was literally the wreck of jewels and the crash of
gems. It was as though some superincumbent stratum of the earth
had been removed in the night, exposing to light a bed of untarnished
crystals. The scene changed at every step, or as the head was inclined
to the right or the left. There were the opal and sapphire and emerald
and jasper and beryl and topaz and ruby.

Such is beauty ever—neither here nor there, now nor then, neither
in Rome nor in Athens, but wherever there is a soul to admire. If I
seek her elsewhere because I do not find her at home, my search will
prove a fruitless one.

Feb. 13

All fear of the world or consequences is swallowed up in a manly
anxiety to do Truth justice.

March 6

How can a man sit down and quietly pare his nails, while the earth
goes gyrating ahead amid such a din of sphere music, whirling him
along about her axis some twenty-four thousand miles between sun
and sun, but mainly in a circle some two millions of miles actual
progress? And then such a hurly-burly on the surface—wind always
blowing—now a zephyr, now a hurricane—tides never idle, ever
fluctuating—no rest for Niagara, but perpetual ran-tan on those lime-
stone rocks—and then that summer simmering which our ears are used
to, which would otherwise be christened confusion worse confounded,
but is now ironically called "silence audible," and above all the
incessant tinkering named "hum of industry," the hurrying to and fro
and confused jabbering of men. Can man do less than get up and shake
himself?

March 14

The mass never comes up to the standard of its best member, but
on the contrary degrades itself to a level with the lowest.

But you are getting all the while further and further from true
society. Your silence was an approach to it, but your conversation is

only a refuge from the encounter of men; as though men were to be satisfied with a meeting of heels, and not heads.

Nor is it better with private assemblies, or meetings together, with a sociable design, of acquaintances so called—that is to say of men and women who are familiar with the lineaments of each other's countenances, who eat, drink, sleep, and transact the business of living within the circuit of a mile.

With a beating heart he fares him forth, by the light of the stars, to this meeting of gods. But the illusion speedily vanishes; what at first seemed to him nectar and ambrosia, is discovered to be plain bohea and short gingerbread.

After all, the field of battle possesses many advantages over the drawing-room. There at least is no room for pretension or excessive ceremony, no shaking of hands or rubbing of noses, which make one doubt your sincerity, but hearty as well as hard hand-play. It at least exhibits one of the faces of humanity, the former only a mask.

Our least deed, like the young of the land crab, wends its way to the sea of cause and effect as soon as born, and makes a drop there to eternity.

If thy neighbor hail thee to inquire how goes the world, feel thyself put to thy trumps to return a true and explicit answer. Plant the feet firmly, and, will he nill he, dole out to him with strict and conscientious impartiality his modicum of a response.

But after all, such a morsel of society as this will not satisfy a man. But like those women of Malamocco and Pelestrina,[1] who when their husbands are fishing at sea, repair to the shore and sing their shrill songs at evening, till they hear the voices of their husbands in reply borne to them over the water, so go we about indefatigably, chanting our stanza of the lay, and awaiting the response of a kindred soul out of the distance.

April 24

Men have been contriving new means and modes of motion. Steamships[2] have been westering during these late days and nights

---

1 [Adriatic villages ultimately amalgamated in Venice.]

2 [The first trans-Atlantic voyages by steam-power alone were made by two British vessels, both reaching New York April 8, 1838.]

on the Atlantic waves—the fuglers of a new evolution to this generation. Meanwhile plants spring silently by the brooksides, and the grim
woods wave indifferent; the earth emits no howl, pot on fire simmers
and seethes, and men go about their business.

July 13

What a hero one can be without moving a finger!

Aug. 4

Whatever of past or present wisdom has published itself to the
world, is palpable falsehood till it come and utter itself by my side.

Aug. 5

Some sounds seem to reverberate along the plain, and then settle
to earth again like dust; such are Noise, Discord, Jargon. But such only
as spring heavenward, and I may catch from steeples and hilltops in
their upward course, which are the more refined parts of the former,
are the true sphere music—pure, unmixed music—in which no wail
mingles.

DIVINE SERVICE IN THE ACADEMY HALL

In dark places and dungeons these words might perhaps strike root
and grow, but utter them in the daylight and their dusky hues are
apparent. From this window I can compare the written with the
preached word: within is weeping, and wailing, and gnashing of teeth;
without, grain fields and grasshoppers, which give those the lie direct.

Aug. 10

The human soul is a silent harp in God's quire, whose strings need
only to be swept by the divine breath to chime in with the harmonies
of creation. Every pulse-beat is in exact time with the cricket's chant,
and the tickings of the death-watch in the wall. Alternate with these
if you can.

Aug. 19

The sound of the Sabbath bell, whose farthest waves are at this
instant breaking on these cliffs, does not awaken pleasing associations
alone. Its muse is wonderfully condescending and philanthropic. One
involuntarily leans on his staff to humor the unusually meditative
mood. It is as the sound of many catechisms and religious books

twanging a canting peal round the world, and seems to issue from some Egyptian temple, and echo along the shore of the Nile, right opposite to Pharaoh's palace and Moses in the bulrushes, startling a multitude of storks and alligators basking in the sun. Not so these larks and pewees of Musketaquid. One is sick at heart of this pagoda worship. It is like the beating of gongs in a Hindoo subterranean temple.[1]

Sept. 3

The only faith that men recognize is a creed. But the true creed which we unconsciously live by, and which rather adopts us than we it, is quite different from the written or preached one. Men anxiously hold fast to their creed, as to a straw, thinking this does them good service because their sheet anchor does not drag.

Sept. 20

It is a luxury to muse by a wall-side in the sunshine of a September afternoon—to cuddle down under a gray stone, and hearken to the siren song of the cricket. Day and night seem henceforth but accidents, and the time is always a still eventide, and as the close of a happy day. Parched fields and mulleins gilded with the slanting rays are my diet. I know of no word so fit to express this disposition of Nature as Alma Natura.[2]

Dec.

All sound is nearly akin to Silence; it is a bubble on her surface which straightway bursts, an emblem of the strength and prolificness of the undercurrent. It is a faint utterance of Silence, and then only agreeable to our auditory nerves when it contrasts itself with the former. In proportion as it does this, and is a heightener and intensifier of the Silence, it is harmony and purest melody.

Feb. 9, 1839

It takes a man to make a room silent.

Feb. 10

THE PEAL OF THE BELLS

When the world grows old by the chimney-side,
Then forth to the youngling rocks I glide,

---

[1] [Thoreau had recently "signed off" from Concord's First Church.]
[2] [Nature as a nursing mother.]

Where over the water, and over the land,
The bells are booming on either hand.

Now up they go ding, then down again dong,
And awhile they swing to the same old song,
And the metal goes round at a single bound,
A-lulling the fields with its measured sound,
Till the tired tongue falls with a lengthened boom
As solemn and loud as the crack of doom.

Then changed is their measure to tone upon tone,
And seldom it is that one sound comes alone,
For they ring out their peals in a mingled throng,
And the breezes waft the loud ding-dong along.

When the echo has reached me in this lone vale,
I am straightway a hero in coat of mail,
I tug at my belt and I march on my post,
And feel myself more than a match for a host.

I am on the alert for some wonderful Thing
Which somewhere's a-taking place;
'Tis perchance the salute which our planet doth ring
When it meeteth another in space.

April 4

Drifting in a sultry day on the sluggish waters of the pond, I almost
cease to live and begin to be. A boatman stretched on the deck of his
craft and dallying with the noon would be as apt an emblem of eternity
for me as the serpent with his tail in his mouth. I am never so prone to
lose my identity. I am dissolved in the haze.

May 17

We say justly that the weak person is flat; for, like all flat substances,
he does not stand in the direction of his strength, that is on his edge,
but affords a convenient surface to put upon.[1] He slides all the way
through life. Most things are strong in one direction—a straw longi-
tudinally, a board in the direction of its edge, a knee transversely to its
grain—but the brave man is a perfect sphere, which cannot fall on its
flat side, and is equally strong every way. The coward is wretchedly

---

[1] [A characteristic pun, "put upon" having a double sense.]

spheroidal at best, too much educated or drawn out on one side commonly and depressed on the other; or he may be likened to a hollow sphere, whose disposition of matter is best when the greatest bulk is intended.

June 4

The words of some men are thrown forcibly against you and adhere like burs.

July 25

There is no remedy for love but to love more.

Sept. 17

Nature never makes haste; her systems revolve at an even pace. The bud swells imperceptibly, without hurry or confusion, as though the short spring days were an eternity. All her operations seem separately, for the time, the single object for which all things tarry. Why, then, should man hasten as if anything less than eternity were allotted for the least deed? Let him consume never so many æons, so that he go about the meanest task well, though it be but the paring of his nails. If the setting sun seems to hurry him to improve the day while it lasts, the chant of the crickets fails not to reassure him, even-measured as of old, teaching him to take his own time henceforth forever. The wise man is restful, never restless or impatient. He each moment abides there where he is, as some walkers actually rest the whole body at each step, while others never relax the muscles of the leg till the accumulated fatigue obliges them to stop short.

Oct. 22

Nature will bear the closest inspection. She invites us to lay our eye level with her smallest leaf, and take an insect view of its plain.

Nov. 5

Common sense is not so familiar with any truth but Genius will represent it in a strange light to it. Let the seer bring down his broad eye to the most stale and trivial fact, and he will make you believe it a new planet in the sky.

All the past is here present to be tried; let it approve itself if it can.

Nov. 13

Make the most of your regrets; never smother your sorrow, but tend and cherish it till it come to have a separate and integral interest. To regret deeply is to live afresh.

Dec. 2

We do all stand in the front ranks of the battle every moment of our lives; where there is a brave man there is the thickest of the fight, there the post of honor.

Dec.

If his fortune deserts him, the brave man in pity still abides by her. Samuel Johnson and his friend Savage, compelled by poverty to pass the night in the streets, resolve that they will stand by their country.

All sounds, and more than all, silence, do fife and drum for us. The least creaking doth whet all our senses and emit a tremulous light, like the aurora borealis, over things. As polishing expresses the vein in marble and the grain in wood, so music brings out what of heroic lurks anywhere.

My friend will be as much better than myself as my aspiration is above my performance.

Jan. 26, 1840

The poet does not need to see how meadows are something else than earth, grass, and water, but how they are thus much. He does not need discover that potato blows are as beautiful as violets, as the farmer thinks, but only how good potato blows are.[1]

Jan. 29

The social condition of genius is the same in all ages. Æschylus was undoubtedly alone and without sympathy in his simple reverence for the mystery of the universe.

Feb. 11

He enjoys true leisure who has time to improve his soul's estate.

---

[1] [Compare, in "Thursday" of *A Week on the Concord and Merrimack Rivers,* "A true account of the actual is the rarest poetry."]

Feb. 14

A very meagre natural history suffices to make me a child. Only their names and genealogy make me love fishes. I would know even the number of their fin-rays, and how many scales compose the lateral line. I fancy I am amphibious and swim in all the brooks and pools in the neighborhood, with the perch and bream, or doze under the pads of our river amid the winding aisles and corridors formed by their stems, with the stately pickerel.

Feb. 28

On the death of a friend, we should consider that the fates through confidence have devolved on us the task of a double living, that we have henceforth to fulfill the promise of our friend's life also, in our own, to the world.

March 4

I learned today that my ornithology had done me no service. The birds I heard, which fortunately did not come within the scope of my science, sung as freshly as if it had been the first morning of creation, and had for background to their song an untrodden wilderness, stretching through many a Carolina and Mexico of the soul.

March 21

The world is a fit theatre today in which any part may be acted. There is this moment proposed to me every kind of life that men lead anywhere, or that imagination can paint. By another spring I may be a mail-carrier in Peru, or a South African planter, or a Siberian exile, or a Greenland whaler, or a settler on the Columbia River, or a Canton merchant, or a soldier in Florida, or a mackerel-fisher off Cape Sable, or a Robinson Crusoe in the Pacific, or a silent navigator of any sea. So wide is the choice of parts, what a pity if the part of Hamlet be left out!

I am freer than any planet; no complaint reaches round the world. I can move away from public opinion, from government, from religion, from education, from society. Shall I be reckoned a ratable poll in the county of Middlesex, or be rated at one spear under the palm trees of Guinea? Shall I raise corn and potatoes in Massachusetts, or figs and olives in Asia Minor? sit out the day in my office in State Street, or ride it out on the steppes of Tartary? For my Brobdingnag I may sail to Patagonia; for my Lilliput, to Lapland. In Arabia and Persia, my day's adventures may surpass the Arabian Nights' Entertainments. I may be a logger on the head waters of the Penobscot, to be recorded in fable hereafter as an amphibious river-god, by as sounding a name as Triton or Proteus; carry furs from Nootka to China, and so be more renowned than Jason and his golden fleece; or go on a South Sea exploring expedition, to be hereafter recounted along with the periplus of Hanno.[1] I may repeat the adventures of Marco Polo or Mandeville.

These are but few of my chances, and how many more things may I do with which there are none to be compared!

Thank Fortune, we are not rooted to the soil, and here is not all the world. The buckeye does not grow in New England; the mockingbird is rarely heard here. Why not keep pace with the day, and not allow of a sunset nor fall behind the summer and the migration of birds? Shall we not compete with the buffalo, who keeps pace with the seasons, cropping the pastures of the Colorado till a greener and sweeter grass awaits him by the Yellowstone? The wild goose is more a cosmopolite than we; he breaks his fast in Canada, takes a luncheon in the Susquehanna, and plumes himself for the night in a Louisiana bayou. The pigeon carries an acorn in his crop from the King of Holland's to Mason and Dixon's line. Yet we think if rail fences are pulled down and stone walls set up on our farms, bounds are henceforth set to our lives and our fates decided. If you are chosen town clerk, forsooth, you can't go to Tierra del Fuego this summer.

But what of all this? A man may gather his limbs snugly within the shell of a mammoth squash, with his back to the northeastern boundary, and not be unusually straitened after all. Our limbs, indeed, have room enough, but it is our souls that rust in a corner. Let us migrate interiorly without intermission, and pitch our tent each day nearer the western horizon. The really fertile soils and luxuriant prairies lie on this side the Alleghenies. There has been no Hanno of the affections. Their domain is untravelled ground, to the Mogul's dominions.

March 22

While I bask in the sun on the shores of Walden Pond, by this heat and this rustle I am absolved from all obligation to the past. The council of nations may reconsider their votes; the grating of a pebble annuls them.

March 30

Pray, what things interest me at present? A long, soaking rain, the drops trickling down the stubble, while I lay drenched on a last year's

[1] [A Carthaginian explorer, *ca.* 500 B.C., alleged to have circumnavigated Africa.]

bed of wild oats, by the side of some bare hill, ruminating. These
things are of moment. To watch this crystal globe just sent from
heaven to associate with me. While these clouds and this sombre
drizzling weather shut all in, we two draw nearer and know one
another. The gathering in of the clouds with the last rush and dying
breath of the wind, and then the regular dripping of twigs and leaves
the country o'er, the impression of inward comfort and sociableness,
the drenched stubble and trees that drop beads on you as you pass,
their dim outline seen through the rain on all sides drooping in
sympathy with yourself. These are my undisputed territory. This is
Nature's English comfort. The birds draw closer and are more familiar
under the thick foliage, composing new strains on their roosts against
the sunshine.

April 4

We look to windward for fair weather.

April 8

How shall I help myself? By withdrawing into the garret, and
associating with spiders and mice, determining to meet myself face to
face sooner or later. Completely silent and attentive I will be this hour,
and the next, and forever. The most positive life that history notices
has been a constant retiring out of life, a wiping one's hands of it,
seeing how mean it is, and having nothing to do with it.

May 14

A kind act or gift lays us under obligation not so much to the giver
as to Truth and Love. We must then be truer and kinder ourselves.
Just in proportion to our sense of the kindness, and pleasure at it, is
the debt paid. What is it to be *grateful* but to be *gratified*—to be *pleased?*
The nobly poor will dissolve all obligations by nobly accepting a
kindness.

June 15

Why always insist that men incline to the moral side of their being?
Our life is not all moral. Surely, its actual phenomena deserve to be
studied impartially.

We have not yet met with a sonnet, genial and affectionate, to
prophane swearing, breaking on the still night air, perhaps, like the

hoarse croak of some bird. Noxious weeds and stagnant waters have
their lovers, and the utterer of oaths must have honeyed lips, and be
another Attic bee after a fashion, for only prevalent and essential
harmony and beauty can employ the laws of sound and of light.

June 16

Would it not be a luxury to stand up to one's chin in some retired
swamp for a whole summer's day, scenting the sweet-fern and bilberry
blows, and lulled by the minstrelsy of gnats and mosquitoes? . . . Say
twelve hours of genial and familiar converse with the leopard frog.
The sun to rise behind alder and dogwood, and climb buoyantly to
his meridian of three hands' breadth, and finally sink to rest behind
some bold western hummock. To hear the evening chant of the mos-
quito from a thousand green chapels, and the bittern begin to boom
from his concealed fort like a sunset gun! Surely, one may as profitably
be soaked in the juices of a marsh for one day, as pick his way dry-shod
over sand. Cold and damp—are they not as rich experience as warmth
and dryness?
So is not shade as good as sunshine, night as day? Why be eagles
and thrushes always, and owls and whip-poor-wills never?

June 18

I should be pleased to meet man in the woods. I wish he were to be
encountered like wild caribou and moose.

June 20

Praise begins when things are seen partially. We begin to praise
when we begin to see that a thing needs our assistance.

June 21

I never feel that I am inspired unless my body is also. It too spurns
a tame and commonplace life. They are fatally mistaken who think,
while they strive with their minds, that they may suffer their bodies
to stagnate in luxury or sloth. The body is the first proselyte the Soul
makes. Our life is but the Soul made known by its fruits, the body. The
whole duty of man may be expressed in one line—Make to yourself a
perfect body.

June 22

When we are shocked at vice we express a lingering sympathy with
it. Dry rot, rust, and mildew shock no man, for none is subject to them.

June 23

Not by constraint or severity shall you have access to true wisdom, but by abandonment, and childlike mirthfulness. If you would know aught, be gay before it.

June 24

Not all the wit of a college can avail to make one harmonious line.

June 25

Let me see no other conflict but with prosperity. If my path run on before me level and smooth, it is all a mirage; in reality it is steep and arduous as a chamois pass. I will not let the years roll over me like a Juggernaut car.

June 26

When a dog runs at you, whistle for him.

Say, Not so, and you will outcircle the philosophers.

June 27

I am living this 27th of June, 1840, a dull, cloudy day and no sun shining. The clink of the smith's hammer sounds feebly over the roofs, and the wind is sighing gently, as if dreaming of cheerfuler days. The farmer is plowing in yonder field, craftsmen are busy in the shops, the trader stands behind the counter, and all works go steadily forward. But I will have nothing to do; I will tell fortune that I play no game with her, and she may reach me in my Asia of serenity and indolence if she can.

For an impenetrable shield, stand inside yourself.

June 30

I sailed from Fair Haven[1] last evening as gently and steadily as the clouds sail through the atmosphere. The wind came blowing blithely from the southwest fields, and stepped into the folds of our sail like a winged horse, pulling with a strong and steady impulse. The sail bends gently to the breeze, as swells some generous impulse of the heart,

[1] [A wide expanse in Sudbury River two miles south of Concord center.]

and anon flutters and flaps with a kind of human suspense. I could watch the motions of a sail forever, they are so rich and full of meaning. I watch the play of its pulse, as if it were my own blood beating there. The varying temperature of distant atmospheres is graduated on its scale. It is a free, buoyant creature, the bauble of the heavens and the earth. A gay pastime the air plays with it. If it wells and tugs, it is because the sun lays his windy finger on it. The breeze it plays with has been outdoors so long. So thin is it, and yet so full of life; so noiseless when it labors hardest, so noisy and impatient when least serviceable. So am I blown on by God's breath, so flutter and flap, and fill gently out with the breeze.

A man's life should be a stately march to a sweet but unheard music, and when to his fellows it shall seem irregular and inharmonious, he will only be stepping to a livelier measure, or his nicer ear hurry him into a thousand symphonies and concordant variations. There will be no halt ever, but at most a marching on his post, or such a pause as is richer than any sound, when the melody runs into such depth and wildness as to be no longer heard, but simplicity consented to with the whole life and being. He will take a false step never, even in the most arduous times, for then the music will not fail to swell into greater sweetness and volume, and itself rule the movement it inspired.

I have a deep sympathy with war, it so apes the gait and bearing of the soul.

July 6

All this worldly wisdom was once the unamiable heresy of some wise man.

Let the daily tide leave some deposit on these pages, as it leaves sand and shells on the shore. So much increase of *terra firma*. This may be a calendar of the ebbs and flows of the soul; and on these sheets as a beach, the waves may cast up pearls and seaweed.

July 11

It is the man determines what is said, not the words. If a mean person uses a wise maxim, I bethink me how it can be interpreted so as to commend itself to his meanness; but if a wise man makes a commonplace remark, I consider what wider construction it will admit.

July 26

When I consider how, after sunset, the stars come out gradually in troops from behind the hills and woods, I confess that I could not have contrived a more curious and inspiring night.

July 27

By the last breath of the May air I inhale I am reminded that the ages never got so far down as this before. The wood thrush is a more modern philosopher than Plato and Aristotle. They are now a dogma, but he preaches the doctrine of this hour.

Nature refuses to sympathize with our sorrow. She seems not to have provided for, but by a thousand contrivances against, it. She has bevelled the margins of the eyelids that the tears may not overflow on the cheek.[1]

Jan. 23, 1841

A day is lapsing. I hear cockerels crowing in the yard, and see them stalking among the chips in the sun. I hear busy feet on the floors, and the whole house jars with industry. Surely the day is well spent, and the time is full to overflowing. Mankind is as busy as the flowers in summer, which make haste to unfold themselves in the forenoon, and close their petals in the afternoon.

The momentous topics of human life are always of secondary importance to the business in hand, just as carpenters discuss politics between the strokes of the hammer while they are shingling a roof.

The squeaking of the pump sounds as necessary as the music of the spheres.

The solidity and apparent necessity of this routine insensibly recommend it to me. It is like a cane or a cushion for the infirm, and in view of it all are infirm. If there were but one erect and solid-standing tree in the woods, all creatures would go to rub against it and make sure of their footing. Routine is a ground to stand on, a wall to retreat to; we cannot draw on our boots without bracing ourselves against it. It is the fence over which neighbors lean when they talk. All this cockcrowing, and hawing and geeing, and business in the streets, is like the spring-board on which tumblers perform and develop their elasticity. Our health requires that we should recline on it from time to

---

[1] [Between this and the following entry belongs the material of the so-called "Lost Journal."]

time. When we are in it, the hand stands still on the face of the clock, and we grow like corn in the genial dankness and silence of the night. Our weakness wants it, but our strength uses it. Good for the body is the work of the body, good for the soul the work of the soul, and good for either the work of the other. Let them not call hard names, nor know a divided interest.

Jan. 24

It is more proper for a spiritual fact to have suggested an analogous natural one, than for the natural fact to have preceded the spiritual in our minds.

By spells seriousness will be forced to cut capers, and drink a deep and refreshing draught of silliness; to turn this sedate day [1] of Lucifer's and Apollo's, into an all fools' day for Harlequin and Cornwallis.[2] The sun does not grudge his rays to either, but they are alike patronized by the gods.   Like overtasked schoolboys, all my members and nerves and sinews petition Thought for a recess, and my very thigh-bones itch to slip away from under me, and run and join the mêlée. I exult in stark inanity, leering on nature and the soul.   We think the gods reveal themselves only to sedate and musing gentlemen. But not so; the buffoon in the midst of his antics catches unobserved glimpses, which he treasures for the lonely hour. When I have been playing tomfool, I have been driven to exchange the old for a more liberal and catholic philosophy.

Jan. 25

We should strengthen, and beautify, and industriously mould our bodies to be fit companions of the soul—assist them to grow up like trees, and be agreeable and wholesome objects in nature. I think if I had had the disposal of this soul of man, I should have bestowed it sooner on some antelope of the plains than upon this sickly and sluggish body.

Jan. 29

Of all strange and unaccountable things this journalizing is the strangest. It will allow nothing to be predicated of it; its good is not good, nor its bad bad. If I make a huge effort to expose my innermost

---

1 [Sunday.]

2 [A merry celebration of the defeat of General Cornwallis at Yorktown, Virginia, on October 19, 1781.]

and richest wares to light, my counter seems cluttered with the meanest homemade stuffs; but after months or years I may discover the wealth of India, and whatever rarity is brought overland from Cathay, in that confused heap, and what perhaps seemed a festoon of dried apple or pumpkin will prove a string of Brazilian diamonds, or pearls from Coromandel.[1]

Jan. 30

Here is the distinct trail of a fox stretching [a] quarter of a mile across the pond. Now I am curious to know what has determined its graceful curvatures, its greater or less spaces and distinctness, and how surely they were coincident with the fluctuations of some mind, why they now lead me two steps to the right, and then three to the left. If these things are not to be called up and accounted for in the Lamb's Book of Life, I shall set them down for careless accountants. Here was one expression of the divine mind this morning. The pond was his journal, and last night's snow made a *tabula rasa*[2] for him. I know which way a mind wended this morning, what horizon it faced, by the setting of these tracks; whether it moved slowly or rapidly, by the greater or less intervals and distinctness, for the swiftest step leaves yet a lasting trace.

Suddenly, looking down the river, I saw a fox some sixty rods off, making across to the hills on my left. As the snow lay five inches deep, he made but slow progress, but it was no impediment to me. So, yielding to the instinct of the chase, I tossed my head aloft and bounded away, snuffing the air like a fox-hound, and spurning the world and the Humane Society at each bound. It seemed the woods rang with the hunter's horn, and Diana and all the satyrs joined in the chase and cheered me on. Olympian and Elean youths were waving palms on the hills. In the meanwhile I gained rapidly on the fox; but he showed a remarkable presence of mind, for, instead of keeping up the face of the hill, which was steep and unwooded in that part, he kept along the slope in the direction of the forest, though he lost ground by it. Notwithstanding his fright, he took no step which was not beautiful. The course on his part was a series of most graceful curves. It was a sort of leopard canter, I should say, as if he were nowise impeded by the snow, but were husbanding his strength all the while. When he doubled I wheeled and cut him off, bounding with fresh vigor, and Antæus-like,

[1] [An old name, now disused, for the eastern coast of India, thought to be rich in pearls.]

[2] [A clean slate.]

recovering my strength each time I touched the snow. Having got near enough for a fair view, just as he was slipping into the wood, I gracefully yielded him the palm. He ran as though there were not a bone in his back, occasionally dropping his muzzle to the snow for a rod or two, and then tossing his head aloft when satisfied of his course. When he came to a declivity he put his fore feet together and slid down it like a cat. He trod so softly that you could not have heard it from any nearness, and yet with such expression that it would not have been quite inaudible at any distance. So, hoping this experience would prove a useful lesson to him, I returned to the village by the highway of the river.

There is all the romance of my youthfulest moment in music. Heaven lies about us, as in our infancy. There is nothing so wild and extravagant that it does not make true. It makes a dream my only real experience, and prompts faith to such elasticity that only the incredible can satisfy it. It tells me again to trust the remotest and finest, as the divinest, instinct. All that I have imagined of heroism, it reminds and reassures me of. It is a life unlived, a life beyond life, where at length my years will pass. I look under the lids of Time.

Feb. 4. Thursday

When you are once comfortably seated at a public meeting, there is something unmanly in the sitting on tiptoe and *qui vive* attitude—the involuntary rising into your throat, as if gravity had ceased to operate—when a lady approaches, with quite godlike presumption, to elicit the miracle of a seat where none is.

Such a state of unrest becomes only a fluttered virtue. When once I have learned my place in the sphere, I will fill it once for all, rather like a fixed star than a planet. I will rest as the mountains do, so that your ladies might as well walk into the midst of the Tyrol, and look for Nature to spread them a green lawn for their disport in the midst of those solemn fastnesses, as that I should fly out of my orbit at their approach and go about eccentric, like a comet, to endanger other systems. No, be true to your instinct, and sit; wait till you can be genuinely polite, if it be till doomsday, and not lose your chance everlastingly by a cowardly yielding to young etiquette. By your look say unto them, The lines have fallen to me in pleasant places, and I will fill that station God has assigned me. As well Miss Cassiopeia[1] up

[1] [Thoreau forgets that the lady of the constellation already has a chair.]

there might ask the brazen-fronted Taurus to draw in his horns, that she might shine in his stead. No, no! not till my cycle is completed.

Feb. 6

"Lu ral lu ral lu" may be more impressively sung than very respectable wisdom talked. It is well-timed, as wisdom is not always.

Feb. 7

The eaves are running on the south side of the house; the titmouse lisps in the poplar; the bells are ringing for church; while the sun presides over all and makes his simple warmth more obvious than all else. What shall I do with this hour, so like time and yet so fit for eternity? Where in me are these russet patches of ground, and scattered logs and chips in the yard? I do not feel cluttered. I have some notion what the John's-wort[1] and life-everlasting[2] may be thinking about when the sun shines on me as on them and turns my prompt thought into just such a seething shimmer. I lie out indistinct as a heath at noonday. I am evaporating and ascending into the sun.

Feb. 8

My Journal is that of me which would else spill over and run to waste, gleanings from the field which in action I reap. I must not live for it, but in it for the gods. They are my correspondent, to whom daily I send off this sheet postpaid. I am clerk in their counting-room, and at evening transfer the account from day-book to ledger. It is as a leaf which hangs over my head in the path. I bend the twig and write my prayers on it; then letting it go, the bough springs up and shows the scrawl to heaven. As if it were not kept shut in my desk, but were as public a leaf as any in nature. It is papyrus by the riverside; it is vellum in the pastures; it is parchment on the hills. I find it everywhere as free as the leaves which troop along the lanes in autumn. The crow, the goose, the eagle carry my quill, and the wind blows the leaves as far as I go. Or, if my imagination does not soar, but gropes in slime and mud, then I write with a reed.

In our holiest moment our devil with a leer stands close at hand. He is a very busy devil. It gains vice some respect, I must confess, thus to be reminded how indefatigable it is. It has at least the merit of

---

1 [Saint-John's-Wort, or Hypericum.]
2 [Cud-weed.]

industriousness. When I go forth with zeal to some good work, my devil is sure to get his robe tucked up the first and arrives there as soon as I, with a look of sincere earnestness which puts to shame my best intent. He is as forward as I to a good work, and as disinterested. He has a winning way of recommending himself by making himself useful. How readily he comes into my best project, and does his work with a quiet and steady cheerfulness which even virtue may take pattern from.

I never was so rapid in my virtue but my vice kept up with me. It always came in by a hand, and never panting, but with a curried coolness halted, as if halting were the beginning not the end of the course. It only runs the swifter because it has no rider. It never was behind me but when I turned to look and so fell behind myself. I never did a charitable thing but there he stood, scarce in the rear, with hat in hand, partner on the same errand, ready to share the smile of gratitude. Though I shut the door never so quick and tell it to stay at home like a good dog, it will out with me, for I shut in my own legs so, and it escapes in the meanwhile and is ready to back and reinforce me in most virtuous deeds. And if I turn and say, "Get thee behind me," he then indeed turns too and takes the lead, though he seems to retire with a pensive and compassionate look, as much as to say, "Ye know not what ye do."

We are double-edged blades, and every time we whet our virtue the return stroke straps our vice.

Feb. 9

I have been breaking silence these twenty-three years and have hardly made a rent in it. Silence has no end; speech is but the beginning of it. My friend thinks I *keep* silence, who am only choked with letting it out so fast. Does he forget that new mines of secrecy are constantly opening in me?

Feb. 18

I do not judge men by anything they can do. Their greatest deed is the impression they make on me. Some serene, inactive men can do everything. Talent only indicates a depth of character in some direction. We do not acquire the ability to do new deeds, but a new capacity for all deeds. My recent growth does not appear in any visible new talent, but its deed will enter into my gaze when I look into the sky, or vacancy. It will help me to consider ferns and everlasting[1].

[1 A popular name for various plants whose flowers keep the appearance of freshness long after they are gathered.]

Feb. 19

We seem but to linger in manhood to tell the dreams of our childhood, and they vanish out of memory ere we learn the language.

Feb. 20

When I am going out for an evening I arrange the fire in my stove so that I do not fail to find a good one when I return, though it would have engaged my frequent attention present. So that, when I know I am to be at home, I sometimes make believe that I may go out, to save trouble. And this is the art of living, too—to leave our life in a condition to go alone, and not to require a constant supervision. We will then sit down serenely to live, as by the side of a stove.

Feb. 23

Let all our stores and munitions be provided for the lone state.[1]

Feb. 26.   Friday

My prickles or smoothness are as much a quality of your hand as of myself. I cannot tell you what I am, more than a ray of the summer's sun. What I am I am, and say not. Being is the great explainer. In the attempt to explain, shall I plane away all the spines, till it is no thistle, but a cornstalk?

If my world is not sufficient without thee, my friend, I will wait till it is and then call thee. You shall come to a palace, not to an almshouse.

My homeliest thought, like the diamond brought from farthest within the mine, will shine with the purest lustre.

To be great, we do as if we would be tall merely, be longer than we are broad, stretch ourselves and stand on tiptoe. But greatness is well proportioned, unstrained, and stands on the soles of the feet.

I who have been sick hear cattle low in the street, with such a healthy ear as prophesies my cure. These sounds lay a finger on my pulse to some purpose. A fragrance comes in at all my senses which proclaims that I am still of Nature the child. The threshing in yonder barn and the tinkling of the anvil come from the same side of Styx with me. If I

---

[1] [Presumably a punning allusion to the Lone Star State.]

were a physician I would try my patients thus. I would wheel them to a window and let Nature feel their pulse. It will soon appear if their sensuous existence is sound. These sounds are but the throbbing of some pulse in me.

Feb. 28

Nothing goes by luck in composition. It allows of no tricks. The best you can write will be the best you are. Every sentence is the result of a long probation. The author's character is read from title-page to end. Of this he never corrects the proofs. We read it as the essential character of a handwriting without regard to the flourishes. And so of the rest of our actions; it runs as straight as a ruled line through them all, no matter how many curvets about it. Our whole life is taxed for the least thing well done; it is its net result. How we eat, drink, sleep, and use our desultory hours, now in these indifferent days, with no eye to observe and no occasion [to] excite us, determines our authority and capacity for the time to come.

March 3

I hear a man blowing a horn this still evening, and it sounds like the plaint of nature in these times. In this, which I refer to some man, there is something greater than any man. It is as if the earth spoke. It adds a great remoteness to the horizon, and its very distance is grand, as when one draws back the head to speak. That which I now hear in the west seems like an invitation to the east. It runs round the earth as a whisper gallery. It is the spirit of the West calling to the spirit of the East, or else it is the rattling of some team lagging in Day's train. Coming to me through the darkness and silence, all things great seem transpiring there. It is friendly as a distant hermit's taper. When it is trilled, or undulates, the heavens are crumpled into time, and successive waves flow across them.

It is a strangely healthy sound for these disjointed times. It is a rare soundness when cow-bells and horns are heard from over the fields. And now I see the beauty and full meaning of that word "sound." Nature always possesses a certain sonorousness, as in the hum of insects, the booming of ice, the crowing of cocks in the morning, and the barking of dogs in the night, which indicates her sound state. God's voice is but a clear bell sound. I drink in a wonderful health, a cordial, in sound. The effect of the slightest tinkling in the horizon measures my own soundness. I thank God for sound; it always mounts, and makes me mount. I think I will not trouble myself for any wealth, when I can be so cheaply enriched. Here I contemplate to drudge that I may own a farm—and may have such a limitless estate for the listening. All good things are cheap: all bad are very dear.

As for these communities, I think I had rather keep bachelor's hall in hell than go to board in heaven. . . . In heaven I hope to bake my own bread and clean my own linen.

March 13

How alone must our life be lived! We dwell on the seashore, and none between us and the sea. Men are my merry companions, my fellow-pilgrims, who beguile the way but leave me at the first turn in the road, for none are travelling *one* road so far as myself.

Each one marches in the van. The weakest child is exposed to the fates henceforth as barely as its parents. Parents and relations but entertain the youth; they cannot stand between him and his destiny. This is the one bare side of every man. There is no fence; it is clear before him to the bounds of space.

March 15

A great cheerfulness have all great wits possessed, almost a prophane levity to such as understood them not, but their religion had the broader basis in proportion as it was less prominent. The religion I love is very laic. The clergy are as diseased, and as much possessed with a devil, as the reformers. They make their topic as offensive as the politician, for our religion is as unpublic and incommunicable as our poetical vein, and to be approached with as much love and tenderness.

March 27 ·

I must not lose any of my freedom by being a farmer and land-holder. Most who enter on any profession are doomed men. The world might as well sing a dirge over them forthwith. The farmer's muscles are rigid. He can do one thing long, not many well. His pace seems determined henceforth; he never quickens it. A very rigid Nemesis is his fate. When the right wind blows or a star calls, I can leave this arable and grass ground, without making a will or settling my estate. I would buy a farm as freely as a silken streamer.

April 1

In reading a work on agriculture, I skip the author's moral reflections, and the words "Providence" and "He" scattered along the page, to come at the profitable level of what he has to say. There is no science in men's religion; it does not teach me so much as the report of the committee on swine. My author shows he has dealt in corn and turnips and can worship God with the hoe and spade, but spare me his morality.

April 4, Sunday

That cheap piece of tinkling brass which the farmer hangs about his cow's neck has been more to me than the tons of metal which are swung in the belfry.

April 5

This lament for a golden age is only a lament for golden men.

April 15

The gods are of no sect; they side with no man. When I imagine that Nature inclined rather to some few earnest and faithful souls, and specially existed for them, I go to see an obscure individual who lives under the hill, letting both gods and men alone, and find that strawberries and tomatoes grow for him too in his garden there, and the sun lodges kindly under his hillside, and am compelled to acknowledge the unbribable charity of the gods.

April 20

Great thoughts hallow any labor. Today I earned seventy-five cents heaving manure out of a pen, and made a good bargain of it. If the ditcher muses the while how he may live uprightly, the ditching spade and turf knife may be engraved on the coat-of-arms of his posterity.

April 22

There are two classes of authors: the one write the history of their times, the other their biography.

April 25

A momentous silence reigns always in the woods, and their meaning seems just ripening into expression. But alas! they make no haste. The rush sparrow,[1] Nature's minstrel of serene hours, sings of an immense leisure and duration.

---

[1] [Now usually called the vesper sparrow.]

Aug. 1, Sunday

The best thought is not only without sombreness, but even without morality. The universe lies outspread in floods of white light to it. The moral aspect of nature is a jaundice reflected from man. To the innocent there are no cherubim nor angels . . . Silent is the preacher about this, and silent must ever be, for he who knows it will not preach.

Aug. 18

The best poets, after all, exhibit only a tame and civil side of nature. They have not seen the west side of any mountain.

How much will some officious men give to preserve an old book, of which perchance only a single [copy] exists, while a wise God is already giving, and will still give, infinitely more to get it destroyed!

Aug. 24

Let us wander where we will, the universe is built round about us, and we are central still. By reason of this, if we look into the heavens, they are concave, and if we were to look into a gulf as bottomless, it would be concave also. The sky is curved downward to the earth in the horizon, because I stand in the plain. I draw down its skirts. The stars so low there seem loth to go away from me, but by a circuitous path to be remembering and returning to me.

Aug. 28

The art which only gilds the surface and demands merely a superficial polish, without reaching to the core, is but varnish and filigree. But the work of genius is rough-hewn from the first, because it anticipates the lapse of time and has an ingrained polish, which still appears when fragments are broken off, an essential quality of its substance. Its beauty is its strength. It breaks with a lustre, and splits in cubes and diamonds. Like the diamond, it has only to be cut to be polished, and its surface is a window to its interior splendors.

Sept. 4.   Saturday

I think I could write a poem to be called "Concord." For argument I should have the River, the Woods, the Ponds, the Hills, the Fields, the Swamps and Meadows, the Streets and Buildings, and the Villagers. Then Morning, Noon, and Evening, Spring, Summer, Autumn, and Winter, Night, Indian Summer, and the Mountains in the Horizon.

Nov. 30

Good poetry seems so simple and natural a thing that when we meet it we wonder that all men are not always poets. Poetry is nothing but healthy speech. . . . The best lines, perhaps, only suggest to me that that man simply saw or heard or felt what seems the commonest fact in my experience.

[Dec.]¹ 12.   Sunday

All music is only a sweet striving to express character. Now that lately I have heard of some traits in the character of a fair and earnest maiden² whom I had only known superficially, but who has gone hence to make herself more known by distance, they sound like strains of a wild harp music. They make all persons and places who had thus forgotten her to seem late and behindhand.

Dec. 15

I seem to see somewhat more of my own kith and kin in the lichens on the rocks than in any books. It does seem as if mine were a peculiarly wild nature, which so yearns toward all wildness. I know of no redeeming qualities in me but a sincere love for some things, and when I am reproved I have to fall back on to this ground. This is my argument in reserve for all cases. My love is invulnerable. Meet me on that ground, and you will find me strong. When I am condemned, and condemn myself utterly, I think straightway, "But I rely on my love for some things." Therein I am whole and entire. Therein I am God-propped.

Dec. 29

These motions everywhere in nature must surely [be] the circulations of God. The flowing sail, the running stream, the waving tree, the roving wind—whence else their infinite health and freedom? I can see nothing so proper and holy as unrelaxed play and frolic in this bower God has built for us. The suspicion of sin never comes to this thought. Oh, if men felt this they would never build temples even of marble or diamond, but it would be sacrilege and prophane, but disport them forever in this paradise.

¹ [Parentheses used throughout this text are Thoreau's; brackets, the editor's.]
² [Probably Ellen Sewall of Scituate, Massachusetts.]

I can at length stretch me when I come to Chaucer's breadth; and I think, "Well, I could be *that* man's acquaintance," for he walked in that low and retired way that I do, and was not too good to live. I am grieved when they hint of any unmanly submissions he may have made, for that subtracts from his breadth and humanity.

Jan. 7, 1842

The great God is very calm withal. How superfluous is any excitement in his creatures! He listens equally to the prayers of the believer and the unbeliever. The moods of man should unfold and alternate as gradually and placidly as those of nature. The sun shines for aye! The sudden revolutions of these times and this generation have acquired a very exaggerated importance. They do not interest me much, for they are not in harmony with the longer periods of nature. The present, in any aspect in which it can be presented to the smallest audience, is always mean. God does not sympathize with the popular movements.

Jan. 8

What offends me most in my compositions is the moral element in them. The repentant say never a brave word. Their resolves should be mumbled in silence. Strictly speaking, morality is not healthy. Those undeserved joys which come uncalled and make us more pleased than grateful are they that sing.

There are in music such strains as far surpass any faith in the loftiness of man's destiny. He must be very sad before he can comprehend them. The clear, liquid notes from the morning fields beyond seem to come through a vale of sadness to man, which gives all music a plaintive air. It hath caught a higher pace than any virtue I know. It is the archreformer. It hastens the sun to his setting. It invites him to his rising. It is the sweetest reproach, a measured satire.

Feb. 20

I am amused to see from my window here how busily man has divided and staked off his domain. God must smile at his puny fences running hither and thither everywhere over the land.

Feb. 23

It is the charm and greatness of all society, from friendship to the drawing-room, that it takes place on a level slightly higher than the actual characters of the parties would warrant; it is an expression of faith. True politeness is only hope and trust in men. It never addresses a fallen or falling man, but salutes a rising generation. It does not flatter but only congratulates. The rays of light come to us in such a curve that every fellow in the street appears higher than he really is. It is the innate civility of nature.

March 13.   Sunday

I am startled that God can make me so rich even with my own cheap stores. It needs but a few wisps of straw in the sun, or some small word dropped, or that has long lain silent in some book.

March 17.   Thursday

I have been making pencils all day, and then at evening walked to see an old schoolmate who is going to help make the Welland Canal navigable for ships round Niagara. He cannot see any such motives and modes of living as I; professes not to look beyond the securing of certain "creature comforts." And so we go silently different ways, with all serenity, I in the still moonlight through the village this fair evening to write these thoughts in my journal, and he, forsooth, to mature his schemes to ends as good, maybe, but different. So are we two made, while the same stars shine quietly over us. If I or he be wrong, Nature yet consents placidly. She bites her lip and smiles to see how her children will agree. So does the Welland Canal get built, and other conveniences, while I live. Well and good, I must confess. Fast sailing ships are hence not detained.

March 22

We cannot well do without our sins; they are the highway of our virtue.

March 26

I must confess I have felt mean enough when asked how I was to act on society, what errand I had to mankind. Undoubtedly I did not feel mean without a reason, and yet my loitering is not without defense. I would fain communicate the wealth of my life to men, would really give them what is most precious in my gift. I would secrete pearls with the shellfish and lay up honey with the bees for them. I will sift the sunbeams for the public good. I know no riches I would keep back. I have no private good, unless it be my peculiar ability to serve the public. This is the only individual property. Each one may thus be innocently rich. I inclose and foster the pearl till it is grown. I wish to communicate those parts of my life which I would gladly live again myself.

March 31

The really efficient laborer will be found not to crowd his day with work, but will saunter to his task surrounded by a wide halo of ease and leisure. There will be a wide margin for relaxation to his day. He is only earnest to secure the kernels of time, and does not exaggerate the value of the husk. Why should the hen set all day? She can lay but one egg, and besides she will not have picked up materials for a new one. Those who work much do not work hard.

April 3

Experience is in the fingers and head. The heart is inexperienced.

Undated

Emerson[1] again is a critic, poet philosopher, with talent not so conspicuous, not so adequate to his task; but his field is still higher, his task more arduous. Lives a far more intense life; seeks to realize a divine life; his affections and intellect equally developed. Has advanced farther, and a new heaven opens to him. Love and Friendship, Religion, Poetry, the Holy are familiar to him. The life of an Artist; more variegated, more observing, finer perception; not so robust, elastic; practical enough in his own field; faithful, a judge of men. There is no such general critic of men and things, no such trustworthy and faithful man. More of the divine realized in him than in any. A poetic critic, reserving the unqualified nouns for the gods.

Emerson has special talents unequalled. The divine in man has had no more easy, methodically distinct expression. His personal influence upon young persons greater than any man's. In his world every man would be a poet, Love would reign, Beauty would take place, Man and Nature would harmonize.

The unlimited anxiety, strain, and care of some persons is one very incurable form of disease. Simple arithmetic might have corrected it; for the life of every man has, after all, an epic integrity, and Nature adapts herself to our weaknesses and deficiencies as well as talents.

[1] [As compared with Carlyle.]

No doubt it is indispensable that we should do *our* work between sun and sun, but only a wise man will know what that is. And yet how much work will be left undone, put off to the next day, and yet the system goes on!

We may waive just so much care of ourselves as we devote of care elsewhere.

> I was born upon thy bank, river,
> My blood flows in thy stream,
> And thou meanderest forever
> At the bottom of my dream.

Every man's success is in proportion to his *average* ability. The meadow flowers spring and bloom where the waters annually deposit their slime, not where they reach in some freshet only. We seem to do ourselves little credit in our own eyes for our performance, which all know must ever fall short of our aspiration and promise, which only we can know entirely; as a stick will avail to reach further than it will strike effectually, since its greatest momentum is a little short of its extreme end. But we do not disappoint our neighbors. A man is not his hope nor his despair, nor his past deed.

I am sometimes made aware of a kindness which may have long since been shown, which surely memory cannot retain, which reflects its light long after its heat. I realize, my friend, that there have been times when thy thoughts of me have been of such lofty kindness that they passed over me like the winds of heaven unnoticed, so pure that they presented no object to my eyes, so generous and universal that I did not detect them. Thou hast loved me for what I was not, but for what I aspired to be. We shudder to think of the kindness of our friend which has fallen on us cold, though in some true but tardy hour we have awakened. There has just reached me the kindness of some acts, not to be forgotten, not to be remembered. I wipe off these scores at midnight, at rare intervals, in moments of insight and gratitude.

By a well-directed silence I have sometimes seen threatening and troublesome people routed. You sit musing as if you were in broad nature again. They cannot stand it. Their position becomes more and more uncomfortable every moment. So much humanity over against one without any disguise—not even the disguise of speech! They cannot stand it nor sit against it.

Scholars have for the most part a diseased way of looking at the world. They mean by it a few cities and unfortunate assemblies of men and women, who might all be concealed in the grass of the prairies. They describe this world as old or new, healthy or diseased, according to the state of their libraries—a little dust more or less on their shelves. When I go abroad from under this shingle or slate roof, I find several things which they have not considered. Their conclusions seem imperfect.

It has not been my design to live cheaply, but only to live as I could, not devoting much time to getting a living. I made the most of what means were already got.

I just looked up at a fine twinkling star and thought that a voyager[1] whom I know, now many days' sail from this coast, might possibly be looking up at that same star with me.   The stars are the apexes of what triangles!

Almost any man knows how to earn money, but not one in a million knows how to spend it. If he had known so much as this, he would never have earned it.

---

1 [Ralph Waldo Emerson, whose second voyage to England began on October 5, 1847. Thoreau used the stars-and-triangles metaphor in several other places, first of all on the back of an envelope amidst notes jotted down in the surveying field.]

1850-51

Little remains, apparently, of Thoreau's journals for the years 1848 and 1849, perhaps because they were largely absorbed into his two books. Some of the undated entries in the present chapter may have been written in those years.

After returning from Walden Pond in the autumn of 1847, Thoreau lived for a year in the home of Emerson, who was travelling in Europe. He then joined his own family in the "yellow house reformed" on Main Street, later owned by Louisa May Alcott, where he lived for the rest of his life.

Thoreau's dominant mood at this time appears to have been a keen delight in the freedom offered him by the open country about Concord and secured by his own drastic solution of the economic problem. Over and over again he tries to express his gratitude for the "flood of life" within and without him. Again and again he gives himself up to the sheer joy of human existence on the simplest terms. "Ecstatic moments," recorded in passages of rhythmic beauty like those concerning his walks by moonlight, are more frequent now than at earlier or later periods. The soundless ethereal music he had heard in his boyhood and youth comes back to him. He discovers in the newly strung telegraph wire his favorite musical instrument. At about this time, though not in the journals, he writes one of his most memorable sentences: "If the day and the night are such that you greet them with joy, and life emits a fragrance like flowers and sweet-scented herbs, is more elastic, more starry, more immortal—that is your success."

Undated, [1850?]

The Hindoos are more serenely and thoughtfully religious than the Hebrews. They have perhaps a purer, more independent and impersonal knowledge of God. Their religious books describe the first inquisitive and contemplative access to God; the Hebrew bible a conscientious return, a grosser and more personal repentance. Repentance is not a free and fair highway to God. A wise man will dispense with repentance. It is shocking and passionate. God prefers that you approach him thoughtful, not penitent, though you are the chief of sinners. It is only by forgetting yourself that you draw near to him.

I do not prefer one religion or philosophy to another. I have no sympathy with the bigotry and ignorance which make transient and partial and puerile distinctions between one man's faith or form of faith and another's—as Christian and heathen. I pray to be delivered from narrowness, partiality, exaggeration, bigotry. To the philosopher all sects, all nations, are alike. I like Brahma, Hari,[1] Buddha, the Great Spirit, as well as God.

I heard a splashing in the shallow and muddy water and stood awhile to observe the cause of it. Again and again I heard and saw the commotion, but could not guess the cause of it—what kind of life had its residence in that insignificant pool. We sat down on the hillside. Ere long a muskrat came swimming by as if attracted by the same disturbance, and then another and another, till three had passed, and I began to suspect that they were at the bottom of it. Still ever and anon I observed the same commotion in the waters over the same spot, and at length I observed the snout of some creature slyly raised above the surface after each commotion, as if to see if it were observed by foes, and then but a few rods distant I saw another snout above the water and began to divine the cause of the disturbance. Putting off my shoes and stockings, I crept stealthily down the hill and waded out slowly and noiselessly about a rod from the firm land, keeping behind the tussocks, till I stood behind the tussock near which I had observed the splashing. Then, suddenly stooping over it, I saw through the shallow but muddy water that there was a mud turtle there, and thrusting in my hand at once caught him by the claw, and, quicker than I can tell it, heaved him high and dry ashore; and there came out with him a large pout just dead and partly devoured, which he held in his jaws. It was the pout in his flurry and the turtle in his struggles to hold him fast which had created the commotion. There he had lain, probably buried in the mud at the bottom up to his eyes, till the pout came sailing over, and then this musky lagune[2] had put forth in the direction of his ventral fins, expanding suddenly under the influence of a more than vernal heat—there are sermons in stones, aye and mud turtles at the bottoms of the pools—in the direction of his ventral fins, his tender white belly, where he kept no eye; and the minister[3] squeaked his last. Oh, what an eye was there, my countrymen! buried in mud up to the lids, meditating on what? sleepless at the bottom of the pool, at the top of the bottom, directed heavenward, in no danger from motes. Pouts expect their foes not from below. Suddenly a mud volcano swallowed him up, seized his midriff; he fell into those relentless jaws from which there is no escape, which relax not their hold even in death. There the pout might calculate on remaining until nine days after the head was cut off. Sculled through Heywood's shallow meadow, not

---

[1] [A name connected with the worship of Vishnu.]
[2] [Lagoon.]
[3] [A popular name for the horned pout or bull-head.]

thinking of foes, looking through the water up into the sky. . . . I had no idea that there was so much going on in Heywood's meadow.

There is a sweet wild world which lies along the strain of the wood thrush—the rich intervals which border the stream of its song—more thoroughly genial to my nature than any other.

June

The life in us is like the water in the river; it may rise this year higher than ever it was known to before and flood the uplands—even this may be the eventful year—and drown out all our muskrats.

There [are] as many strata at different levels of life as there are leaves in a book. Most men probably have lived in two or three. When on the higher levels we can remember the lower levels, but when on the lower we cannot remember the higher.

My imagination, my love and reverence and admiration, my sense of the miraculous, is not so excited by any event as by the remembrance of my youth. Men talk about Bible miracles because there is no miracle in their lives. Cease to gnaw that crust. There is ripe fruit over your head.

June 20

And then for my afternoon walks I have a garden, larger than any artificial garden that I have read of and far more attractive to me—mile after mile of embowered walks, such as no nobleman's grounds can boast, with animals running free and wild therein as from the first—varied with land and water prospect, and, above all, so retired that it is extremely rare that I meet a single wanderer in its mazes.

Undated

I find the actual to be far less real to me than the imagined. Why this singular prominence and importance is given to the former, I do not know. In proportion as that which possesses my thoughts is removed from the actual, it impresses me.

I am sure that my acquaintances mistake me. I am not the man they take me for. On a little nearer view they would find me out. They ask my advice on high matters, but they do not even know how poorly on't I am for hats and shoes. I have hardly a shift. Just as shabby as I am in my outward apparel—aye, and more lamentably shabby, for nakedness is not so bad a condition after all—am I in my inward apparel. If I should turn myself inside out, my rags and meanness would appear. I am something to him that made me, undoubtedly, but not much to any other that he has made. All I can say is that I live and breathe and have my thoughts.

What is peculiar in the life of a man consists not in his obedience, but his opposition, to his instincts. In one direction or another he strives to live a supernatural life.

As to conforming outwardly, and living your own life inwardly, I have not a very high opinion of that course.

I can easily walk ten, fifteen, twenty, any number of miles, commencing at my own door, without going by any house, without crossing a road except where the fox and the mink do. Concord is the oldest inland town in New England,[1] perhaps in the States, and the walker is peculiarly favored here. There are square miles in my vicinity which have no inhabitant. First along by the river, and then the brook, and then the meadow and the woodside. Such solitude! From a hundred hills I can see civilization and abodes of man afar. These farmers and their works are scarcely more obvious than woodchucks.

Sept.

I saw a delicate flower had grown up two feet high
Between the horses' path and the wheel-track,
Which Dakin's and Maynard's wagons had
Passed over many a time.
An inch more to right or left had sealed its fate,
Or an inch higher. And yet it lived and flourished
As much as if it had a thousand acres
Of untrodden space around it, and never
Knew the danger it incurred.
It did not borrow trouble nor invite an
Evil fate by apprehending it.
For though the distant market-wagon
Every other day inevitably rolled
This way, it just as inevitably rolled
In those ruts. And the same

[1] [Wethersfield and Windsor are older.]

Charioteer who steered the flower
Upward guided the horse and cart aside from it.
There were other flowers which you would say
Incurred less danger, grew more out of the way,
Which no cart rattled near, no walker daily passed,
But at length one rambling deviously—
For no rut restrained—plucked them,
And then it appeared that they stood
Directly in his way, though he had come
From farther than the market-wagon.

A neat herd of cows approached, of unusually fair proportions and smooth, clean skins, evidently petted by their owner, who must have carefully selected them. One more confiding heifer, the fairest of the herd, did by degrees approach as if to take some morsel from our hands, while our hearts leaped to our mouths with expectation and delight. She by degrees drew near with her fair limbs progressive, making pretense of browsing; nearer and nearer, till there was wafted toward us the bovine fragrance—cream of all the dairies that ever were or will be—and then she raised her gentle muzzle toward us, and snuffed an honest recognition within hand's reach. I saw 'twas possible for his herd to inspire with love the herdsman. She was as delicately featured as a hind. Her hide was mingled white and fawn-color, and on her muzzle's tip there was a white spot not bigger than a daisy, and on her side toward me the map of Asia plain to see.

Farewell, dear heifer! Though thou forgettest me, my prayer to heaven shall be that thou may'st not forget thyself. There was a whole bucolic in her snuff. I saw her name was Sumach. And by the kindred spots I knew her mother, more sedate and matronly, with full-grown bag; and on her sides was Asia, great and small, the plains of Tartary, even to the pole, while on her daughter it was Asia Minor. She not disposed to wanton with the herdsman.

And as I walked, she followed me, and took an apple from my hand, and seemed to care more for the hand than apple. So innocent a face as I have rarely seen on any creature, and I have looked in face of many heifers. And as she took the apple from my hand, I caught the apple of her eye. She smelled as sweet as the clethra[1] blossom. There was no sinister expression. And for horns, though she had them, they were so well disposed in the right place, bent neither up nor down, I do not now remember she had any. No horn was held toward me.

---

[1] [The white alder or sweet pepper-bush.]

Sept. 11

Autumnal mornings, when the feet of countless sparrows are heard like rain-drops on the roof by the boy who sleeps in the garret.

Villages with a single long street lined with trees, so straight and wide that you can see a chicken run across it a mile off.

Oct.

Cultivate poverty like sage, like a garden herb. Do not trouble yourself to get new things, whether clothes or friends. That is dissipation. Turn the old; return to them. Things do not change; we change. If I were confined to a corner in a garret all my days, like a spider, the world would be just as large to me while I had my thoughts.

Oct. 31

I am wont to think that I could spend my days contentedly in any retired country house that I see; for I see it to advantage now and without incumbrance; I have not yet imported my humdrum thoughts, my prosaic habits, into it to mar the landscape. What is this beauty in the landscape but a certain fertility in me? I look in vain to see it realized but in my own life.

Undated

My dear, my dewy sister,[1] let thy rain descend on me. I not only love thee, but I love the best of thee; that is to love thee rarely. I do not love thee every day. Commonly I love those who are less than thou. I love thee only on great days. Thy dewy words feed me like the manna of the morning. I am as much thy sister as thy brother. Thou art as much my brother as my sister. It is a portion of thee and a portion of me which are of kin. Thou dost not have to woo me. I do not have to woo thee. O my sister! O Diana, thy tracks are on the eastern hills. Thou surely passedst that way. I, the hunter, saw them in the morning dew. My eyes are the hounds that pursue thee. Ah, my friend, what if I do not answer thee? I hear thee. Thou canst speak; I cannot. I hear and forget to answer. I am occupied with hearing. I awoke and thought of thee; thou wast present to my mind. How camest thou there? Was I not present to thee likewise?

What does education often do? It makes a straight-cut ditch of a free, meandering brook.

[1] [The person here addressed cannot be certainly identified.]

Nov. 11

Some circumstantial evidence is very strong, as when you find a trout in the milk.

A people who would begin by burning the fences and let the forest stand! I saw the fences half consumed, their ends lost in the middle of the prairie, and some worldly miser with a surveyor looking after his bounds, while heaven had taken place around him, and he did not see the angels around, but was looking for an old post-hole in the midst of paradise. I looked again and saw him standing in the middle of a boggy Stygian fen, surrounded by devils, and he had found his bounds without a doubt, three little stones where a stake had been driven, and, looking nearer, I saw that the Prince of Darkness was his surveyor.[1]

Nov. 16

In literature it is only the wild that attracts us. Dullness is only another name for tameness. It is the untamed, uncivilized, free, and wild thinking in Hamlet, in the Iliad, and in all the scriptures and mythologies that delights us—not learned in the schools, not refined and polished by art. A truly good book is something as wildly natural and primitive, mysterious and marvellous, ambrosial and fertile, as a fungus or a lichen.

My Journal should be the record of my love. I would write in it only of the things I love, my affection for any aspect of the world, what I love to think of. I have no more distinctness or pointedness in my yearnings than an expanding bud, which does indeed point to flower and fruit, to summer and autumn, but is aware of the warm sun and spring influence only. I feel ripe for something, yet do nothing, can't discover what that thing is. I feel fertile merely. It is seedtime with me. I have lain fallow long enough.

Notwithstanding a sense of unworthiness which possesses me, not without reason, notwithstanding that I regard myself as a good deal of a scamp, yet for the most part the spirit of the universe is unaccountably kind to me, and I enjoy perhaps an unusual share of happiness.

Dec. 24

Our thoughts are with those among the dead into whose sphere we are rising, or who are now rising into our own. Others we inevitably forget, though they be brothers and sisters. Thus the departed may be

[1] [At this time Thoreau was himself working as a surveyor.]

nearer to us than when they were present. At death our friends and relations either draw nearer to us and are found out, or depart further from us and are forgotten. Friends are as often brought nearer together as separated by death.

Jan. 7, 1851

The knowledge of an unlearned man is living and luxuriant like a forest, but covered with mosses and lichens and for the most part inaccessible and going to waste; the knowledge of the man of science is like timber collected in yards for public works, which still supports a green sprout here and there, but even this is liable to dry rot.

Jan. 10

Perhaps I am more than usually jealous of my freedom. I feel that my connections with and obligations to society are at present very slight and transient. Those slight labors which afford me a livelihood, and by which I am serviceable to my contemporaries, are as yet a pleasure to me, and I am not often reminded that they are a necessity. So far I am successful, and only he is successful in his business who makes that pursuit which affords him the highest pleasure sustain him. But I foresee that if my wants should be much increased the labor required to supply them would become a drudgery. If I should sell both my forenoons and afternoons to society, neglecting my peculiar calling, there would be nothing left worth living for. I trust that I shall never thus sell my birthright for a mess of pottage.

Undated·

English literature from the days of the minstrels to the Lake Poets, Chaucer and Spenser and Shakspeare and Milton included, breathes no quite fresh and, in this sense, wild strain. It is an essentially tame and civilized literature, reflecting Greece and Rome. Her wilderness is a greenwood, her wild man a Robin Hood. There is plenty of genial love of nature in her poets, but not so much of nature herself. Her chronicles inform us when her wild animals, but not when the wild man in her, became extinct. There was need of America.

Feb.

My desire for knowledge is intermittent; but my desire to commune with the spirit of the universe, to be intoxicated with the fumes, call it, of that divine nectar, to bear my head through atmospheres and over heights unknown to my feet, is perennial and constant.

Feb. 13

As for antiquities, one of our old deserted country roads, marked only by the parallel fences and cellar-hole with its bricks where the last inhabitant died, the victim of intemperance, fifty years ago, with its bare and exhausted fields stretching around, suggests to me an antiquity greater and more remote from the America of the news-papers than the tombs of Etruria.

Feb. 14

We shall see but little way if we require to understand what we see. How few things can a man measure with the tape of his understanding! How many greater things might he be seeing in the meanwhile!

Feb. 18

There is little or nothing to be remembered written on the subject of getting an honest living. Neither the New Testament nor Poor Richard speaks to our condition. I cannot think of a single page which entertains, much less answers, the questions which I put to myself on this subject. How to make the getting our living poetic! for if it is not poetic, it is not life but death that we get. Is it that men are too dis-gusted with their experience to speak of it? or that commonly they do not question the common modes? The most practically important of all questions, it seems to me, is how shall I get my living, and yet I find little or nothing said to the purpose in any book. Those who are living on the interest of money inherited, or dishonestly, i.e. by false methods, acquired, are of course incompetent to answer it. I consider that society with all its arts, has done nothing for us in this respect. One would think, from looking at literature, that this question had never disturbed a solitary individual's musings. Cold and hunger seem more friendly to my nature than those methods which men have adopted and advise to ward them off. If it were not that I desire to do something here—accomplish some work—I should certainly prefer to suffer and die rather than be at the pains to get a living by the modes men propose.

Undated

The lecturer is wont to describe the Nineteenth Century, the American [of] the last generation, in an off-hand and triumphant strain, wafting him to paradise, spreading his fame by steam and telegraph, recounting the number of wooden stopples he has whittled. But who does not perceive that this is not a sincere or pertinent account of any man's or nation's life? It is the hip-hip-hurrah and mutual-admiration-society style. Cars go by, and we know their substance as well as their shadow. They stop and we get into them. But those sublime thoughts passing on high do not stop, and we never get into them. Their conductor is not like one of us.

I feel that the man who, in his conversation with me about the life of man in New England, lays much stress on railroads, telegraphs, and such enterprises does not go below the surface of things. He treats the shallow and transitory as if it were profound and enduring. In one of the mind's avatars, in the interval between sleeping and waking, aye, even in one of the interstices of a Hindoo dynasty, perchance, such things as the Nineteenth Century, with all its improvements, may come and go again. Nothing makes a deep and lasting impression but what is weighty.

March 30

The man for whom law exists—the man of forms, the conservative— is a tame man.

May 1

Nations! What are nations? Tartars! and Huns! and Chinamen! Like insects they swarm. The historian strives in vain to make them memorable. It is for want of a man that there are so many men. It is individuals that populate the world.

May 6

If a low use is to be served, one man will do nearly or quite as well as another; if a high one, individual excellence is to be regarded. Any man can stop a hole to keep the wind away, but no other man can serve that use which the author of this illustration did.[1]

He approaches the study of mankind with great advantages who is accustomed to the study of nature.

May 24

Our most glorious experiences are a kind of regret. Our regret is so sublime that we may mistake it for triumph. It is the painful,

---

[1] [See Shakespeare's *Hamlet*, Act V, Scene 1, line 235.]

plaintively sad surprise of our Genius remembering our past lives and contemplating what is possible.

June 7

It is a certain faeryland where we live. You may walk out in any direction over the earth's surface, lifting your horizon, and everywhere your path, climbing the convexity of the globe, leads you between heaven and earth, not away from the light of the sun and stars and the habitations of men. I wonder that I ever get five miles on my way, the walk is so crowded with events and phenomena. How many questions there are which I have not put to the inhabitants!

June 12

Listen to music religiously, as if it were the last strain you might hear.

June 13

We do not commonly live our life out and full; we do not fill all our pores with our blood; we do not inspire and expire fully and entirely enough, so that the wave, the comber, of each inspiration shall break upon our extremest shores, rolling till it meets the sand which bounds us, and the sound of the surf come back to us. Might not a bellows assist us to breathe? That our breathing should create a wind in a calm day! We live but a fraction of our life. Why do we not let on the flood, raise the gates, and set all our wheels in motion? He that hath ears to hear, let him hear.

June 22

To be calm, to be serene! There is the calmness of the lake when there is not a breath of wind; there is the calmness of a stagnant ditch. So is it with us. Sometimes we are clarified and calmed healthily, as we never were before in our lives, not by an opiate, but by some unconscious obedience to the all-just laws, so that we become like a still lake of purest crystal and without an effort our depths are revealed to ourselves. All the world goes by us and is reflected in our deeps. Such clarity! obtained by such pure means! by simple living, by honesty of purpose. We live and rejoice. I awoke into a music which no one about me heard. Whom shall I thank for it? The luxury of wisdom! the luxury of virtue! Are there any intemperate in these things? I feel my Maker blessing me. To the sane man the world is a musical instrument. The very touch affords an exquisite pleasure.

June 29

At a distance in the meadow I hear still, at long intervals, the hurried commencement of the bobolink's strain, the bird just dashing into song, which is as suddenly checked, as it were, by the warder of the seasons, and the strain is left incomplete forever. Like human beings they are inspired to sing only for a short season.

July 2

A traveller! I love his title. A traveller is to be reverenced as such. His profession is the best symbol of our life. Going from —— toward ——; it is the history of every one of us. I am interested in those that travel in the night.

July 6

There is some advantage in being the humblest, cheapest, least dignified man in the village, so that the very stable boys shall damn you. Methinks I enjoy that advantage to an unusual extent. There is many a coarsely well-meaning fellow, who knows only the skin of me, who addresses me familiarly by my Christian name. I get the whole good of him and lose nothing myself. There is "Sam," the jailer[1]— whom I never call Sam, however—who exclaimed last evening: "Thoreau, are you going up the street pretty soon? Well, just take a couple of these handbills along and drop one in at Hoar's piazza and one at Holbrook's, and I'll do as much for you another time." I am not above being used, aye abused, sometimes.

July 7

The moon is now more than half full. When I come through the village at 10 o'clock this cold night, cold as in May, the heavy shadows of the elms covering the ground with their rich tracery impress me as if men had got so much more than they had bargained for, not only trees to stand in the air, but to checker the ground with their shadows. At night they lie along the earth. They tower, they arch, they droop over the streets like chandeliers of darkness.

I can express adequately only the thought which I *love* to express. All the faculties in repose but the one you are using, the whole energy concentrated in that. Be ever so little distracted, your thoughts so little

1 [Samuel Staples.]

confused, your engagements so few, your attention so free, your existence so mundane, that in all places and in all hours you can hear the sound of crickets in those seasons when they are to be heard. It is a mark of serenity and health of mind when a person hears this sound much.

July 10

I am always struck by the centrality of the observer's position. He always stands fronting the middle of the arch, and does not suspect at first that a thousand observers on a thousand hills behold the sunset sky from equally favorable positions.

July 12, 8 P.M.

Now at least the moon is full, and I walk alone, which is best by night, if not by day always. Your companion must sympathize with the present mood. The conversation must be located where the walkers are, and vary exactly with the scene and events and the contour of the ground. Farewell to those who will talk of nature unnaturally, whose presence is an interruption. . . .

I start a sparrow from her three eggs in the grass, where she had settled for the night. The earliest corn is beginning to show its tassels now, and I scent it as I walk—its peculiar dry scent. (This afternoon I gathered ripe blackberries, and felt as if the autumn had commenced.) Now perchance many sounds and sights only remind me that they once said something to me, and are so by association interesting. I go forth to be reminded of a previous state of existence, if perchance any memento of it is to be met with hereabouts. I have no doubt that Nature preserves her integrity. Nature is in as rude health as when Homer sang. We may at last by our sympathies be well. I see a skunk on Bear Garden Hill stealing noiselessly away from me, while the moon shines over the pitch pines, which send long shadows down the hill. Now, looking back, I see it shining on the south side of farm-houses and barns with a weird light, for I pass here half an hour later than last night. I smell the huckleberry bushes. I hear a human voice— some laborer singing after his day's toil—which I do not often hear. Loud it must be, for it is far away. Methinks I should know it for a white man's voice. Some strains have the melody of an instrument. Now I hear the sound of a bugle in the "Corner,"[1] reminding me of poetic wars; a few flourishes and the bugler has gone to rest. At the foot of the Cliff hill I hear the sound of the clock striking nine, as

---

[1] [Nine Acre Corner, near Concord's southern boundary.]

distinctly as within a quarter of a mile usually, though there is no wind. The moonlight is more perfect than last night; hardly a cloud in the sky—only a few fleecy ones. There is more serenity and more light. I hear that sort of throttled or chuckling note as of a bird flying high, now from this side, then from that. Methinks when I turn my head I see Wachusett from the side of the hill. I smell the butter-and-eggs as I walk. I am startled by the rapid transit of some wild animal across my path, a rabbit or a fox—or you hardly know if it be not a bird. Looking down from the cliffs, the leaves of the tree-tops shine more than ever by day. Here and there a lightning-bug shows his greenish light over the tops of the trees.

As I return through the orchard, a foolish robin bursts away from his perch unnaturally, with the habits of man. The air is remarkably still and unobjectionable on the hilltop, and the whole world below is covered as with a gossamer blanket of moonlight. It is just about as yellow as a blanket. It is a great dimly burnished shield with darker blotches on its surface. You have lost some light, it is true, but you have got this simple and magnificent stillness, brooding like genius.

July 16, Wednesday

Methinks my present experience is nothing; my past experience is all in all. I think that no experience which I have today comes up to, or is comparable with, the experiences of my boyhood. And not only this is true, but as far back as I can remember I have unconsciously referred to the experiences of a previous state of existence, "For life is a forgetting," etc. Formerly, methought, nature developed as I developed, and grew up with me. My life was ecstasy. In youth, before I lost any of my senses, I can remember that I was all alive, and inhabited my body with inexpressible satisfaction; both its weariness and its refreshment were sweet to me. This earth was the most glorious instrument, and I was audience to its strains. To have such sweet impressions made on us, such ecstasies begotten of the breezes! I can remember how I was astonished. I said to myself—I said to others— "There comes into my mind such an indescribable, infinite, all-absorbing, divine, heavenly pleasure, a sense of elevation and expansion, and [I] have had nought to do with it. I perceive that I am dealt with by superior powers. This is a pleasure, a joy, an existence which I have not procured myself. I speak as a witness on the stand, and tell what I have perceived." The morning and the evening were sweet to me, and I led a life aloof from society of men. I wondered if a mortal had ever known what I knew. I looked in books for some recognition of a kindred experience, but, strange to say, I found none. Indeed, I was slow to discover that other men had had this experience, for it had been possible to read books and to associate with men on other grounds. The maker of me was improving me. When I detected this interference I was profoundly moved. For years I marched as to a music in comparison with which the military music of the streets is noise and discord. I was daily intoxicated, and yet no man could call me intemperate. With all your science can you tell how it is, and whence it is, that light comes into the soul?

July 19

Here I am thirty-four years old,[1] and yet my life is almost wholly unexpanded. How much is in the germ! There is such an interval between my ideal and the actual in many instances that I may say I am unborn. There is the instinct for society, but no society. Life is not long enough for one success. Within another thirty-four years that miracle can hardly take place. Methinks my seasons revolve more slowly than those of nature; I am differently timed. I am contented. This rapid revolution of nature, even of nature in me, why should it hurry me? Let a man step to the music which he hears, however measured. Is it important that I should mature as soon as an apple tree? aye, as soon as an oak? May not my life in nature, in proportion as it is supernatural, be only the spring and infantile portion of my spirit's life? Shall I turn my spring to summer? May I not sacrifice a hasty and petty completeness here to entireness there? If my curve is large, why bend it to a smaller circle? My spirit's unfolding observes not the pace of nature. The society which I was made for is not here. Shall I, then, substitute for the anticipation of that this poor reality? I would [rather] have the unmixed expectation of that than this reality. If life is a waiting, so be it. I will not be shipwrecked on a vain reality.

July 20

The clap which waked me last night was as if some one was moving lumber in an upper apartment, some vast hollow hall, tumbling it down and dragging it over the floor; and ever and anon the lightning filled the damp air with light, like some vast glow-worm in the fields of ether opening its wings.[2]

---

1 [His birthday was July 12. He had eleven years yet to live.]

2 [The beauty of this image is scarcely lessened by Thoreau's confusion of the wingless glowworm with the firefly.]

July 21, 8 A.M.

Now I yearn for one of those old, meandering, dry, uninhabited roads, which lead away from towns, which lead us away from temptation, which conduct to the outside of earth, over its uppermost crust; where you may forget in what country you are travelling; where no farmer can complain that you are treading down his grass, no gentleman who has recently constructed a seat in the country that you are trespassing; on which you can go off at half-cock and wave adieu to the village; along which you may travel like a pilgrim, going nowhither; where travellers are not too often to be met; where my spirit is free; where the walls and fences are not cared for; where your head is more in heaven than your feet are on earth; which have long reaches where you can see the approaching traveller half a mile off and be prepared for him; not so luxuriant a soil as to attract men; some root and stump fences which do not need attention; where travellers have no occasion to stop, but pass along and leave you to your thoughts; where it makes no odds which way you face, whether you are going or coming, whether it is morning or evening, mid-noon or midnight; where earth is cheap enough by being public; where you can walk and think with least obstruction, there being nothing to measure progress by; where you can pace when your breast is full, and cherish your moodiness; where you are not in false relations with men, are not dining nor conversing with them; by which you may go to the uttermost parts of the earth. It is wide enough, wide as the thoughts it allows to visit you. Sometimes it is some particular half-dozen rods which I wish to find myself pacing over, as where certain airs blow; then my life will come to me, methinks; like a hunter I walk in wait for it. When I am against this bare promontory of a huckleberry hill, then forsooth my thoughts will expand. Is it some influence, as a vapor which exhales from the ground, or something in the gales which blow there, or in all things there brought together agreeably to my spirit? The walls must not be too high, imprisoning me, but low, with numerous gaps. The trees must not be too numerous, nor the hills too near, bounding the view, nor the soil too rich, attracting the attention to the earth. It must simply be the way and the life—a way that was never known to be repaired, nor to need repair, within the memory of the oldest inhabitant. I cannot walk habitually in those ways that are liable to be mended; for sure it was the devil only that wore them. Never by the heel of thinkers (of thought) were they worn; the zephyrs could repair that damage. The saunterer wears out no road, even though he travel on it, and therefore should pay no highway, or rather *low* way, tax. He may be taxed to construct a higher way than men travel. A way which no geese defile, nor hiss along it, but only sometimes their wild brethren fly far overhead; which the kingbird and the swallow twitter over, and the song sparrow sings on its rails; where the small red butterfly is at home on the yarrow, and no boys threaten it with imprisoning hat. There I can walk and stalk and pace and plod. Which nobody but Jonas Potter travels beside me; where no cow but his is tempted to linger for the herbage by its side; where the guide-board is fallen, and now the hand points to heaven significantly—to a Sudbury and Marlborough in the skies. That's a road I can travel, that the particular Sudbury I am bound for, six miles an hour, or two, as you please; and few there be that enter thereon. There I can walk, and recover the lost child that I am without any ringing of a bell.

There is no glory so bright but the veil of business can hide it effectually. With most men life is postponed to some trivial business, and so therefore is heaven. Men think foolishly they may abuse and misspend life as they please and when they get to heaven turn over a new leaf.

Men are very generally spoiled by being so civil and well-disposed. You can have no profitable conversation with them, they are so conciliatory, determined to agree with you. They exhibit such long-suffering and kindness in a short interview. I would meet with some provoking strangeness, so that we may be guest and host and refresh one another. It is possible for a man wholly to disappear and be merged in his manners. The thousand and one gentlemen whom I meet, I meet despairingly, and but to part from them, for I am not cheered by the hope of any rudeness from them. A cross man, a coarse man, an eccentric man, a silent, a man who does not drill well—of him there is some hope. Your gentlemen, they are all alike.

There is always a kind of fine æolian harp music to be heard in the air. I hear now, as it were, the mellow sound of distant horns in the hollow mansions of the upper air, a sound to make all men divinely insane that hear it, far away overhead, subsiding into my ear. To ears that are expanded what a harp this world is! The occupied ear thinks that beyond the cricket no sound can be heard, but there is an immortal melody that may be heard morning, noon, and night, by ears that can attend, and from time to time this man or that hears it, having ears that were made for music. To hear this the hardhack and the meadow-sweet *aspire*. They are thus beautifully painted, because they are tinged in the lower stratum of that melody.

July 23

You must walk so gently as to hear the finest sounds, the faculties being in repose. Your mind must not perspire. True, out of doors my thought is commonly drowned, as it were, and shrunken, pressed down by stupendous piles of light ethereal influences, for the pressure of the atmosphere is still fifteen pounds to a square inch. I can do little more than preserve the equilibrium and resist the pressure of the atmosphere. I can only nod like the ryeheads in the breeze. I expand more surely in my chamber, as far as expression goes, as if that pressure were taken off; but here outdoors is the place to store up influences.

But this habit of close observation—in Humboldt, Darwin, and others. Is it to be kept up long, this science? Do not tread on the heels of your experience. Be impressed without making a minute of it. Poetry puts an interval between the impression and the expression—waits till the seed germinates naturally.

Aug. 5

I hear now from Bear Garden Hill—I rarely walk by moonlight without hearing—the sound of a flute, or a horn, or a human voice. It is a performer I never see by day; should not recognize him if pointed out; but you may hear his performance in every horizon. He plays but one strain and goes to bed early, but I know by the character of that single strain that he is deeply dissatisfied with the manner in which he spends his day. He is a slave who is purchasing his freedom. He is Apollo watching the flocks of Admetus on every hill, and this strain he plays every evening to remind him of his heavenly descent. It is all that saves him—his one redeeming trait. It is a reminiscence; he loves to remember his youth. He is sprung of a noble family. He is highly related, I have no doubt; was tenderly nurtured in his infancy, poor hind as he is. That noble strain he utters, instead of any jewel on his finger, or precious locket fastened to his breast, or purple garments that came with him. The elements recognize him, and echo his strain. All the dogs know him their master, though lords and ladies, rich men and learned, know him not. He is the son of a rich man, of a famous man who served his country well. He has heard his sire's stories. I thought of the time when he would discover his parentage, obtain his inheritance, and sing a strain suited to the morning hour. He cherishes hopes. I never see the man by day who plays that clarinet.

May I love and revere myself above all the gods that men have ever invented. May I never let the vestal fire go out in my recesses.

This coolness comes to condense the dews and clear the atmosphere. The stillness seems more deep and significant. Each sound seems to come from out a greater thoughtfulness in nature, as if nature had acquired some character and mind. The cricket, the gurgling stream, the rushing wind amid the trees, all speak to me soberly yet encouragingly of the steady onward progress of the universe. My heart leaps into my mouth at the sound of the wind in the woods. I, whose life was but yesterday so desultory and shallow, suddenly recover my spirits, my spirituality, through my hearing. I see a goldfinch go twittering through the still, louring day, and am reminded of the peeping flocks which will soon herald the thoughtful season. Ah! if I could so live that there should be no desultory moment in all my life! that in the trivial season, when small fruits are ripe, my fruits might be ripe also! that I could match nature always with my moods! that in each season when some part of nature especially flourishes, then a corresponding part of me may not fail to flourish! Ah, I would walk, I would sit and sleep, with natural piety! What if I could pray aloud or to myself as I went along by the brook-sides a cheerful prayer like the birds! For joy I could embrace the earth; I shall delight to be buried in it. And then to think of those I love among men, who will know that I love them though I tell them not! I sometimes feel as if I were rewarded merely for expecting better hours. I did not despair of worthier moods, and now I have occasion to be grateful for the flood of life that is flowing over me. I am not so poor: I can smell the ripening apples; the very rills are deep; the autumnal flowers, the *Trichostema dichotomum*[1]— not only its bright blue flower above the sand, but its strong wormwood scent which belongs to the season—feed my spirit, endear the earth to me, make me value myself and rejoice; the quivering of pigeons' wings reminds me of the tough fibre of the air which they rend. I thank you, God. I do not deserve anything, I am unworthy of the least regard; and yet I am made to rejoice. I am impure and worthless, and yet the world is gilded for my delight and holidays are prepared for me, and my path is strewn with flowers. But I cannot thank the Giver; I cannot even whisper my thanks to those human friends I have.

---

[1] [Bastard pennyroyal.]

It seems to me that I am more rewarded for my expectations than for anything I do or can do. Ah, I would not tread on a cricket in whose song is such a revelation, so soothing and cheering to my ear! Oh, keep my senses pure! And why should I speak to my friends? for how rarely is it that I am I; and are they, then, they? We will meet, then, far away. The seeds of the summer are getting dry and falling from a thousand nodding heads. If I did not know you through thick and thin, how should I know you at all? Ah, the very brooks seem fuller of reflections than they were! Ah, such provoking sibylline sentences they are! The shallowest is all at once unfathomable. How can that depth be fathomed where a man may see himself reflected? The rill I stopped to drink at I drink in more than I expected. I satisfy and still provoke the thirst of thirsts. Nut Meadow Brook where it crosses the road beyond Jenny Dugan's that was. I do not drink in vain. I mark that brook as if I had swallowed a water snake that would live in my stomach. I have swallowed something worth the while. The day is not what it was before I stooped to drink. Ah, I shall hear from that draught! It is not in vain that I have drunk. I have drunk an arrowhead. It flows from where all fountains rise.

Aug. 19

The way in which men cling to old institutions after the life has departed out of them, and out of themselves, reminds me of those monkeys which cling by their tails—aye, whose tails contract about the limbs, even the dead limbs, of the forest, and they hang suspended beyond the hunter's reach long after they are dead. It is of no use to argue with such men. They have not an apprehensive intellect, but merely, as it were a prehensile tail. . . . The tail itself contracts around the dead limb even after they themselves are dead, and not till sensible corruption takes place do they fall.

I fear that the character of my knowledge is from year to year becoming more distinct and scientific; that, in exchange for views as wide as heaven's cope, I am being narrowed down to the field of the microscope. I see details, not wholes nor the shadow of the whole. I count some parts, and say, "I know."

Aug. 21

What a faculty must that be which can paint the most barren landscape and humblest life in glorious colors! It is pure and invigorated senses reacting on a sound and strong imagination. Is not that the poet's case? The intellect of most men is barren. They neither fertilize nor are fertilized. It is the marriage of the soul with Nature that makes the intellect fruitful, that gives birth to imagination. When we were dead and dry as the highway, some sense which has been healthily fed will put us in relation with Nature, in sympathy with her; some grains of fertilizing pollen, floating in the air, fall on us, and suddenly the sky is all one rainbow, is full of music and fragrance and flavor. The man of intellect only, the prosaic man, is a barren, staminiferous flower; the poet is a fertile and perfect flower. Men are such confirmed arithmeticians and slaves of business that I cannot easily find a blank-book that has not a red line or a blue one for the dollars and cents, or some such purpose.

There is some advantage, intellectually and spiritually, in taking wide views with the bodily eye and not pursuing an occupation which holds the body prone. There is some advantage, perhaps, in attending to the general features of the landscape over studying the particular plants and animals which inhabit it. A man may walk abroad and no more see the sky than if he walked under a shed. The poet is more in the air than the naturalist, though they may walk side by side. Granted that you are out-of-doors; but what if the outer door *is* open, if the inner door is shut! You must walk sometimes perfectly free, not prying nor inquisitive, not bent upon seeing things. Throw away a whole day for a single expansion, a single inspiration of air.

Aug. 22

It is the fault of some excellent writers—De Quincey's first impressions on seeing London suggest it to me—that they express themselves with too great fullness and detail. They give the most faithful, natural, and lifelike account of their sensations, mental and physical, but they lack moderation and sententiousness. They do not affect us by an in-effectual earnestness and a reserve of meaning, like a stutterer; they say all they mean. Their sentences are not concentrated and nutty. Sentences which suggest far more than they say, which have an atmosphere about them, which do not merely report an old, but make a new, impression; sentences which suggest as many things and are as durable as a Roman aqueduct; to frame these, that is the *art* of writing. Sentences which are expensive, towards which so many volumes, so much life, went; which lie like boulders on the page, up and down or across; which contain the seed of other sentences, not mere repetition, but creation; which a man might sell his grounds and castles to build. If De

Quincey had suggested each of his pages in a sentence and passed on, it would have been far more excellent writing. His style is nowhere kinked and knotted up into something hard and significant, which you could swallow like a diamond, without digesting.

Aug. 23

I sometimes reproach myself because I do not find anything attractive in certain mere trivial employments of men—that I skip men so commonly, and their affairs—the professions and the trades—do not elevate them at least in my thought and get some material for poetry out of them directly. I will not avoid, then, to go by where these men are repairing the stone bridge—see if I cannot see poetry in that, if that will not yield me a reflection. It is narrow to be confined to woods and fields and grand aspects of nature only. The greatest and wisest will still be related to men. Why not see men standing in the sun and casting a shadow, even as trees? May not some light be reflected from them as from the stems of trees? I will try to enjoy them as animals, at least. They are perhaps better animals than men. Do not neglect to speak of men's low life and affairs with sympathy, though you ever so speak as to suggest a contrast between them and the ideal and divine.

I saw a snake by the roadside and touched him with my foot to see if he were alive. He had a toad in his jaws, which he was preparing to swallow with his jaws distended to three times his width, but he relinquished his prey in haste and fled; and I thought, as the toad jumped leisurely away with his slime-covered hind-quarters glistening in the sun, as if I, his deliverer, wished to interrupt his meditations—without a shriek or fainting—I thought what a healthy indifference he manifested. Is not this the broad earth still? he said.

Aug. 28

The poet is a man who lives at last by watching his moods. An old poet comes at last to watch his moods as narrowly as a cat does a mouse.

I omit the unusual—the hurricanes and earthquakes—and describe the common. This has the greatest charm and is the true theme of poetry. You may have the extraordinary for your province, if you will let me have the ordinary. Give me the obscure life, the cottage of the poor and humble, the workdays of the world, the barren fields, the smallest share of all things, but poetic perception. Give me but the eyes to see the things which you possess.

How rich, like what we love to read of South American primitive forests, is the scenery of this river! What luxuriance of weeds, what depth of mud along its sides! These old antehistoric, geologic, antediluvian rocks, which only primitive wading birds, still lingering among us, are worthy to tread. The season which we seem to *live* in anticipation of is arrived. The water, indeed, reflects heaven because my mind does; such is its own serenity, its transparency and stillness.

With what sober joy I stand to let the water drip from me and feel my fresh vigor, who have been bathing in the same tub which the muskrat uses! Such a medicated bath as only nature furnishes. A fish leaps, and the dimple he makes is observed now. How ample and generous was nature! My inheritance is not narrow. Here is no other this evening. Those resorts which I most love and frequent, numerous and vast as they are, are as it were given up to me, as much as if I were an autocrat or owner of the world, and by my edicts excluded men from my territories. Perchance there is some advantage here not enjoyed in older countries. There are said to be two thousand inhabitants in Concord, and yet I find such ample space and verge, even miles of walking every day in which I do not meet nor see a human being, and often not very recent traces of them. So much of man as there is in your mind, there will be in your eye. Methinks that for a great part of the time, as much as it is possible, I walk as one possessing the advantages of human culture, fresh from society of men, but turned loose into the woods, the only man in nature, walking and meditating to a great extent as if man and his customs and institutions were not. The catbird, or the jay, is sure of the whole of your ear now. Each noise is like a stain on pure glass. The rivers now, these great blue subterranean heavens, reflecting the supernal skies and red-tinted clouds.

Sept. 1

Is not disease the rule of existence? There is not a lily pad floating on the river but has been riddled by insects. Almost every shrub and tree has its gall, oftentimes esteemed its chief ornament and hardly to be distinguished from the fruit. If misery loves company, misery has company enough. Now, at midsummer, find me a perfect leaf or fruit.

Sept. 2

We cannot write well or truly but what we write with gusto. The body, the senses, must conspire with the mind. Expression is the act of the whole man, that our speech may be vascular. The intellect is powerless to express thought without the aid of the heart and liver and of every member. Often I feel that my head stands out too dry, when it should be immersed. A writer, a man writing, is the scribe of all nature; he is the corn and the grass and the atmosphere writing. It is always essential that we love to do what we are doing, do it with a heart. The maturity of the mind, however, may perchance consist with a certain dryness.

Sept. 3

As I went under the new telegraph wire, I heard it vibrating like a harp high overhead. It was as the sound of a far-off glorious life, a supernal life, which came down to us, and vibrated the lattice-work of this life of ours.

Sept. 4

To have a hut here, and a footpath to the brook! For roads, I think that a poet cannot tolerate more than a footpath through the fields; that is wide enough, and for purposes of winged poesy suffices. It is not for the muse to speak of cart-paths. I would fain travel by a footpath round the world. I do not ask the railroads of commerce, not even the cart-paths of the farmer. Pray, what other path would you have than a footpath? What else should wear a path? This is the track of man alone. What more suggestive to the pensive walker? One walks in a wheel-track with less emotion; he is at a greater distance from man; but this footpath was, perchance, worn by the bare feet of human beings, and he cannot but think with interest of them.

Sept. 5

All perception of truth is the detection of an analogy; we reason from our hands to our head.

Sept. 6

How much of the life of certain men *goes* to sustain, to make respected, the institutions of society! They are the ones who pay the heaviest tax. Here are certain valuable institutions which can only be sustained by a wonderful strain which appears all to come upon certain Spartans who volunteer. Certain men are always to be found—especially the children of our present institutions—who are born with an instinct to perceive them. They are, in effect, supported by a fund which society possesses for that end, or they receive a pension and their life *seems* to be a sinecure—but it is not. The unwritten laws are the most stringent. They are required to wear a certain dress. What an array of gentlemen whose sole employment—and it is no sinecure—is to support their dignity, and with it the dignity of so many indispensable institutions!

Sept. 7

We sometimes experience a mere fullness of life, which does not find any channels to flow into. We are stimulated, but to no obvious purpose. I feel myself uncommonly prepared for *some* literary work, but I can select no work. I am prepared not so much for contemplation, as for forceful expression. I am braced both physically and intellect- ually. It is not so much the music as the marching to the music that I feel. I feel that the juices of the fruits which I have eaten, the melons and apples, have ascended to my brain and are stimulating it. They give me a heady force. Now I can write nervously. Carlyle's writing is for the most part of this character.

What shall we say of these timid folk who carry the principle of thinking nothing and doing nothing and being nothing to such an extreme? . . . They atone for their producing nothing by a brutish respect for something. They are as simple as oxen, and as guiltless of thought and reflection. Their reflections are reflected from other minds. The creature of institutions, bigoted and a conservatist, can say nothing hearty. He cannot meet life with life, but only with words. He rebuts you by avoiding you. He is shocked like a woman.

Our ecstatic states, which appear to yield so little fruit, have this value at least: though in the seasons when our genius reigns we may be powerless for expression, yet, in calmer seasons, when our talent is active, the memory of those rarer moods comes to color our picture and is the permanent paint-pot, as it were, into which we dip our brush. Thus no life or experience goes unreported at last; but if it be not solid gold it is gold-leaf, which gilds the furniture of the mind.

My profession is to be always on the alert to find God in nature, to know his lurking-places, to attend all the oratorios, the operas, in nature.

Sept. 11

The habit of looking at men in the gross makes their lives have less of human interest for us. But though there are crowds of laborers before us, yet each one leads his little epic life each day. There is the stone- mason, who, methought, was simply a stony man that hammered stone from breakfast to dinner, and dinner to supper, and then went to his slumbers. But he, I find, is even a man like myself, for he feels the heat of the sun and has raised some boards on a frame to protect him. And now, at mid-forenoon, I see his wife and child have come and brought him drink and meat for his lunch and to assuage the stoniness of his labor, and sit to chat with him.

Sept. 12

At the entrance to the Deep Cut,[1] I heard the telegraph wire vibrating like an æolian harp. It reminded me suddenly—reservedly, with a beautiful paucity of communication, even silently, such was its effect on my thoughts—it reminded me, I say, with a certain pathetic moderation, of what finer and deeper stirrings I was susceptible, which grandly set all argument and dispute aside, a triumphant though transient exhibition of the truth. It told me by the faintest imaginable strain, it told me by the finest strain that a human ear can hear, yet conclusively and past all refutation, that there were higher, infinitely higher, planes of life which it behooved me never to forget. As I was entering the Deep Cut, the wind, which was conveying a message to me from heaven, dropped it on the wire of the telegraph which it vibrated as it passed. I instantly sat down on a stone at the foot of the telegraph pole, and attended to the communication. It merely said: "Bear in mind, Child, and never for an instant forget, that there are higher planes, infinitely higher planes, of life than this thou art now travelling on. Know that the goal is distant, and is upward, and is worthy of all your life's effort to attain to." And then it ceased, and though I sat some minutes longer I heard nothing more.

Sept. 20, 3 P.M.

To Cliffs *via* Bear Hill.
As I go through the fields, endeavoring to recover my tone and sanity and to perceive things truly and simply again, after having been perambulating the bounds of the town all the week, and dealing with the most commonplace and worldly-minded men, and emphatically *trivial* things, I feel as if I had committed suicide in a sense. I am again forcibly struck with the truth of the fable of Apollo serving King Admetus, its universal applicability. A fatal coarseness is the result of mixing in the trivial affairs of men. Though I have been associating even with the *select* men of this and the surrounding towns, I feel inexpressibly begrimed. My Pegasus has lost his wings; he has

1 [Made for the railroad, near Thoreau's hut at Walden Pond.]

turned a reptile and gone on his belly. Such things are compatible only with a cheap and superficial life.

The poet must keep himself unstained and aloof. Let him perambulate the bounds of Imagination's provinces, the realms of faery, and not the insignificant boundaries of towns. The excursions of the imagination are so boundless, the limits of towns are so petty.

Sept. 22

Yesterday and today the stronger winds of autumn have begun to blow, and the telegraph harp has sounded loudly. I heard it especially in the Deep Cut this afternoon, the tone varying with the tension of different parts of the wire. The sound proceeds from near the posts, where the vibration is apparently more rapid. I put my ear to one of the posts, and it seemed to me as if every pore of the wood was filled with music, labored with the strain—as if every fibre was affected and being seasoned or timed, rearranged according to a new and more harmonious law. Every swell and change or inflection of tone pervaded and seemed to proceed from the wood, the divine tree or wood, as if its very substance was transmuted. What a recipe for preserving wood, perchance—to keep it from rotting—to fill its pores with music! How this wild tree from the forest, stripped of its bark and set up here, rejoices to transmit this music! When no music proceeds from the wire, on applying my ear I hear the hum within the entrails of the wood—the oracular tree acquiring, accumulating, the prophetic fury.

The resounding wood! how much the ancients would have made of it! To have a harp on so great a scale, girdling the very earth, and played on by the winds of every latitude and longitude, and that harp were, as it were, the manifest blessing of heaven on a work of man's! Shall we not add a tenth Muse to the immortal Nine? And that the invention thus divinely honored and distinguished—on which the Muse has condescended to smile—is this magic medium of communication for mankind!

Sept. 23

The telegraph harp sounds strongly today, in the midst of the rain. I put my ear to the trees and I hear it working terribly within, and anon it swells into a clear tone, which seems to concentrate in the core of the tree, for all the sound seems to proceed from the wood. It is as if you had entered some world-famous cathedral, resounding to some vast organ. The fibres of all things have their tension, and are strained like the strings of a lyre. I feel the very ground tremble under my feet as I stand near the post. This wire vibrates with great power, as if it would strain and rend the wood. What an awful and fateful music it must be to the worms in the wood. No better vermifuge were needed. No danger that worms will attack this wood; such vibrating music would thrill them to death.

Sept. 30

As the wood of an old Cremona, its very fibre, perchance, harmoniously transposed and educated to resound melody, has brought a great price, so methinks these telegraph posts should bear a great price with musical instrument makers. It is prepared to be the material of harps for ages to come, as it were put asoak in and seasoning in music.

Oct. 1, 5 P.M.

Just put a fugitive slave, who has taken the name of Henry Williams, into the cars for Canada. He escaped from Stafford County, Virginia, to Boston last October; has been in Shadrach's place at the Cornhill Coffee-House; had been corresponding through an agent with his master, who is his father, about buying himself, his master asking $600, but he having been able to raise only $500. Heard that there were writs out for two Williamses, fugitives, and was informed by his fellow-servants and employer that Augerhole Burns and others of the police had called for him when he was out. Accordingly fled to Concord last night on foot, bringing a letter to our family from Mr. Lovejoy of Cambridge and another which Garrison had formerly given him on another occasion. He lodged with us, and waited in the house till funds were collected with which to forward him. Intended to dispatch him at noon through to Burlington, but when I went to buy his ticket, saw one at the depot who looked and behaved so much like a Boston policeman that I did not venture that time. An intelligent and very well-behaved man, a mulatto.

Oct. 4

Minott is, perhaps, the most poetical farmer—who most realizes to me the poetry of the farmer's life—that I know. He does nothing with haste and drudgery, but as if he loved it. He makes the most of his labor, and takes infinite satisfaction in every part of it. He is not looking forward to the sale of his crops or any pecuniary profit, but he is paid by the constant satisfaction which his labor yields him. He has not too much land to trouble him—too much work to do—no hired man nor boy—but simply to amuse himself and live. He cares not so much to raise a large crop as to do his work well. He knows every pin and nail in his barn. If another linter[1] is to be floored, he lets no hired man rob him of that amusement, but he goes slowly to the woods and, at his leisure, selects a pitch pine tree, cuts it, and hauls it or gets it hauled to the mill; and so he knows the history of his barn floor.

Farming is an amusement which has lasted him longer than gunning or fishing. He is never in a hurry to get his garden planted and yet [it] is always planted soon enough, and none in the town is kept so beautifully clean.

He always prophesies a failure of the crops, and yet is satisfied with what he gets. His barn floor is fastened down with oak pins, and he prefers them to iron spikes, which he says will rust and give way. He handles and amuses himself with every ear of his corn crop as much as a child with its playthings, and so his small crop goes a great way. He might well cry if it were carried to market. The seed of weeds is no longer in his soil.

He loves to walk in a swamp in windy weather and hear the wind groan through the pines. He keeps a cat in his barn to catch the mice. He indulges in no luxury of food or dress or furniture, yet he is not penurious but merely simple. If his sister dies before him, he may have to go to the almshouse in his old age; yet he is not poor, for he does not want riches. He gets out of each manipulation in the farmers' operations a fund of entertainment which the speculating drudge hardly knows. With never-failing rheumatism and trembling hands, he seems yet to enjoy perennial health. Though he never reads a book—since he has finished the "Naval Monument"—he speaks the best of English.

Oct. 8

By the side of J. P. Brown's grain-field I picked up some white oak acorns in the path by the wood-side, which I found to be unexpectedly sweet and palatable, the bitterness being scarcely perceptible. To my taste they are quite as good as chestnuts. No wonder the first men lived on acorns. Such as these are no mean food, such as they are represented to be. Their sweetness is like the sweetness of bread, and to have discovered this palatableness in this neglected nut, the whole world is to me the sweeter for it. I am related again to the first men. What can be handsomer, wear better to the eye, than the color of the acorn, like the leaves on which they fall polished, or varnished? To find that

[1] [A lean-to.]

acorns are edible—it is a greater addition to one's stock of life than would be imagined. I should be at least equally pleased if I were to find that the grass tasted sweet and nutritious. It increases the number of my friends; it diminishes the number of my foes. How easily at this season I could feed myself in the woods! There is mast for me too, as well as for the pigeon and the squirrel. This Dodonean[1] fruit.

Oct. 12

I seem to be more constantly merged in nature; my intellectual life is more obedient to nature than formerly, but perchance less obedient to spirit. I have less memorable seasons. I exact less of myself. I am getting used to my meanness, getting to accept my low estate. O if I could be discontented with myself! If I could feel anguish at each descent!

Oct. 27

The obstacles which the heart meets with are like granite blocks which one alone cannot move. She[2] who was as the morning light to me is now neither the morning star nor the evening star. We meet but to find each other further asunder, and the oftener we meet the more rapid our divergence. So a star of the first magnitude pales in the heavens, not from any fault in the observer's eye nor from any fault in itself, perchance, but because its progress in its own system has put a greater distance between.

My friend will be bold to conjecture; he will guess bravely at the significance of my words.

Nov. 1

It is a rare qualification to be able to state a fact simply and adequately, to digest some experience cleanly, to say "yes" and "no" with authority, to make a square edge, to conceive and suffer the truth to pass through us living and intact, even as a waterfowl an eel, as it flies over the meadows, thus stocking new waters. First of all a man must see, before he can say. Statements are made but partially. Things are said with reference to certain conventions or existing institutions, not absolutely. A fact truly and absolutely stated is taken out of the region of common sense and acquires a mythologic or universal significance. Say it and have done with it. Express it without expressing yourself. See not with the eye of science, which is barren, nor of youthful poetry, which is impotent. But taste the world and digest it. It

1 [Referring to the sacred grove of oaks at Dodona in ancient Greece.]
2 [Possibly Mrs. Ralph Waldo Emerson.]

would seem as if things got said but rarely and by chance. As you *see*, so at length will you *say*. When facts are seen superficially, they are seen as they lie in relation to certain institutions, perchance. But I would have them expressed as more deeply seen, with deeper references; so that the hearer or reader cannot recognize them or apprehend their significance from the platform of common life, but it will be necessary that he be in a sense translated in order to understand them; when the truth respecting his things shall naturally exhale from a man like the odor of the muskrat from the coat of the trapper. At first blush a man is not capable of reporting truth; he must be drenched and saturated with it first. What was *enthusiasm* in the young man must become *temperament* in the mature man. Without excitement, heat, or passion, he will survey the world which excited the youth and threw him off his balance. As all things are significant, so all words should be significant. It is a fault which attaches to the speaker, to speak flippantly or superficially of anything. Of what use are words which do not move the hearer—are not oracular and fateful? A style in which the matter is all in all, and the manner nothing at all.

Man recognizes laws little enforced, and he condescends to obey them. In the moment that he feels his superiority to them as compulsatory, he, as it were, courteously re-enacts them but to obey them.

Nov. 7

The glorious sandy banks far and near, caving and sliding—far sandy slopes, the forts of the land—where you see the naked flesh of New England, her garment being blown aside like that of the priests (of the Levites?) when they ascend to the altar. Seen through this November sky, these sands are dear to me, worth all the gold of California, suggesting Pactolus, while the Saxonville factory-bell sounds o'er the woods. That sound perchance it is that whets my vision. The shore suggests the seashore, and two objects at a distance near the shore look like seals on a sand-bar. Dear to me to lie in, this sand; fit to preserve the bones of a race for thousands of years to come. And this is my home, my native soil; and I am a New-Englander. Of thee, O earth, are my bone and sinew made; to thee, O sun, am I brother.

Nov. 9

In our walks C.[1] takes out his note-book sometimes and tries to write as I do, but all in vain. He soon puts it up again, or contents

[1] [William Ellery Channing, the younger.]

himself with scrawling some sketch of the landscape. Observing me still scribbling, he will say that he confines himself to the ideal, purely ideal remarks; he leaves the facts to me. Sometimes, too, he will say a little petulantly, "I am universal; I have nothing to do with the particular and definite. . . ."

I, too, would fain set down something beside facts. Facts should only be as the frame to my pictures; they should be material to the mythology which I am writing; not facts to assist men to make money, farmers to farm profitably, in any common sense; facts to tell who I am, and where I have been or what I have thought: as now the bell rings for evening meeting, and its volumes of sound, like smoke which rises from where a cannon is fired, make the tent in which I dwell. My facts shall be falsehoods to the common sense. I would so state facts that they shall be significant, shall be myths or mythologic. Facts which the mind perceived, thoughts which the body thought—with these I deal. I, too, cherish vague and misty forms, vaguest when the cloud at which I gaze is dissipated quite and naught but the skyey depths are seen.

Nov. 11

Today you may write a chapter on the advantages of travelling, and tomorrow you may write another chapter on the advantages of not travelling. The horizon has one kind of beauty and attraction to him who has never explored the hills and mountains in it, and another, I fear a less ethereal and glorious one, to him who has. That blue mountain in the horizon is certainly the most heavenly, the most elysian, which we have not climbed, on which we have not camped for a night. But only our horizon is moved thus further off, and if our whole life should prove thus a failure, the future which is to atone for all, where still there must be some success, will be more glorious still.

Nov. 12

Write often, write upon a thousand themes, rather than long at a time, not trying to turn too many feeble somersets in the air—and so come down upon your head at last. Antæus-like, be not long absent from the ground. Those sentences are good and well discharged which are like so many little resiliencies from the spring floor of our life—a distinct fruit and kernel itself, springing from *terra firma*. Let there be as many distinct plants as the soil and the light can sustain. Take as many bounds in a day as possible. Sentences uttered with your back to the wall.

Nov. 13

Just spent a couple of hours (eight to ten) with Miss Mary Emerson [1] at Holbrook's. The wittiest and most vivacious woman that I know, certainly that woman among my acquaintance whom it is most profitable to meet, the least frivolous, who will most surely provoke to good conversation and the expression of what is in you. She is singular, among women at least, in being really and perseveringly interested to know what thinkers think. She relates herself surely to the intellectual where she goes. It is perhaps her greatest praise and peculiarity that she, more surely than any other woman, gives her companion occasion to utter his best thought. In spite of her own biases, she can entertain a large thought with hospitality, and is not prevented by any intellectuality in it, as women commonly are. In short, she is a genius, as woman seldom is, reminding you less often of her sex than any woman whom I know. In that sense she is capable of a masculine appreciation of poetry and philosophy. I never talked with any other woman who I thought accompanied me so far in describing a poetic experience. Miss Fuller is the only woman I think of in this connection, and of her rather from her fame than from any knowledge of her. Miss Emerson expressed tonight a singular want of respect for her own sex, saying that they were frivolous almost without exception, that woman was the weaker vessel, etc.; that into whatever family she might go, she depended more upon the "clown" for society than upon the lady of the house. Men are more likely to have opinions of their own.

Nov. 14

In the evening went to a party. It is a bad place to go to—thirty or forty persons, mostly young women, in a small room, warm and noisy. Was introduced to two young women. The first one was as lively and loquacious as a chickadee; had been accustomed to the society of watering-places, and therefore could get no refreshment out of such a dry fellow as I. The other was said to be pretty-looking, but I rarely look people in their faces, and, moreover, I could not hear what she said, there was such a clacking—could only see the motion of her lips when I looked that way. I could imagine better places for conversation, where there should be a certain degree of silence surrounding you, and less than forty talking at once. Why, this afternoon, even, I did better. There was old Mr. Joseph Hosmer and I ate our luncheon of cracker and cheese together in the woods. I heard all he said, though it was

---

[1] [Aunt of Ralph Waldo Emerson. She was at this time seventy-five years old.]

not much, to be sure, and he could hear me. And then he talked out of such a glorious repose, taking a leisurely bite at the cracker and cheese between his words; and so some of him was communicated to me, and some of me to him, I trust.

These parties, I think, are a part of the machinery of modern society, that young people may be brought together to form marriage connections.

I confess that I am lacking a sense, perchance, in this respect, and I derive no pleasure from talking with a young woman half an hour simply because she has regular features. The society of young women is the most unprofitable I have ever tried. They are so light and flighty that you can never be sure whether they are there or not there. I prefer to talk with the more staid and settled, *settled for life*, in every sense.

Nov. 15

I think it would be a good discipline for Channing, who writes poetry in a sublimo-slipshod style, to write Latin, for then he would be compelled to say something always, and frequently have recourse to his grammar and dictionary. Methinks that what a man might write in a dead language could be more surely translated into good sense in his own language, than his own language could be translated into good Latin, or the dead language.

Nov. 16, Sunday

It is remarkable that the highest intellectual mood which the world tolerates is the perception of the truth of the most ancient revelations, now in some respects out of date; but any direct revelation, any original thoughts, it hates like virtue. The fathers and the mothers of the town would rather hear the young man or young woman at their tables express reverence for some old statement of the truth than utter a direct revelation themselves. They don't want to have any prophets born into their families—damn them! So far as thinking is concerned, surely original thinking is the divinest thing. Rather we should reverently watch for the least motions, the least scintillations, of thought in this sluggish world, and men should run to and fro on the occasion more than at an earthquake. We check and repress the divinity that stirs within us, to fall down and worship the divinity that is dead without us. I go to see many a good man or good woman, so called, and utter freely that thought which alone it was given to me to utter; but there was a man who lived a long, long time ago, and his name was Moses, and another whose name was Christ, and if your thought does not, or does not appear to, coincide with what they said, the good man or the good woman has no ears to hear you. They think they love God! It is only his old clothes, of which they make scarecrows for the children. Where will they come nearer to God than in those very children?

Nov. 20

Hard and steady and engrossing labor with the hands, especially out of doors, is invaluable to the literary man and serves him directly. Here I have been for six days surveying in the woods, and yet when I get home at evening, somewhat weary at last, and beginning to feel that I have nerves, I find myself more susceptible than usual to the finest influences, as music and poetry. The very air can intoxicate me, or the least sight or sound, as if my finer senses had acquired an appetite by their fast.

Dec. 12

Ah, dear nature, the mere remembrance, after a short forgetfulness, of the pine woods! I come to it as a hungry man to a crust of bread.

Dec. 20

It is wonderful, wonderful, the unceasing demand that Christendom makes on you that you speak *from a moral point of view*. Though you be a babe, the cry is, Repent, repent. The Christian world will not admit that a man has a just perception of any truth, unless at the same time he cries, "Lord be merciful to me a sinner."

Dec. 22

If I am thus seemingly cold compared with my companion's warm, who knows but mine is a less transient glow, a steadier and more equable heat, like that of the earth in spring, in which the flowers spring and expand? It is not words that I wish to hear or to utter, but relations that I seek to stand in; and it oftener happens, methinks, that I go away unmet, unrecognized, ungreeted in my offered relation, than that you are disappointed of words. If I can believe that we are re-lated to one another as truly and gloriously as I have imagined, I ask nothing more, and words are not required to convince me of this. I am disappointed of relations, you of words.

Dec. 23

It would give me such joy to know that a friend had come to see me, and yet that pleasure I seldom if ever experience.

Dec. 30

This afternoon, being on Fair Haven Hill, I heard the sound of a saw, and soon after from the Cliff saw two men sawing down a noble pine beneath, about forty rods off. I resolved to watch it till it fell, the last of a dozen or more which were left when the forest was cut and for fifteen years have waved in solitary majesty over the sproutland. I saw them like beavers or insects gnawing at the trunk of this noble tree, the diminutive manikins with their cross-cut saw which could scarcely span it. It towered up a hundred feet as I afterward found by measurement, one of the tallest probably in the township and straight as an arrow, but slanting a little toward the hillside, its top seen against the frozen river and the hills of Conantum. I watch closely to see when it begins to move. Now the sawers stop, and with an axe open it a little on the side toward which it leans, that it may break the faster. And now their saw goes again. Now surely it is going; it is inclined one quarter of the quadrant, and, breathless, I expect its crashing fall. But no, I was mistaken; it has not moved an inch; it stands at the same angle as at first. It is fifteen minutes yet to its fall. Still its branches wave in the wind, as if it were destined to stand for a century, and the wind soughs through its needles as of yore; it is still a forest tree, the most majestic tree that waves over Musketaquid. The silvery sheen of the sunlight is reflected from its needles; it still affords an inaccessible crotch for the squirrel's nest; not a lichen has forsaken its mast-like stem, its raking mast—the hill is the hulk. Now, now's the moment! The manikins at its base are fleeing from their crime. They have dropped the guilty saw and axe. How slowly and majestically it starts! as if it were only swayed by a summer breeze, and would return without a sigh to its location in the air. And now it fans the hillside with its fall, and it lies down to its bed in the valley, from which it is never to rise, as softly as a feather, folding its green mantle about it like a warrior, as if, tired of standing, it embraced the earth with silent joy, returning its elements to the dust again. But hark! there you only saw, but did not hear. There now comes up a deafening crash to these rocks, advertising you that even trees do not die without a groan. It rushes to embrace the earth, and mingle its elements with the dust. And now all is still once more and forever, both to eye and ear.

I went down and measured it. It was about four feet in diameter where it was sawed, about one hundred feet long. Before I had reached it the axemen had already half divested it of its branches. Its gracefully spreading top was a perfect wreck on the hillside as if it had been made of glass, and the tender cones of one year's growth upon its summit appealed in vain and too late to the mercy of the chopper. Already he has measured it with his axe, and marked off the mill-logs it will make. And the space it occupied in upper air is vacant for the next two centuries. It is lumber. He has laid waste the air. When the fish hawk in the spring revisits the banks of the Musketaquid, he will circle in vain to find his accustomed perch, and the hen-hawk will mourn for the pines lofty enough to protect her brood. A plant which it has taken two centuries to perfect, rising by slow stages into the heavens, has this afternoon ceased to exist. It sapling top had expanded to this January thaw as the forerunner of summers to come. Why does not the village bell sound a knell? I hear no knell tolled. I see no procession of mourners in the streets, or the woodland aisles. The squirrel has leaped to another tree; the hawk has circled further off, and has now settled upon a new eyrie, but the woodman is preparing [to] lay his axe at the root of that also.

Dec. 31

This night I heard Mrs. S—— lecture on womanhood. The most important fact about the lecture was that a woman said it, and in that respect it was suggestive. Went to see her afterward, but the interview added nothing to the previous impression, rather subtracted. She was a woman in the too common sense after all. You had to fire small charges: I did not have a finger in once, for fear of blowing away all her works and so ending the game. You had to substitute courtesy for sense and argument. It requires nothing less than a chivalric feeling to sustain a conversation with a lady. I carried her lecture for her in my pocket wrapped in her handkerchief; my pocket exhales cologne to this moment. The championess of woman's rights still asks you to be a ladies' man. I can't fire a salute, even, for fear some of the guns may be shotted. I had to unshot all the guns in truth's battery and fire powder and wadding only. Certainly the heart is only for rare occasions; the intellect affords the most unfailing entertainment. It would only do to let her feel the wind of the ball. I fear that to the last woman's lectures will demand mainly courtesy from man.

1852

This is the most fruitful year of Thoreau's journalizing. He has come to the noon of his life and his powers have reached not only their zenith but something like harmony. The poet and naturalist in him have worked out a temporary truce. Thought and feeling, sight and insight, wit and humor, even the sense of life's tragedy and the spirit of laughter, find it possible to inhabit the same skin. The preacher descends from the pulpit and shows that he can talk like people of this world, or as they would like to talk if they were able. The veteran writer overcomes for a while his inveterate vices—scarcely separable from his virtues—of calculated exaggeration, straining for point, perversity, dogmatism, and scolding. We might say, in Yeats's language, that Thoreau now doffs the ostentatiously ragged coat of homespun he has made for himself, having found that "there's more enterprise in going naked."

Aware that maturity is coming upon him, Thoreau has already reminded himself, in the highly illuminating meditation of November 1, 1851, that "what was enthusiasm in the young man must become temperament in the mature man. Without excitement, heat, or passion, he will survey the world which excited the youth and threw him off his balance." Now passion and heat are not wholly absent from the journal of 1852. Thoreau is still extremely severe, as he will continue to be, with society and its institutions. More observable, however, is the growing warmth of his interest in some of his neighbors: in Mary Moody Emerson, his feminine counterpart; in Johnny Riordan, child of Irish immigrants; in various farmers, woodsmen, hunters, and one woodchuck. Best of all in the work of this year, and clearly one of Thoreau's masterpieces, is the requiem for Bill Wheeler, the town drunkard.

Jan. 8, 1852

Reading from my manuscripts to Miss Emerson this evening and using the word "god," in one instance, in perchance a merely heathenish sense, she inquired hastily in a tone of dignified anxiety, "Is that god spelt with a little *g*?" Fortunately it was. (I had brought in the word "god" without any solemnity of voice or connection.) So I went on as if nothing had happened.

Jan. 15

We have heard a deal about English comfort. But may you not trace these stories home to some wealthy Sardanapalus who was able to pay for obsequious attendance and for every luxury? How far does it describe merely the tact and selfishness of the wealthy class? Ask the great mass of Englishmen and travellers, whose vote alone is conclusive, concerning the comfort they enjoyed in second and third class accommodations in steamboats and railroads and eating and lodging houses. Lord Somebody-or-other may have made himself comfortable, but the very style of his living makes it necessary that the great majority of his countrymen should be uncomfortable.

Jan. 16

Bill Wheeler had two clumps for feet and progressed slowly, by short steps, having frozen his feet once, as I understood. Him I have been sure to meet once in five years, progressing into the town on his stubs, holding the middle of the road as if he drove an invisible herd before him, especially on a military day—out of what confines, whose hired man having been, I never knew—in what remote barn having quartered all these years. He seemed to belong to a different caste from other men, and reminded me of both the Indian Pariah and martyr. I understood that somebody was found to give him his drink for the few chores he could do. His meat was never referred to, he had so sublimed his life. One day since this, not long ago, I saw in my walk a kind of shelter such as woodmen might use, in the woods by the Great Meadows, made of meadow-hay cast over a rude frame. Thrusting my head in at a hole, as I am wont to do in such cases, I found Bill Wheeler there curled up asleep on the hay, who, being suddenly wakened from a sound sleep, rubbed his eyes and inquired if I found any game, thinking I was sporting. I came away reflecting much on that man's life—how he communicated with none; how now, perchance, he did chores for none; how low he lived, perhaps from a deep principle, that he might be some mighty philosopher, greater than Socrates or Diogenes, simplifying life, returning to nature, having turned his back on towns; how many things he had put off—luxuries, comforts, human society, even his feet—wrestling with his thoughts. I felt even as Diogenes when he saw the boy drinking out of his hands, and threw away his cup. Here was one who went alone, did no work, and had no relatives that I knew of, was not ambitious that I could see, did not depend on the good opinion of men. Must he not see things with an impartial eye, disinterested, as a toad observes the gardener? Perchance here is one of a sect of philosophers, the only one, so simple, so abstracted in thought and life from his contemporaries, that his wisdom is indeed foolishness to them. Who knows but in his solitary meadow-hay bunk he indulges, in thought, only in triumphant satires on men? Who knows but here is a superiority to literature and such things, unexpressed and inexpressible? Who has resolved to humble and mortify himself as never man was humbled and mortified. Whose very vividness of perception, clear knowledge, and insight have made him dumb, leaving no common consciousness and ground of parlance with his kind—or, rather, his unlike kindred! Whose news plainly is not my news nor yours. I was not sure for a moment but here was a philosopher who had left far behind him the philosophers of Greece and India, and I envied him his advantageous point of view. I was not to be deceived by a few stupid words, of course, and apparent besottedness. It was his position and career that I contemplated.

A month or two after this, as I heard, he was found dead among the brush over back of the hill—so far decomposed that his coffin was carried to his body and it was put into it with pitchforks. I have my misgivings still that he may have died a Brahmin's death, dwelling at the roots of trees at last, and been absorbed into the spirit of Brahm; though I have since been assured that he suffered from disappointed love—was what is called love-cracked—than which can there be any nobler suffering, any fairer death, for a human creature?—that that made him to drink, froze his feet, and did all the rest for him. Why have not the world the benefit of his long trial?

Jan. 22

To set down such choice experiences that my own writings may inspire me and at last I may make wholes of parts. Certainly it is a distinct profession to rescue from oblivion and to fix the sentiments and thoughts which visit all men more or less generally, that the contemplation of the unfinished picture may suggest its harmonious completion. Associate reverently and as much as you can with your loftiest thoughts. Each thought that is welcomed and recorded is a nest egg, by the side of which more will be laid. Thoughts accidentally thrown together become a frame in which more may be developed and exhibited. Perhaps this is the main value of a habit of writing, of keeping a journal—that so we remember our best hours and stimulate ourselves. My thoughts are my company. They have a certain individuality and separate existence, aye, personality. Having by chance recorded a few disconnected thoughts and then brought them into juxtaposition, they suggest a whole new field in which it was possible to labor and to think. Thought begat thought.

Jan. 24

If thou art a writer, write as if thy time were short, for it is indeed short at the longest. Improve each occasion when thy soul is reached.

Drain the cup of inspiration to its last dregs. Fear no intemperance in that, for the years will come when otherwise thou wilt regret opportunities unimproved. The spring will not last forever. These fertile and expanding seasons of thy life, when the rain reaches thy root, when thy vigor shoots, when thy flower is budding, shall be fewer and farther between. Again I say, Remember thy Creator in the days of thy youth. Use and commit to life what you cannot commit to memory. I hear the tones of my sister's piano below. It reminds me of strains which once I heard more frequently, when, possessed with the inaudible rhythm, I sought my chamber in the cold and communed with my own thoughts. I feel as if I then received the gifts of the gods with too much indifference. Why did I not cultivate those fields they introduced me to? Does nothing withstand the inevitable march of time? Why did I not use my eyes when I stood on Pisgah? Now I hear those strains but seldom. My rhythmical mood does not endure. I cannot draw from it and return to it in my thought as to a well all the evening or the morning. I cannot dip my pen in it. I cannot work the vein, it is so fine and volatile. Ah, sweet, ineffable reminiscences!

Jan. 27

As I stand under the hill beyond J. Hosmer's and look over the plains westward toward Acton and see the farmhouses nearly half a mile apart, few and solitary, in these great fields between these stretching woods, out of the world, where the children have to go far to school; the still, stagnant, heart-eating, life-everlasting and gone-to-seed country, so far from the post-office where the weekly paper comes, wherein the new-married wife cannot live for loneliness, and the young man has to depend upon his horse for society; see young J. Hosmer's house, whither he returns with his wife in despair after living in the city—I standing in Tarbell's road, which he alone cannot break out— the world in winter for most walkers reduced to a sled track winding far through the drifts, all springs sealed up and no digressions; where the old man thinks he may possibly afford to rust it out, not having long to live, but the young man pines to get nearer the post-office and the Lyceum, is restless and resolves to go to California, because the depot is a mile off (he hears the rattle of the cars at a distance and thinks the world is going by and leaving him); where rabbits and partridges multiply, and muskrats are more numerous than ever, and none of the farmer's sons are willing to be farmers, and the apple trees are decayed, and the cellar-holes are more numerous than the houses, and the rails are covered with lichens, and the old maids wish to sell out and move into the village, and have waited twenty years in vain for this purpose and never finished but one room in the house, never plastered nor painted, inside or out, lands which the Indian was long since dispossessed [of], and now the farms are run out, and what were forests are grain-fields, what were grain-fields, pastures; dwellings which only those Arnolds of the wilderness,[1] those *coureurs de bois*, the baker and the butcher visit, to which at least the latter penetrates for the annual calf—and as he returns the cow lows after—whither the villager never penetrates, but in huckleberry time, perchance, and if he does not, who does?—where some men's breaths smell of rum, having smuggled in a jugful to alleviate their misery and solitude; where the owls give a regular serenade;—I say, standing there and seeing these things, I cannot realize that this is that hopeful young America which is famous throughout the world for its activity and enterprise, and this is the most thickly settled and Yankee part of it. What must be the condition of the *old* world! The *sphagnum*[2] must by this time have concealed it from the eye.

In new countries men are scattered broadcast; they do not wait for roads to place their houses on, but roads seek out the houses, and each man is a prince in his principality and depends on himself. Perchance when the virgin soil is exhausted, a reaction takes place, and men concentrate in villages again, become social and commercial, and leave the steady and moderate few to work the country's mines.

I do not know but thoughts written down thus in a journal might be printed in the same form with greater advantage than if the related ones were brought together into separate essays. They are now allied to life, and are seen by the reader not to be far-fetched. It is more simple, less artful. I feel that in the other case I should have no proper frame for my sketches. Mere facts and names and dates communicate more than we suspect. Whether the flower looks better in the nosegay than in the meadow where it grew and we had to wet our feet to get it! Is the scholastic air any advantage?

Jan. 28

Perhaps I can never find so good a setting for my thoughts as I shall thus have taken them out of. The crystal never sparkles more brightly than in the cavern. The world have always loved best the fable with the moral. The children could read the fable alone, the grown-up read both. The truth so told has the best advantages of the most

[1] [Probably a reference to Benedict Arnold's march from Cambridge to Quebec in 1775.]

[2] [Bog or peat moss.]

abstract statement, for it is not the less universally applicable. Where else will you ever find the true cement for your thoughts? How will you ever rivet them together without leaving the marks of the file? Yet Plutarch did not so; Montaigne did not so. Men have written travels in this form, but perhaps no man's daily life has been rich enough to be journalized.

They showed me Johnny Riordan today, with one thickness of ragged cloth over his little shirt for all this cold weather, with shoes with large holes in the toes, into which the snow got, as he said, without an outer garment, to walk a mile to school every day over the bleakest of causeways—the clothes with countless patches, which hailed from, claimed descent from, were originally identical with, pantaloons of mine, which set as if his mother had fitted them to a tea-kettle first. This little mass of humanity, this tender gobbet for the fates, cast into a cold world with a torn lichen leaf wrapped about him—oh, I should rather hear that America's first-born were all slain than that his little fingers and toes should feel cold while I am warm. Is man so cheap that he cannot be clothed but with a mat, a rag, that we should bestow on him our *cold* victuals? Are there any fellow-creatures to whom we abandon our rags, to whom we give our old clothes and shoes when they will not fend the weather from ourselves? Let the mature rich wear the rags and insufficient clothing; let the infant poor wear the purple and fine linen. I shudder when I think of the fate of innocency. Our charitable institutions are an insult to humanity. A charity which dispenses the crumbs that fall from its overloaded tables, which are left after its feasts![1]

Jan. 30, Friday

I doubt if Emerson could trundle a wheelbarrow through the streets, because it would be out of character. One needs to have a comprehensive character.

I am afraid to travel much or to famous places, lest it might completely dissipate the mind. Then I am sure that what we observe at home, if we observe anything, is of more importance than what we observe abroad. The far-fetched is of the least value. What we observe in travelling are to some extent the accidents of the body, but [what] we observe when sitting at home are, in the same proportion, phenomena of the mind itself. A wakeful night will yield as much thought as a long journey. If I try thoughts by their quality, not their quantity, I may find that a restless night will yield more than the longest journey.

[1] [Compare the entry for February 8 of this year.]

Jan. 31

In the East, women religiously conceal that they have faces; in the West, that they have legs. In both cases they make it evident that they have but little brains.

I hear my friend say, "I have lost my faith in men; there are none true, magnanimous, holy," etc., etc., meaning, all the while, that I do not possess those unattainable virtues; but, worm as I am, this is not wise in my friend, and I feel simply discouraged so far as my relation to him is concerned. We must have infinite faith in each other. If we have not, we must never let it leak out that we have not. He erects his want of faith as a barrier between us. When I hear a grown man or woman say, "Once I had faith in men; now I have not," I am inclined to ask, "Who are you whom the world has disappointed? Have not you rather disappointed the world? There is the same ground for faith now that ever there was. It needs only a little love in you who complain so to ground it on." For my own part, I am thankful that there are those who come so near being my friends that they can be estranged from me. I had faith before they would destroy the little I have. The mason asks but a narrow shelf to spring his brick from; man requires only an infinitely narrower one to spring the arch of faith from.

Feb. 1

One of little faith looks for his rewards and punishments to the next world, and, despairing of this world, behaves accordingly in it; another thinks the present a worthy occasion and arena, sacrifices to it, and expects to hear sympathizing voices. The man who believes in another world and not in this is wont to put me off with Christianity. The present moment in which we talk is of a little less value to him than the next world. So we are said to hope in proportion as we do not realize. It is all hope deferred. But one grain of realization, of instant life, on which we stand, is equivalent to acres of the leaf of hope hammered out to gild our prospect.

Feb. 5

I suspect that the child plucks its first flower with an insight into its beauty and significance which the subsequent botanist never retains.

Feb. 8

Carried a new cloak to Johnny Riordan. I found that the shanty was warmed by the simple social relations of the Irish. On Sunday

they come from the town and stand in the doorway and so keep out
the cold. One is not cold among his brothers and sisters. What if there
is less fire on the hearth, if there is more in the heart!

Feb. 10

Now if there are any who think that I am vainglorious, that I set
myself up above others and crow over their low estate, let me tell them
that I could tell a pitiful story respecting myself as well as them, if
my spirits held out to do it; I could encourage them with a sufficient
list of failures, and could flow as humbly as the very gutters themselves;
I could enumerate a list of as rank offenses as ever reached the nostrils
of heaven; that I think worse of myself than they can possibly think of
me, being better acquainted with the man. I put the best face on the
matter. I will tell them this secret, if they will not tell it to anybody
else.

Write while the heat is in you. When the farmer burns a hole in his
yoke, he carries the hot iron quickly from the fire to the wood, for every
moment it is less effectual to penetrate (pierce) it. It must be used
instantly, or it is useless. The writer who postpones the recording of his
thoughts uses an iron which has cooled to burn a hole with. He cannot
inflame the minds of his audience.

Feb. 11

I have lived some thirty-odd years on this planet, and I have yet to
hear the first syllable of valuable or even earnest advice from my
seniors. They have told me nothing, and probably can tell me nothing
to the purpose. There is life, an experiment untried by me, and it does
not avail me that you have tried it. If I have any valuable experience,
I am sure to reflect that this my mentors said nothing about. What
were mysteries to the child remain mysteries to the old man.

Feb. 13

Talking with Rice this afternoon about the bees which I discovered
the other day, he told me something about his bee-hunting. He and
Pratt go out together once or twice a year. He takes a little tin box with
a little refined sugar and water about the consistency of honey, or some
honey in the comb, which comes up so high only in the box as to let
the lid clear a bee's back, also some little bottles of paint—red, blue,
white, etc.—and a compass properly prepared to line the bees with,

the sights perhaps a foot apart. Then they ride off (this is in the fall)
to some extensive wood, perhaps the west side of Sudbury. They go to
some buckwheat-field or a particular species of late goldenrod which
especially the bees frequent at that season, and they are sure to find
honey-bees enough. They catch one by putting the box under the
blossoms and then covering him with the lid, at the same time cutting
off the stalk of the flower. They then set down the box, and after a
while raise the lid slightly to see if the bee is feeding; if so, they take
off the lid, knowing that he will not fly away till he gets ready, and
catch another; and so on till they get a sufficient number. Then they
thrust sticks into their little paint-bottles, and, with these, watching
their opportunity, they give the bees each a spot of a particular color
on his body—they spot him distinctly—and then, lying about a rod
off, not to scare them, and watching them carefully all the while, they
wait till one has filled his sac, and prepares to depart to his hive. They
are careful to note whether he has a red or a blue jacket or what color.
He rises up about ten feet and then begins to circle rapidly
round and round with a hum, sometimes a circle twenty feet in diameter
before he has decided which way to steer, and then suddenly shoots off
in a bee-line to his hive. The hunters lie flat on their backs and watch
him carefully all the while. If blue-jacket steers toward the open land
where there are known to be hives, they forthwith leave out of the box
all the blue-jackets, and move off a little and open the box in a new
place to get rid of that family. And so they work till they come to a
bee, red-jacket perhaps, that steers into the wood or swamp or in a
direction to suit them. They take the point of compass exactly, and
wait perhaps till red-jacket comes back, that they may ascertain his
course more exactly, and also judge by the time it has taken for him to
go and return, using their watches, how far off the nest is, though
sometimes they are disappointed in their calculations, for it may take
the [bee] more or less time to crawl into its nest, depending on its
position in the tree. By the third journey he will commonly bring some
of his companions. Our hunters then move forward a piece, from time
to time letting out a bee to make sure of their course. After the bees
have gone and come once, they generally steer straight to their nest
at once without circling round first. Sometimes the hunters, having
observed this course carefully on the compass, go round a quarter of a
circle and, letting out another bee, observe the course from that point,
knowing that where these two lines intersect must be the nest. Rice
thinks that a bee-line does not vary more than fifteen or twenty feet
from a straight one in going half a mile. They frequently trace the
bees thus to their hives more than a mile.

Color, which is the poet's wealth, is so expensive that most take to mere outline or pencil sketches and become men of science.

Feb. 18

I have a commonplace-book for facts and another for poetry, but I find it difficult always to preserve the vague distinction which I had in my mind, for the most interesting and beautiful facts are so much the more poetry and that is their success. They are *translated* from earth to heaven. I see that if my facts were sufficiently vital and significant— perhaps transmuted more into the substance of the human mind—I should need but one book of poetry to contain them all.

It is impossible for the same person to see things from the poet's point of view and that of the man of science. The poet's second love may be science, not his first—when use has worn off the bloom. I realize that men may be born to a condition of mind at which others arrive in middle age by the decay of their poetic faculties.

Feb. 26

We are told today that civilization is making rapid progress; the tendency is ever upward; substantial justice is done even by human courts; you may trust the good intentions of mankind. We read to-morrow in the newspapers that the French nation is on the eve of going to war with England to give employment to her army. What is the influence of men of principle, or how numerous are they? How many moral teachers has society? This Russian war is popular. Of course so many as she has will resist her. How many resist her? How many have I heard speak with warning voice? utter wise warnings? The preacher's standard of morality is no higher than that of his audience. He studies to conciliate his hearers and never to offend them. Does the threatened war between France and England[1] evince any more enlightenment than a war between two savage tribes, as the Iroquois and the Hurons? Is it founded in better reason?

March 1

After having read various books on various subjects for some months, I take up a report on Farms by a committee of Middlesex Husbandmen, and read of the number of acres of bog that some farmer has redeemed, and the number of rods of stone wall that he has

---

[1] [Referring to events leading to the Crimean War.]

built, and the number of tons of hay he now cuts, or of bushels of corn or potatoes he raises there, and I feel as if I had got my foot down on to the solid and sunny earth, the basis of all philosophy, and poetry, and religion even. I have faith that the man who redeemed some acres of land the past summer redeemed also some parts of his character. I shall not expect to find him ever in the almshouse or the prison. He is, in fact, so far on his way to heaven. When he took the farm there was not a grafted tree on it, and now he realizes something handsome from the sale of fruit. These, in the absence of other facts, are evidence of a certain moral worth.

March 4

It is discouraging to talk with men who will recognize no principles. How little use is made of reason in this world! You argue with a man for an hour, he agrees with you step by step, you are approaching a triumphant conclusion, you think that you have converted him; but ah, no, he has a habit, he takes a pinch of snuff, he remembers that he entertained a different opinion at the commencement of the controversy, and his reverence for the past compels him to reiterate it now. You began at the butt of the pole to curve it, you gradually bent it round according to rule, and planted the other end in the ground, and already in imagination saw the vine curling round this segment of an arbor, under which a new generation was to recreate itself; but when you had done, just when the twig was bent, it sprang back to its former stubborn and unhandsome position like a bit of whalebone.

I love that the rocks should appear to have some spots of blood on them, Indian blood at least; to be convinced that the earth has been crowded with men, living, enjoying, suffering, that races passed away have stained the rocks with their blood, that the mould I tread on has been animated, aye, humanized. I am the more at home. I farm the dust of my ancestors, though the chemist's analysis may not detect it. I go forth to redeem the meadows they have become. I compel them to take refuge in turnips.

March 5

I find myself inspecting little granules, as it were, on the bark of trees, little shields or apothecia springing from a thallus, such is the mood of my mind, and I call it studying lichens. That is merely the prospect which is afforded me. It is short commons and innutritious. Surely I might take wider views. The habit of looking at things microscopically, as the lichens on the trees and rocks, really prevents my seeing aught else in a walk. Would it not be noble to study the shield of the sun on the thallus of the sky, cerulean, which scatters its infinite sporules of light through the universe? To the lichenist is not the shield (or rather the apothecium) of a lichen disproportionately large compared with the universe? The minute apothecium of the pertusaria, which the woodchopper never detected, occupies so large a space in my eye at present as to shut out a great part of the world.

April 1

He is in the lowest scale of laborers who is merely an able-bodied man and can compete with others only in physical strength. Woodchoppers in this neighborhood get but fifty cents a cord, but, though many can chop two cords in a day in pleasant weather and under favorable circumstances, yet most do not average more than seventy-five cents a day, take the months together. But one among them of only equal physical strength and skill as a chopper, having more wit, buys a cross-cut saw for four dollars, hires a man to help him at a dollar a day, and saws down trees all winter at ten cents apiece and thirty or forty a day, and clears two or more dollars a day by it. Yet as long as the world may last few will be found to buy the cross-cut saw, and probably the wages of the sawyer will never be reduced to a level with those of the chopper.

Gilpin's *Forest Scenery* is a pleasing book,[1] so moderate, temperate, graceful, roomy, like a gladed wood; not condensed; with a certain religion in its manners and respect for all the good of the past, rare in more recent books; and it is grateful to read after them. Somewhat spare indeed in the thoughts as in the sentences. Some of the cool wind of the copses converted into grammatical and graceful sentences, without heat. Not one of those humors come to a head which some modern books are, but some of the natural surface of a healthy mind.

April 2

In the promulgated views of man, in institutions, in the common sense, there is narrowness and delusion. It is our weakness that so exaggerates the virtues of philanthropy and charity and makes it the highest human attribute. The world will sooner or later tire of philanthropy and all religions based on it mainly. They cannot long sustain my spirit. In order to avoid delusions, I would fain let man go by and behold a universe in which man is but as a grain of sand. I am sure that those of my thoughts which consist, or are contemporaneous, with

1 [Written and illustrated by William Gilpin (1724–1804), an English clergyman.]

social personal connections, however humane, are not the wisest and widest, most universal. What is the village, city, State, nation, aye the civilized world, that it should concern a man so much? the thought of them affects me in my wisest hours as when I pass a woodchuck's hole. It is a comfortable place to nestle, no doubt, and we have friends, some sympathizing ones, it may be, and a hearth, there; but I have only to get up at midnight, aye to soar or wander a little in my thought by day, to find them all slumbering. Look at our literature. What a poor, puny, social thing, seeking sympathy! The author troubles himself about his readers—would fain have one before he dies. He stands too near his printer; he corrects the proofs. Not satisfied with defiling one another in this world, we would all go to heaven together. To be a good man, that is, a good neighbor in the widest sense, is but little more than to be a good citizen. Mankind is a gigantic institution; it is a community to which most men belong. It is a test I would apply to my companion—can he forget man? can he see this world slumbering?

I do not value any view of the universe into which man and the institutions of man enter very largely and absorb much of the attention. Man is but the place where I stand, and the prospect hence is infinite. It is not a chamber of mirrors which reflect me. When I reflect, I find that there is other than me. Man is a past phenomenon to philosophy. The universe is larger than enough for man's abode. Some rarely go outdoors, most are always at home at night, very few indeed have stayed out all night once in their lives, fewer still have gone behind the world of humanity, seen its institutions like toadstools by the wayside.

April 4, Sunday

I have got to that pass with my friend that our words do not pass with each other for what they are worth. We speak in vain; there is none to hear. He finds fault with me that I walk alone, when I pine for want of a companion; that I commit my thoughts to a diary even on my walks, instead of seeking to share them generously with a friend; curses my practice even. Awful as it is to contemplate, I pray that, if I am the cold intellectual skeptic whom he rebukes, his curse may take effect, and wither and dry up those sources of my life, and my journal no longer yield me pleasure nor life.

April 11

If I am too cold for human friendship, I trust I shall not soon be too cold for natural influences. It appears to be a law that you cannot have a deep sympathy with both man and nature. Those qualities which bring you near to the one estrange you from the other.

Every man will be a poet if he can; otherwise a philosopher or man of science. This proves the superiority of the poet.

At what an expense any valuable work is performed! At the expense of a life! If you do one thing well, what else are you good for in the meanwhile?

April 12

I am made somewhat sad this afternoon by the coarseness and vulgarity of my companion, because he is one with whom I have made myself intimate. He inclines latterly to speak with coarse jesting of facts which should always be treated with delicacy and reverence. I lose my respect for the man who can make the mystery of sex the subject of a coarse jest, yet, when you speak earnestly and seriously on the subject, is silent. I feel that this is to be truly irreligious. Whatever may befall me, I trust that I may never lose my respect for purity in others. The subject of sex is one on which I do not wish to meet a man at all unless I *can* meet him on the most inspiring ground—if his view degrades, and does not elevate. I would preserve purity in act and thought, as I would cherish the memory of my mother. A companion can possess no worse quality than vulgarity. If I find that *he* is not habitually reverent of the fact of sex, I, even I, will not associate with [him]. I will cast this first stone. . . . A man's speech on this subject should, of course, be ever as reverent and chaste and simple as if it were to be heard by the ears of maidens.

April 15

Channing calls our walks along the banks of the river, taking a boat for convenience at some distant point, *riparial* excursions. It is a pleasing epithet, but I mistrust such, even as good as this, in which the mere name is so agreeable, as if it would ring hollow ere long; and rather the thing should make the true name poetic at last. Alcott wished me to name my book *Sylvania*!

April 16

How many there are who advise you to print! How few who advise you to lead a more interior life! In the one case there is all the world to advise you, in the other there is none to advise you but yourself. Nobody ever advised me not to print but myself. The public persuade the author to print, as the meadow invites the brook to fall into it.

Only he can be trusted with gifts who can present a face of bronze to expectations.[1]

As I turned round the corner of Hubbard's Grove, saw a woodchuck, the first of the season, in the middle of the field, six or seven rods from the fence which bounds the wood, and twenty rods distant. I ran along the fence and cut him off, or rather overtook him, though he started at the same time. When I was only a rod and a half off, he stopped, and I did the same; then he ran again, and I ran up within three feet of him, when he stopped again, the fence being between us. I squatted down and surveyed him at my leisure. His eyes were dull black and rather inobvious, with a faint chestnut (?) iris, with but little expression and that more of resignation than of anger. The general aspect was a coarse grayish brown, a sort of grisel (?). A lighter brown next the skin, then black or very dark brown and tipped with whitish rather loosely. The head between a squirrel and a bear, flat on the top and dark brown, and darker still or black on the tip of the nose. The whiskers black, two inches long. The ears very small and roundish, set far back and nearly buried in the fur. Black feet, with long and slender claws for digging. It appeared to tremble, or perchance shivered with cold. When I moved, it gritted its teeth quite loud, sometimes striking the under jaw against the other chatteringly, sometimes grinding one jaw on the other, yet as if more from instinct than anger. Whichever way I turned, that way it headed. I took a twig a foot long and touched its snout, at which it started forward and bit the stick, lessening the distance between us to two feet, and still it held all the ground it gained. I played with it tenderly awhile with the stick, trying to open its gritting jaws. Ever its long incisors, two above and two below, were presented. But I thought it would go to sleep if I stayed long enough. It did not sit upright as sometimes, but *standing* on its fore feet with its head down, i.e. half sitting, half standing. We sat looking at one another about half an hour, till we began to feel mesmeric influences. When I was tired, I moved away, wishing to see him run, but I could not start him. He would not stir as long as I was looking at him or could see him. I walked round him; he turned as fast and fronted me still. I sat down by his side within a foot. I talked to him *quasi* forest lingo, baby-talk, at any rate in a conciliatory tone, and thought that I had some influence on him. He gritted his teeth less. I chewed checkerberry leaves and presented them to his nose at last without a grit; though I saw that by so much gritting of the teeth he had worn them rapidly and they were covered with a fine white powder,

---

[1] [*Walden,* ready for printing, had not yet found a publisher.]

which, if you measured it thus, would have made his anger terrible. He did not mind any noise I might make. With a little stick I lifted one of his paws to examine it, and held it up at pleasure. I turned him over to see what color he was beneath (darker or more purely brown), though he turned himself back again sooner than I could have wished. His tail was also all brown, though not very dark, rat-tail like, with loose hairs standing out on all sides like a caterpillar brush. He had a rather mild look. I spoke to him kindly. I reached checkerberry leaves to his mouth. I stretched my hands over him, though he turned up his head and still gritted a little. I laid my hand on him, but immediately took it off again, instinct not being wholly overcome. If I had had a few fresh bean leaves, thus in advance of the season, I am sure I should have tamed him completely. It was a frizzly tail. His is a humble, terrestrial color like the partridge's, well concealed where dead wiry grass rises above darker brown or chestnut dead leaves—a modest color. If I had had some food, I should have ended with stroking him at my leisure. Could easily have wrapped him in my handkerchief. He was not fat nor particularly lean. I finally had to leave him without seeing him move from the place. A large, clumsy, burrowing squirrel. *Arctomys*, bearmouse. I respect him as one of the natives. He lies there, by his color and habits so naturalized amid the dry leaves, the withered grass, and the bushes. A sound nap, too, he has enjoyed in his native fields, the past winter. I think I might learn some wisdom of him. His ancestors have lived here longer than mine. He is more thoroughly acclimated and naturalized than I. Bean leaves the red man raised for him, but he can do without them.

April 19

Stopped in the barn on the Baker Farm.[1] Sat in the dry meadow-hay, where the mice nest. To sit there, rustling the hay, just beyond reach of the rain while the storm roars without, it suggests an inexpressible dry stillness, the quiet of the haymow in a rainy day; such stacks of quiet and undisturbed thought, when there is not even a cricket to stir in the hay, but all without is wet and tumultuous, and all within is dry and quiet. Oh, what reams of thought one might have here! The crackling of the hay makes silence audible. It is so deep a bed, it makes one dream to sit on it, to think of it.

April 21

The birds are singing in the rain about the small pond in front, the inquisitive chickadee that has flown at once to the alders to recon-

---

1 [A place near Fair Haven Bay which Thoreau had once thought of buying.]

noitre us, the blackbirds, the song sparrow, telling of expanding buds. But above all the robin sings here too, I know not at what distance in the wood. "Did he sing thus in Indian days?" I ask myself; for I have always associated this sound with the village and the clearing, but now I do detect the aboriginal wildness in his strain, and can imagine him a woodland bird, and that he sang thus when there was no civilized ear to hear him, a pure forest melody even like the wood thrush. Every genuine thing retains this wild tone, which no true culture displaces. I heard him even as he might have sounded to the Indian, singing at evening upon the elm above his wigwam, with which was associated in the red man's mind the events of an Indian's life, his childhood. Formerly I had heard in it only those strains which tell of the white man's village life; now I heard those strains which remembered the red man's life, such as fell on the ears of Indian children —as he sang when these arrowheads, which the rain has made shine so on the lean stubble-field, were fastened to their shaft.

We have heard enough nonsense about the Pyramids. If Congress should vote to rear such structures on the prairies today, I should not think it worth the while, nor be interested in the enterprise. It was the foolish undertaking of some tyrant. . . . Men are wont to speak as if it were a noble work to build a pyramid—to set, forsooth, a hundred thousand Irishmen at work at fifty cents a day to piling stone. As if the good joints could ennoble it, if a noble motive was wanting! To ramble round the world to see that pile of stones which ambitious Mr. Cheops, an Egyptian booby, like some Lord Timothy Dexter,[1] caused a hundred thousand poor devils to pile up for low wages, which contained for all treasure the thigh-bone of a cow. The tower of Babel has been a good deal laughed at. It was just as sensible an undertaking as the Pyramids, which, because they were completed and have stood to this day, are admired.

April 24

I know two species of men. The vast majority are men of society. They live on the surface; they are interested in the transient and fleeting; they are like driftwood on the flood. They ask forever and only the news, the froth and scum of the eternal sea. They use policy; they make up for want of matter with manner. They have many letters to write. Wealth and the approbation of men is to them success. The enterprises of society are something final and sufficing for them. The world advises them, and they listen to its advice. They live wholly an

[1] [A wealthy and eccentric Massachusetts merchant who crowded one of his gardens with colossal wooden statues, one representing himself.]

evanescent life, creatures of circumstance. It is of prime importance to them who is the president of the day. They have no knowledge of truth, but by an exceedingly dim and transient instinct, which stereotypes the church and some other institutions. They dwell, they are ever, right in my face and eyes like gnats; they are like motes, so near the eyes that, looking beyond, they appear like blurs; they have their being between my eyes and the end of my nose. The *terra firma* of my existence lies far beyond, behind them and their improvements. If they write, the best of them deal in "elegant literature." Society, man, has no prize to offer me that can tempt me; not one. That which interests a town or city or any large number of men is always something trivial, as politics. It is impossible for me to be interested in what interests men generally. Their pursuits and interests seem to me frivolous. When I am most myself and see the clearest, men are least to be seen; they are like *muscæ volitantes*, and that they are seen at all is the proof of imperfect vision.

April 29

The art of life, of a poet's life, is, not having anything to do, to do something.

May 5

As I went up the Groton road, I saw a dim light at a distance, where no house was, which appeared to come from the earth. Could it be a traveller with a lanthorn? Could it be a will-o'-the-wisp? (Who ever saw one? Are not they a piece of modern mythology?) You wonder if you will ever reach it; already it seems to recede. Is it the reflection of the evening star in water? or what kind of phosphorescence? But now I smell the burning. I see the sparks go up in the dark. It is a heap of stumps half covered with earth, left to smoulder and consume in the newly plowed meadow, now burst forth into dull internal flames. Looks like a gipsy encampment. I sit on the untouched end of a stump, and warm me by it, and write by the light, the moon not having risen. What a strange, Titanic thing this Fire, this Vulcan, here at work in the night in this bog, far from men, dangerous to them, consuming earth, gnawing at its vitals! The heap glows within. Here sits hungry Fire with the forest in his mouth. On the one side is the solid wood; on the other, smoke and sparks. Thus he works. The farmer designs to consume, to destroy, this wood, remains of trees. He gives them to his dog, or vulture, Fire. They burn like spunk, and I love the smell of the smoke. The frogs peep and dream around. Within are fiery caverns, incrusted with fire as a cave with saltpetre. No wonder at salamanders. It suggests a creature that lives in it, generated by it.

I hear Barrett's sawmill running by night to improve the high water. Then water is at work, another devourer of wood. These two wild forces let loose against nature. It is a hollow, galloping sound; makes tearing work, taming timber, in a rude Orphean fashion preparing it for dwellings of men and musical instruments, perchance. I can imagine the sawyer, with his lanthorn and his bar in hand, standing by, amid the shadows cast by his light. There is a sonorous vibration and ring to it, as if from the nerves of the tortured log. Tearing its entrails.

May 9

It is impossible to remember a week ago. A river of Lethe flows with many windings the year through, separating one season from another. The heavens for a few days have been lost. It has been a sort of *paradise* instead. As with the seashore, so is it with the universal earthshore, not in summer can you look far into the ocean of the ether. They who come to this world as to a watering-place in the summer for coolness and luxury never get the far and fine November views of heaven. Is not all the summer akin to a paradise? We have to bathe in ponds to brace ourselves. The earth is blue now—the near hills, in this haze.

May 14

Most men can be easily transplanted from here there, for they have so little root—no tap-root—or their roots penetrate so little way, that you can thrust a shovel quite under them and take them up, roots and all.

June 9

For a week past we have had *washing* days.[1] The grass waving, the trees having leaved out, their boughs wave and feel the effect of the breeze. Thus new life and motion is imparted to the trees. The season of waving boughs; and the lighter under sides of the new leaves are exposed. This is the first half of June. Already the grass is not so fresh and liquid-velvety a green, having much of it blossom[ed] and some even gone to seed, and it is mixed with reddish ferns and other plants, but the general leafiness, shadiness, and waving of grass and boughs in the breeze characterize the season. The wind is not quite agreeable,

---

[1] [Days on which washing hung out-of-doors would soon dry.]

because it prevents your hearing the birds sing. Meanwhile the crickets are strengthening their quire. The weather is very clear, and the sky bright. The river shines like silver. Methinks this is a traveller's month. The locust in bloom. The waving, undulating rye. The deciduous trees have filled up the intervals between the evergreens, and the woods are bosky now.

A child loves to strike on a tin pan or other ringing vessel with a stick, because, its ears being fresh, sound, attentive, and percipient, it detects the finest music in the sound, at which all nature assists. Is not the very cope of the heavens the sounding-board of the infant drummer? So clear and unprejudiced ears hear the sweetest and most soul-stirring melody in tinkling cowbells and the like (dogs baying the moon), not to be referred to association, but intrinsic in the sound itself; those cheap and simple sounds which men despise because their ears are dull and debauched. Ah, that I were so much a child that I could unfailingly draw music from a quart pot! Its little ears tingle with the melody. To it there is music in sound alone.

June 12

Boys are bathing at Hubbard's Bend, playing with a boat (I at the willows). The color of their bodies in the sun at a distance is pleasing, the not often seen flesh-color. I hear the sound of their sport borne over the water. As yet we have not man in nature. What a singular fact for an angel visitant to this earth to carry back in his note-book, that men were forbidden to expose their bodies under the severest penalties! A pale pink, which the sun would soon tan. White men! There are no white men to contrast with the red and the black; they are of such colors as the weaver gives them. I wonder that the dog knows his master when he goes in to bathe and does not stay by his clothes.

The steam whistle at a distance sounds even like the hum of a bee in a flower. So man's works fall into nature.

June 15

I hear the scream of a great hawk, sailing with a ragged wing against the high wood-side, apparently to scare his prey and so detect it—shrill, harsh, fitted to excite terror in sparrows and to issue from his split and curved bill. I see his open bill the while against the sky. Spit with force from his mouth with an undulatory quaver imparted to it from his wings or motion as he flies. A hawk's ragged wing will grow whole again, but so will not a poet's.

8 P.M.—On river.

No moon. A deafening sound from the toads, and intermittingly from
bullfrogs.

It is candle-light. The fishes leap. The meadows sparkle with the
coppery light of fireflies. The evening star, multiplied by undulating
water, is like bright sparks of fire continually ascending. The reflections
of the trees are grandly indistinct. There is a low mist slightly enlarging
the river, through which the arches of the stone bridge are just visible,
as a vision. The mist is singularly bounded, collected here, while there
is none there; close up to the bridge on one side and none on the other,
depending apparently on currents of air. A dew in the air it is, which in
time will wet you through. See stars reflected in the bottom of our
boat, it being a quarter full of water. There is a low crescent of northern
light and shooting stars from time to time. (We go only from Channing's
to the ash above the railroad.) I paddle with a bough, the Nile boatman's oar, which is rightly pliant, and you do not labor much. Some
dogs bay. A sultry night.

June 17

The sound of the crickets at dawn after these first sultry nights
seems like the dreaming of the earth still continued into the daylight.
I love that early twilight hour when the crickets still creak right on
with such faith and promise, as if it were still night—expressing the
innocence of morning—when the creak of the cricket is fresh and be-
dewed. While the creak of the cricket has that ambrosial sound, no
crime can be committed. It buries Greece and Rome past resurrection.
The earth-song of the cricket! Before Christianity was, it is. Health!
health! health! is the burden of its song. It is, of course, that man,
refreshed with sleep, is thus innocent and healthy and hopeful. When
we hear that sound of the crickets in the sod, the world is not so much
with us.

I hear the universal cock-crowing with surprise and pleasure, as if I
never heard it before. What a tough fellow! How native to the earth!
Neither wet nor dry, cold nor warm, kills him.

June 19

It requires considerable skill in crossing a country to avoid the
houses and too cultivated parts—somewhat of the engineer's or gunner's
skill—so to pass a house, if you must go near it through high grass—
pass the enemy's lines where houses are thick—as to make a hill or
wood screen you—to shut every window with an apple tree. For that
route which most avoids the houses is not only the one in which you

will be least molested, but it is by far the most agreeable. Saw the handsomest large maple west of this hill that I ever saw. We crawled through the end of a swamp on our bellies, the bushes were so thick, to screen us from a house forty rods off whose windows completely commanded the open ground, leaping some broad ditches, and when we emerged into the grass ground, some apple trees near the house beautifully screened us. It is rare that you cannot avoid a grain-field or piece of English mowing by skirting a corn-field or nursery near by, but if you must go through high grass, then step lightly and in each other's tracks.

June 25

One man lies in his words, and gets a bad reputation; another in his manners, and enjoys a good one.

June 30

Nature must be viewed humanly to be viewed at all; that is, her scenes must be associated with humane affections, such as are associated with one's native place, for instance. She is most significant to a lover. A lover of Nature is preëminently a lover of man. If I have no friend, what is Nature to me? She ceases to be morally significant.

July 2

Nature is reported not by him who goes forth consciously as an observer, but in the fullness of life. To such a one she rushes to make her report. To the full heart she is all but a figure of speech.

July 5

The wood thrush's is no opera music; it is not so much the composition as the strain, the tone—cool bars of melody from the atmosphere of everlasting morning or evening.[1] It is the quality of the song, not the sequence. In the peawai's note there is some sultriness, but in the thrush's, though heard at noon, there is the liquid coolness of things that are just drawn from the bottom of springs. The thrush alone declares the immortal wealth and vigor that is in the forest. Here is a bird in whose strain the story is told, though Nature waited for the science of æsthetics to discover it to man. Whenever a man hears it, he is young, and Nature is in her spring. Wherever he hears it, it is a new world and a free country, and the gates of heaven are not shut against him. Most other birds sing from the level of my ordinary cheer-

[1] [Apparently Thoreau did not distinguish the wood thrush from the hermit thrush.]

ful hours—a carol; but this bird never fails to speak to me out of an ether purer than that I breathe, of immortal beauty and vigor. He deepens the significance of all things seen in the light of his strain. He sings to make men take higher and truer views of things. He sings to amend their institutions; to relieve the slave on the plantation and the prisoner in the dungeon, the slave in the house of luxury and the prisoner of his own low thoughts.

July 7, 4 A.M.

The first really foggy morning. Yet before I rise I hear the song of birds from out it, like the bursting of its bubbles with music, the bead on liquids just uncorked. Their song gilds thus the frostwork of the morning. As if the fog were a great sweet froth on the surface of land and water, whose fixed air escaped, whose bubbles burst with music. The sound of its evaporation, the fixed air of the morning just brought from the cellars of the night escaping. The morning twittering of birds in perfect harmony with it. I came near awaking this morning. I am older than last year; the mornings are further between; the days are fewer. Any excess—to have drunk too much water, even, the day before— is fatal to the morning's clarity, but in health the sound of a cow-bell is celestial music.

July 11

What is called genius is the abundance of life or health, so that whatever addresses the senses, as the flavor of these berries, or the lowing of that cow, which sounds as if it echoed along a cool mountain-side just before night, where odoriferous dews perfume the air, and there is everlasting vigor, serenity, and expectation of perpetual untarnished morning—each sight and sound and scent and flavor— intoxicates with a healthy intoxication. The shrunken stream of life overflows its banks, makes and fertilizes broad intervals, from which generations derive their sustenances. This is the true overflowing of the Nile. So exquisitely sensitive are we, it makes us embrace our fates, and, instead of suffering or indifference, we enjoy and bless. If we have not dissipated the vital, the divine, fluids, there is, then, a circulation of vitality beyond our bodies. The cow is nothing. Heaven is not there, but in the condition of the hearer. I am thrilled to think that I owe a perception to the commonly gross sense of taste, that I have been inspired through the palate, that these berries have fed my brain. After I had been eating these simple, wholesome, ambrosial fruits on this high hillside, I found my senses whetted, I was young again, and whether I stood or sat I was not the same creature.

July 12

Now for another fluvial walk. There is always a current of air above the water, blowing up or down the course of the river, so that this is the coolest highway. Divesting yourself of all clothing but your shirt and hat, which are to protect your exposed parts from the sun, you are prepared for the fluvial excursion. You choose what depths you like, tucking your toga higher or lower, as you take the deep middle of the road or the shallow sidewalks. Here is a road where no dust was ever known, no intolerable drouth. Now your feet expand on a smooth sandy bottom, now contract timidly on pebbles, now slump in genial fatty mud—greasy, saponaceous—amid the pads. You scare out whole schools of small breams and perch, and sometimes a pickerel, which have taken shelter from the sun under the pads. This river is so clear compared with the South Branch, or main stream, that all their secrets are betrayed to you. Or you meet with and interrupt a turtle taking a more leisurely walk up the stream. Ever and anon you cross some furrow in the sand, made by a muskrat, leading off to right or left to their galleries in the bank, and you thrust your foot into the entrance, which is just below the surface of the water and is strewn with grass and rushes, of which they make their nests. In shallow water near the shore, your feet at once detect the presence of springs in the bank emptying in, by the sudden coldness of the water, and there, if you are thirsty, you dig a little well in the sand with your hands, and when you return, after it has settled and clarified itself, get a draught of pure cold water there. The fishes are very forward to find out such places, and I have observed that a frog will occupy a cool spring, however small.

July 14

A writer who does not speak out of a full experience uses torpid words, wooden or lifeless words, such words as "humanitary," which have a paralysis in their tails.

The youth gets together his materials to build a bridge to the moon, or perchance a palace or temple on the earth, and at length the middle-aged man concludes to build a wood-shed with them.

July 18

When I think of the London *Times* and the reviews here, the *Revue des Deux Mondes,* and of the kind of life which it is possible to live here, I perceive that this, the natural side, has not got into literature. Think of an essay on human life, through all which was heard the note of the huckleberry-bird[1] still ringing, as here it rings ceaselessly. As if it were the muse invoked! The *Revue des Deux Mondes* does not embrace this view of things, nor imply it.

July 24

It would be well if the false preacher of Christianity were always met and balked by a superior, more living and elastic faith in his audience; just as some missionaries in India are balked by the easiness with which the Hindoos believe every word of the miracles and prophecies, being only surprised "that they are so much less wonderful than those of their own scripture, which ,also they implicitly believe."

Just after sunrise this morning I noticed Hayden walking beside his team, which was slowly drawing a heavy hewn stone swung under the axle, surrounded by an atmosphere of industry, his day's work begun. Honest, peaceful industry, conserving the world, which all men respect, which society has consecrated. A reproach to all sluggards and idlers. Pausing abreast the shoulders of his oxen and half turning round, with a flourish of his merciful whip, while they gained their length on him. And I thought, such is the labor which the American Congress exists to protect—honest, manly toil. His brow has commenced to sweat. Honest as the day is long. One of the sacred band doing the needful but irksome drudgery. Toil that makes his bread taste sweet, and keeps society sweet. The day went by, and at evening I passed a rich man's yard, who keeps many servants and foolishly spends much money while he adds nothing to the common stock, and there I saw Hayden's stone lying beside a whimsical structure intended to adorn this Lord Timothy Dexter's mansion, and the dignity forthwith departed from Hayden's labor, in my eyes. I am frequently invited to survey farms in a rude manner, a very [*sic*] and insignificant labor, though I manage to get more out of it than my employers; but I am never invited by the community to do anything quite worth the while to do. How much of the industry of the boor, traced to the end, is found thus to be subserving some rich man's foolish enterprise! There is a coarse, boisterous, money-making fellow in the north part of the town who is going to build a bank wall under the hill along the edge of his meadow. The powers have put this into his head to keep him out of mischief, and he wishes me to spend three weeks digging there with

[1] [The field sparrow.]

him. The result will be that he will perchance get a little more money to hoard, or leave for his heirs to spend foolishly when he is dead. Now, if I do this, the community will commend me as an industrious and hard-working man; but, as I choose to devote myself to labors which yield more real profit, though but little money, they regard me as a loafer. But, as I do not need this police of meaningless labor to regulate me, and do not see anything absolutely praiseworthy in his undertaking, however amusing it may be to him, I prefer to finish my education at a different school.

July 26

By my intimacy with nature I find myself withdrawn from man. My interest in the sun and the moon, in the morning and the evening, compels me to solitude.

The grandest picture in the world is the sunset sky. In your higher moods what man is there to meet? You are of necessity isolated. The mind that perceives clearly any natural beauty is in that instant withdrawn from human society. My desire for society is infinitely increased; my fitness for any actual society is diminished.

July 27

I am sure that if I call for a companion in my walk I have relinquished in my design some closeness of communion with Nature. The walk will surely be more commonplace. The inclination for society indicates a distance from Nature. I do not design so wild and mysterious a walk.

How cool and assuaging the thrush's note after the fever of the day! I doubt if they have anything so richly wild in Europe. So long a civilization must have banished it. It will only be heard in America, perchance, while our star is in the ascendant. I should be very much surprised if I were to hear in the strain of the nightingale such unexplored wildness and fertility, reaching to sundown, inciting to emigration. Such a bird must itself have emigrated long ago.

Aug. 3

A thrumming of piano-strings beyond the gardens and through the elms. At length the melody steals into my being. I know not when it began to occupy me. By some fortunate coincidence of thought or circumstance I am attuned to the universe, I am fitted to hear, my being moves in a sphere of melody, my fancy and imagination are excited to an inconceivable degree. This is no longer the dull earth on which I stood. It is possible to live a grander life here; already the steed is stamping, the knights are prancing; already our thoughts bid a proud farewell to the so-called actual life and its humble glories. Now this is the verdict of a soul in health. But the soul diseased says that its own vision and life alone is true and sane. What a different aspect will courage put upon the face of things!

Aug. 5

I can tell the extent to which a man has heard music by the faith he retains in the trivial and mean, even by the importance he attaches to what is called the actual world. Any memorable strain will have unsettled so low a faith and substituted a higher. Men profess to be lovers of music, but for the most part they give no evidence in their opinions and lives that they have heard it. It would not leave them narrow-minded and bigoted.

Aug. 7

When I think of the thorough drilling to which young men are subjected in the English universities, acquiring a minute knowledge of Latin prosody and of Greek particles and accents, so that they can not only turn a passage of Homer into English prose or verse, but readily a passage of Shakespeare into Latin hexameters or elegiacs—that this and the like of this is to be liberally educated—I am reminded how different was the education of the actual Homer and Shakespeare. The worthies of the world and liberally educated have always, in this sense, got along with little Latin and less Greek.

Aug. 8

The entertaining a single thought of a certain elevation makes all men of one religion. It is always some base alloy that creates the distinction of sects. Thought greets thought over the widest gulfs of time with unerring freemasonry. I know, for instance, that Sadi[1] entertained once identically the same thought that I do, and thereafter I can find no essential difference between Sadi and myself. He is not Persian, he is not ancient, he is not strange to me. By the identity of his thoughts with mine he still survives. It makes no odds what atoms serve us. Sadi possessed no greater privacy or individuality than is thrown open to me. He had no more interior and essential and sacred self than can come naked into my thought this moment. Truth

[1] [Sa'di (1184–1292), foremost poet of Persia, was highly valued by Emerson.]

and a true man is something essentially public, not private. If Sadi were to come back to claim a *personal* identity with the historical Sadi, he would find there were too many of us; he could not get a skin that would contain us all. The symbol of a personal identity preserved in this sense is a mummy from the catacombs—a whole skin, it may [be], but no life within it. By living the life of a man is made common property. By sympathy with Sadi I have embowelled him. In his thought I have a sample of *him*, a slice from his core, which makes it unimportant where certain bones which the thinker once employed may lie; but I could not have got this without being equally entitled to it with himself. The difference between any man and that posterity amid whom he is famous is too insignificant to sanction that he should be set up again in any world as distinct from them. Methinks I can be as intimate with the essence of an ancient worthy as, so to speak, he was with himself.

I only know myself as a human entity, the scene, so to speak, of thoughts and affections, and am sensible of a certain doubleness by which I can stand as remote from myself as from another. However intense my experience, I am conscious of the presence and criticism of a part of me which, as it were, is not a part of me, but spectator, sharing no experience, but taking note of it, and that is no more I than it is you. When the play—it may be the tragedy of life—is over, the spectator goes his way. It was a kind of fiction, a work of the imagination only, so far as he was concerned.

Aug. 23

I live so much in my habitual thoughts, a routine of thought, that I forget there is any outside to the globe, and am surprised when I behold it as now—yonder hills and river in the moonlight, the monsters. Yet it is salutary to deal with the surface of things. What are these rivers and hills, these hieroglyphics which my eyes behold? There is something invigorating in this air, which I am peculiarly sensible is a real wind, blowing from over the surface of a planet. I look out at my eyes, I come to my window, and I feel and breathe the fresh air. It is a fact equally glorious with the most inward experience. Why have we ever slandered the outward? The perception of surfaces will always have the effect of miracle to a sane sense.

Aug. 24

How far we can be apart and yet attract each other! There is one who almost wholly misunderstands me and whom I too probably misunderstand, toward whom, nevertheless, I am distinctly drawn. I have the utmost human good-will toward that one, and yet I know not what mistrust keeps us asunder. I am so much and so exclusively the friend of my friend's virtue that I am compelled to be silent for the most part, because his vice is present. I am made dumb by this third party. I only desire *sincere* relations with the worthiest of my acquaintance, that they may give me an opportunity once in a year to speak the truth. They invite me to see them, and do not show themselves. . . . I leave my friends early; I go away to cherish my idea of friendship.

Sept. 13

I must walk more with free senses. It is as bad to *study* stars and clouds as flowers and stones. I must let my senses wander as my thoughts, my eyes see without looking. Carlyle said that how to observe was to look, but I say that it is rather to see, and the more you look the less you will observe. I have the habit of attention to such excess that my senses get no rest, but suffer from a constant strain. Be not preoccupied with looking. Go not to the object; let it come to you. When I have found myself ever looking down and confining my gaze to the flowers, I have thought it might be well to get into the habit of observing the clouds as a corrective; but no! that study would be just as bad. What I need is not to look at all, but a true sauntering of the eye.

Sept. 23

In love we impart, each to each, in subtlest immaterial form of thought or atmosphere, the best of ourselves, such as commonly vanishes or evaporates in aspirations, and mutually enrich each other. The lover alone perceives and dwells in a certain human fragrance. To him humanity is not only a flower, but an aroma and a flavor also.

Oct. 20

Many a man, when I tell him that I have been on to a mountain, asks if I took a glass with me. No doubt, I could have seen further with a glass, and particular objects more distinctly—could have counted more meeting-houses; but this has nothing to do with the peculiar beauty and grandeur of the view which an elevated position affords. It was not to see a few particular objects, as if they were near at hand, as I had been accustomed to see them, that I ascended the mountain, but to see an infinite variety far and near in their relation to each other, thus reduced to a single picture. The facts of science, in comparison

with poetry, are wont to be as vulgar as looking from the mountain
with a telescope. It is a counting of meeting-houses.[1]

Oct. 23

What men call social virtues, good fellowship, is commonly but the
virtue of pigs in a litter, which lie close together to keep each other
warm. It brings men together in crowds and mobs in barrooms and
elsewhere, but it does not deserve the name of virtue.

Oct. 28

After whatever revolutions in my moods and experiences, when I
come forth at evening, as if from years of confinement to the house, I
see the few stars which make the constellation of the Lesser Bear in
the same relative position—the everlasting geometry of the stars. How
incredible to be described are these bright points which appear in the
blue sky as the darkness increases, said to be other worlds, like the
berries on the hills when the summer is ripe! Even the ocean of birds,
even the regions of the ether, are studded with isles. Far in this ethereal
sea lie the Hesperian isles, unseen by day, but when the darkness comes
their fires are seen from this shore, as Columbus saw the fires of San
Salvador.

Nov. 4

Must be out-of-doors enough to get experience of wholesome reality,
as a ballast to thought and sentiment. Health requires this relaxation,
this aimless life. This life in the present. Let a man have thought what
he will of Nature in the house, she will still be novel outdoors. I keep
out of doors for the sake of the mineral, vegetable, and animal in me.

My thought is a part of the meaning of the world, and hence I use a
part of the world as a symbol to express my thought.

Dec. 28

It is worth the while to apply what wisdom one has to the conduct
of his life, surely. I find myself oftenest wise in little things and foolish
in great ones. That I may accomplish some particular pretty affair
well, I live my whole life coarsely. A broad margin of leisure is as
beautiful in a man's life as in a book. Haste makes waste, no less in life
than in housekeeping. Keep the time, observe the hours of the universe, not of the cars. What are threescore years and ten hurriedly

---

[1] [In 1854 Thoreau bought a small spyglass for birdwatching.]

and coarsely lived to moments of divine leisure in which your life is coincident with the life of the universe? We live too fast and coarsely, just as we eat too fast, and do not know the true savor of our food. We consult our will and understanding and the expectation of men, not our genius. I can impose upon myself tasks which will crush me for life and prevent all expansion, and this I am but too inclined to do.

One moment of life costs many hours, hours not of business but of preparation and invitation. Yet the man who does not betake himself at once and desperately to sawing is called a loafer, though he may be knocking at the doors of heaven all the while, which shall surely be opened to him. That aim in life is highest which requires the highest and finest discipline. How much, what infinite, leisure it requires, as of a lifetime, to appreciate a single phenomenon! You must camp down beside it as for life, having reached your land of promise, and give yourself wholly to it. It must stand for the whole world to you, symbolical of all things. The least partialness is your own defect of sight and cheapens the experience fatally. Unless the humming of a gnat is as the music of the spheres, and the music of the spheres is as the humming of a gnat, they are naught to me. It is not communications to serve for a history—which are sciences—but the great story itself, that cheers and satisfies us.

1853-54

Having found for himself a way of keeping fully alive while earning a liveli-
hood, Thoreau was concerned in these years with the plight of those who had
discovered no such solution. His journal entries on this theme were brought
together in the posthumous essay called "Life Without Principle," a badly
organized but powerful protest against the notion summed up in the famous
words: "America's business is business."

The Fugitive Slave Law of 1850 had jolted Thoreau out of his habitual
indifference to politics. In 1851 he had helped an escaping slave to reach Canada,
and probably he took every later opportunity to commit the same crime. During
the excitement in Boston over the remanding of Anthony Burns, he wrote in his
journal for 1853 a fierce denunciation of government later delivered as a speech
entitled "Slavery in Massachusetts." Taken together with his "Civil Dis-
obedience," oddly contemporary in 1848 with the "Communist Manifesto,"
these pronouncements show that Thoreau was no longer, if he ever had been, a
"hermit."

He did not, however, take an active part in any of the societies working for
the abolition of slavery, and the professional reformers drifting in and out of
Concord had cold greetings from him. Characteristically, he thought of the
national crisis not in national terms but only as it was related to his state, town,
neighbors, and himself. Feeling personally besmirched by the iniquity of human
bondage, he preferred to fight it single-handed.

Over 700 unsold copies of Thoreau's first book were returned to him by the
publisher in 1853. Undismayed by this rebuff, he published Walden *less than*
a year later.

Jan. 1, 1853

Being at Cambridge day before yesterday, Sibley told me that
Agassiz told him that Harris[1] was the greatest entomologist in the
world, and gave him permission to repeat his remark. As I stood on
the top of a ladder, he[2] came along with his hand full of papers and
inquired, "Do you value autographs?" "No, I do not," I answered
slowly and gravely. "Oh, I didn't know but you did. I had some of
Governor Dunlap," said he, retreating.

After talking with Uncle Charles the other night about the worthies

---

[1] [Thaddeus William Harris, Harvard Librarian, 1831–36. John Sibley, his
assistant, succeeded him.]

[2] [That is, Harris.]

of this country, Webster and the rest, as usual, considering who were geniuses and who not, I showed him up to bed, and when I had got into bed myself, I heard his chamber door opened, after eleven o'clock, and he called out, in an earnest, stentorian voice, loud enough to wake the whole house, "Henry! was John Quincy Adams a genius?" "No, I think not," was my reply. "Well, I didn't think he was," answered he.

Jan. 2

The bells are particularly sweet this morning. I hear more, methinks, than ever before. How much more religion in their sound than they ever call men together to! Men obey their call and go to the stove-warmed church, though God exhibits himself to the walker in a frosted bush today as much as in a burning one to Moses of old.

Jan. 3

I love Nature partly *because* she is not man, but a retreat from him. None of his institutions control or pervade her. There a different kind of right prevails. In her midst I can be glad with an entire gladness. If this world were all man, I could not stretch myself, I should lose all hope. He is constraint, she is freedom to me. He makes me wish for another world. She makes me content with this. None of the joys she supplies is subject to his rules and definitions. What he touches he taints. In thought he moralizes. One would think that no free, joyful labor was possible to him. How infinite and pure the least pleasure of which Nature is basis, compared with the congratulation of mankind! The joy which Nature yields is like [that] afforded by the frank words of one we love.

> Man, man is the devil,
> The source of all evil.

Methinks that these prosers, with their saws and their laws, do not know how glad a man can be. What wisdom, what warning, can prevail against gladness? There is no law so strong which a little gladness may not transgress. I have a room all to myself; it is nature. It is a place beyond the jurisdiction of human governments. Pile up your books, the records of sadness, your saws[1] and your laws. Nature is glad outside, and her merry worms within will ere long topple them down. There is a prairie beyond your law. Nature is a prairie for outlaws. There are two worlds, the post-office and nature. I know them both. I continually forget mankind and their institutions, as I do a bank.

---

[1] [Moralistic proverbs.]

Jan. 9, 3 P.M.

To Walden and Cliffs.
The telegraph harp again. Always the same unrememberable revelation it is to me. It is something as enduring as the worm that never dies. Before the [*sic*] it was, and will be after. I never hear it without thinking of Greece. How the Greeks *harped* upon the words immortal, ambrosial! They are what it says. It stings my ear with everlasting truth. It allies Concord to Athens, and both to Elysium. It always intoxicates me, makes me sane, reverses my views of things. I am pledged to it. I get down the railroad till I hear that which makes all the world a lie. When the zephyr, or west wind, sweeps this wire, I rise to the height of my being. A period—a semicolon, at least—is put to my previous and habitual ways of viewing things. This wire is my redeemer. It always brings a special and a general message to me from the Highest. Day before yesterday I looked at the mangled and blackened bodies of men which had been blown up by powder,[1] and felt that the lives of men were not innocent, and that there was an avenging power in nature. Today I hear this immortal melody, while the west wind is blowing balmily on my cheek, and methinks a roseate sunset is preparing. Are there not two powers?

Jan. 14

I am often reminded that the farmer living far inland has not thought of plows and carts alone. Here, when getting his fuel, he cuts the roots or limbs of some sturdier [tree] with reference to the uses it may serve in the construction of a ship. The farmer not only gets out wood to burn, but ship-timber. It was he who decided the destiny [of] some mighty oak, that it should become the keel of a famous ship. It is he who says, "Ye shall become ships to plow the sea," when he says, "Ye shall become money to me." It is in the woods and in the farmer's yard that the vessel is first put upon the stocks. He burns the hewings in his ample fireplace; he teams the rest to Medford with the same yokes that plow his fields. With bars and chains he clutches and binds the wheels, and with numerous yokes drags it over the hills to the nearest port. He learns as well as the engineer what hills are steep, what ground ascends. By repeated strains and restings on the terraces, he at length surmounts every difficulty. Think of the difficulties which the farmer silently overcomes, who conveys the keel or mast of a man-of-war from his woods to the nearest port, which would have defied the skill of a tribe of savages to overcome!

[1] [In a powder mill four miles west of Concord.]

Men's ignorance is made as useful as their knowledge. If one knew more, he would admire less. In the winter how many farmers help build ships where men grow up who never saw the ocean!

Jan. 21

Silence alone is worthy to be heard. Silence is of various depth and fertility, like soil. Now it is a mere Sahara, where men perish of hunger and thirst, now a fertile bottom, or prairie, of the West. As I leave the village, drawing nearer to the woods, I listen from time to time to hear the hounds of Silence baying the Moon—to know if they are on the track of any game. If there's no Diana in the night, what is it worth? I hark the goddess Diana. The silence rings; it is musical and thrills me. A night in which the silence was audible. I hear the unspeakable.

Jan. 25

The pickerel of Walden! when I see them lying on the ice, or in the well which the fisherman cuts in the ice, I am always surprised by their rare beauty, as if they were a fabulous fish, they are so foreign to the streets, or even the woods; handsome as flowers and gems, golden and emerald—a transcendent and dazzling beauty which separates [them] by a wide interval from the cadaverous cod and haddock, at least a day old, which we see. They are as foreign as Arabia to our Concord life, as if the two ends of the earth had come together. These are not green like the pines, or gray like the stones, or blue like the sky; but they have, if possible, to my eye, yet rarer colors, like precious stones. It is surprising that these fishes are caught here. They are something tropical. That in this deep and capacious spring, far beneath the rattling teams and chaises and tinkling sleighs that travel the Walden road, this great gold and emerald fish swims! They are true topazes, inasmuch as you can only conjecture what place they come from. The pearls of Walden, some animalized Walden water. I never chanced to see this kind of fish in any market. With a few convulsive quirks they give up their diluted ghosts.

Jan. 26

It is surprising how much room there is in nature—if a man will follow his proper path. In these broad fields, in these extensive woods, on this stretching river, I never meet a walker. Passing behind the farmhouses, I see no man out. Perhaps I do not meet so many men as I should have met three centuries ago, when the Indian hunter roamed these woods. I enjoy the retirement and solitude of an early settler. Men have cleared some of the earth, which no doubt is an advantage to the walker. I see a man sometimes chopping in the woods, or planting or hoeing in a field, at a distance; and yet there may be a lyceum in the evening, and there is a book-shop and library in the village, and five times a day I can be whirled to Boston within an hour.

Jan. 27

Trench[1] says a wild man is a *willed* man. Well, then, a man of will who does what he wills or wishes, a man of hope and of the future tense, for not only the obstinate is willed, but far more the constant and persevering. The obstinate man, properly speaking, is one who will not. The perseverance of the saints is positive willedness, not a mere passive willingness. The fates are wild, for they *will*; and the Almighty is wild above all, as fate is.

What are our fields but *felds* or *felled* woods.[2] They bear a more recent name than the woods, suggesting that previously the earth was covered with woods. Always in the new country a field is a clearing.

Jan. 31

A man is wise with the wisdom of his time only, and ignorant with its ignorance. Observe how the greatest minds yield in some degree to the superstitions of their age.

Feb. 11

While surveying on the Hunt farm the other day, behind Simon Brown's house I heard a remarkable echo. In the course of surveying, being obliged to call aloud to my assistant from every side and almost every part of a farm in succession, and at various hours of a day, I am pretty sure to discover an echo if any exists, and the other day it was encouraging and soothing to hear it. After so many days of comparatively insignificant drudgery with stupid companions, this leisure, this sportiveness, this generosity in nature, sympathizing with the better part of me; somebody I could talk with—one degree, at least, better than talking with one's self. Ah! Simon Brown's premises harbor a hired man and a hired maid he wots not of. Some voice of somebody I pined to hear, with whom I could form a community. I did wish,

---

[1] [Richard Chevenix Trench (1807–96), Anglican archbishop, poet, and etymologist. Thoreau had in hand his book *The Study of Words*, 1851.]

[2] [This derivation, like many or most of those proposed by Thoreau, is purely fanciful.]

rather, to linger there and call all day to the air and hear my words repeated, but a vulgar necessity dragged me along round the bounds of the farm, to hear only the stale answers of my chain-man shouted back to me.

I am surprised that we make no more ado about echoes. They are almost the only kindred voices that I hear. I wonder that the traveller does not oftener remark upon a remarkable echo—he who observes so many things. There needs some actual doubleness like this in nature, for if the voices which we commonly hear were all that we ever heard, what then? Has it to do with the season of the year? I have since heard an echo on Moore's farm.

It was the memorable event of the day, that echo I heard, not anything my companions said, or the travellers whom I met, or my thoughts, for they were all mere repetitions or echoes in the worst sense of what I had heard and thought before many times; but this echo was accompanied with novelty, and by its repetition of my voice it did more than double that. It was a profounder Socratic method of suggesting thoughts unutterable to me the speaker. There was one I heartily loved to talk with. Under such favorable auspices I could converse with myself, could reflect; the hour, the atmosphere, and the conformation of the ground permitted it.

Feb. 23

I think myself in a wilder country, and a little nearer to primitive times, when I read in old books which spell the word savages with an *l* (salvages), like John Smith's *General Historie of Virginia, etc.*, reminding me of the derivation of the word from *sylva*. There is some of the wild wood and its bristling branches still left in their language. The savages they described are really *salvages*, men of the *woods*.

March 5

The Secretary of the Association for the Advancement of Science[1] requests me, as he probably has thousands of others, by a printed circular letter from Washington the other day, to fill the blank against certain questions, among which the most important one was what branch of science I was specially interested in, using the term science in the most comprehensive sense possible. Now, though I could state to a select few that department of human inquiry which engages me, and should be rejoiced at an opportunity to do so, I felt that it would be to make myself the laughing-stock of the scientific community to

[1] [Founded in 1848 and still active. Thoreau never joined it.]

describe or attempt to describe to them that branch of science which specially interests me, inasmuch as they do not believe in a science which deals with the higher law. So I was obliged to speak to their condition and describe to them that poor part of me which alone they can understand. The fact is I am a mystic, a transcendentalist, and a natural philosopher to boot. Now I think of it, I should have told them at once that I was a transcendentalist. That would have been the shortest way of telling them that they would not understand my explanations.

How absurd that, though I probably stand as near to nature as any of them, and am by constitution as good an observer as most, yet a true account of my relation to nature should excite their ridicule only! If it had been the secretary of an association of which Plato or Aristotle was the president, I should not have hesitated to describe my studies at once and particularly.

March 12

It is essential that a man confine himself to pursuits—a scholar, for instance, to studies—which lie next to and conduce to his life, which do not go against the grain, either of his will or his imagination. The scholar finds in his experience some studies to be most fertile and radiant with light, others dry, barren, and dark. If he is wise, he will not persevere in the last, as a plant in a cellar will strive toward the light. He will confine the observations of his mind as closely as possible to the experience or life of his senses. His thought must live with and be inspired with the life of the body.[1]

March 13

All enterprises must be self-supporting, must pay for themselves. The great art of life is how to turn the surplus life of the soul into life for the body—that so the life be not a failure. For instance, a poet must sustain his body with his poetry. As is said of the merchants, in ninety-nine cases out of a hundred the life of men is a failure, and bankruptcy may be surely prophesied. You must get your living by loving. To be supported by the charity of friends or a government pension is to go into the almshouse. To inherit property is not to be born—is to be still-born rather.

March 21

Ah! then, as I was rising this crowning road, just beyond the old lime-kiln, there leaked into my open ear the faint peep of a hyla from

---

[1] [One of Thoreau's central intuitions.]

some far pool. One little hyla somewhere in the fens, aroused by the genial season, crawls up the bank or a bush, squats on a dry leaf, and essays a note or two, which scarcely rends the air, does no violence to the zephyr, but yet breaks through all obstacles, thick-planted maples, and far over the downs to the ear of the listening naturalist, who will never see that piper in this world—nor even the next, it may be—as it were the first faint cry of the new-born year, notwithstanding the notes of birds. Where so long I have heard only the brattling and moaning of the wind, what means this tenser, far-piercing sound? All nature rejoices with one joy. If the hyla has revived again, may not I?

Whatever your sex or position, life is a battle in which you are to show your pluck, and woe be to the coward. Whether passed on a bed of sickness or a tented field, it is ever the same fair play and admits no foolish distinction. Despair and postponement are cowardice and defeat. Men were born to succeed, not to fail.

March 23

Man cannot afford to be a naturalist, to look at Nature directly, but only with the side of his eye. He must look through and beyond her. To look at her is fatal as to look at the head of Medusa. It turns the man of science to stone. I feel that I am dissipated by so many observations. I should be the magnet in the midst of all this dust and filings.

Without being the owner of any land, I find that I have a civil right in the river—that, if I am not a land-owner I am a water-owner. It is fitting, therefore, that I should have a boat, a cart, for this my farm. Since it is almost wholly given up to a few of us, while the other high-ways are much travelled, no wonder that I improve it. Such a one as I will choose to dwell in a township where there are most ponds and rivers and our range is widest. In relation to the river, I find my natural rights least infringed on. It is an extensive "common" still left. Certain savage liberties still prevail in the oldest and most civilized countries. . . . Nobody legislates for me, for the way would be not to legislate at all.

I am surprised as well as delighted when any one wishes to know what I think. It is such a rare use they would make of me, as if they were acquainted with the tool. Commonly, if men want anything of me, it is only to know how many acres I make of their land, or, at most, what trivial news I have burdened myself with. They never will go to law for my meat. They prefer the shell.

March 26

Saw about 10 A.M. a gaggle of geese, forty-three in number, in a very perfect harrow flying northeasterly. One side [of] the harrow was a little longer than the other. They appeared to be four or five feet apart. At first I heard faintly, as I stood by Minott's gate, borne to me from the southwest through the confused sounds of the village, the indistinct honking of geese. I was somewhat surprised to find that Mr. Loring at his house should have heard and seen the same flock. I should think that the same flock was commonly seen and heard from the distance of a mile east and west. It is remarkable that we commonly see geese go over in the spring about 10 o'clock in the morning, as if they were accustomed to stop for the night at some place southward whence they reached us at that time.

March 28

My Aunt Maria asked me to read the life of Dr. Chalmers, which, however, I did not promise to do. Yesterday, Sunday, she was heard through the partition shouting to my Aunt Jane, who is deaf, "Think of it! He stood half an hour today to hear the frogs croak, and he wouldn't read the life of Chalmers." [1]

March 30

Ah, those youthful days! are they never to return? when the walker does not too curiously observe particulars, but sees, hears, scents, tastes, and feels only himself—the phenomena that show themselves in him—his expanding body, his intellect and heart. No worm or insect, quadruped or bird, confined his view, but the unbounded universe was his. A bird is now become a mote in his eye.

April 3

I have no time to read newspapers. If you chance to live and move and have your being in that thin stratum in which the events which make the news transpire—thinner than the paper on which it is printed—then these things will fill the world for you; but if you soar above or dive below that plane, you cannot remember nor be reminded of them.

---

[1] [The *Memoirs of Thomas Chalmers*, Scottish theologian, published in four volumes, 1849–52.]

April 4

The other day, when I had been standing perfectly still some ten minutes, looking at a willow which had just blossomed, some rods in the rear of Martial Miles's house, I felt eyes on my back and, turning round suddenly, saw the heads of two men who had stolen out of the house and were watching me over a rising ground as fixedly as I the willow. They were studying man, which is said to be the proper study of mankind, I nature, and yet, when detected, they felt the cheapest of the two.

May 9

I have devoted most of my day to Mr. Alcott.[1] He is broad and genial, but indefinite; some would say feeble; forever feeling about vainly in his speech and touching nothing. But this is a very negative account of him, for he thus suggests far more than the sharp and definite practical mind. The feelers of his thought diverge—such is the breadth of their grasp—not converge; and in his society almost alone I can express at my leisure, with more or less success, my vaguest but most cherished fancy or thought. There are never any obstacles in the way of our meeting. He has no creed. He is not pledged to any institution. The sanest man I ever knew; the fewest crotchets, after all, has he.

It has occurred to me, while I am thinking with pleasure of our day's intercourse, "Why should I not think aloud to you?" Having each some shingles of thought well dried, we walk and whittle them, trying our knives, and admiring the clear yellowish grain of the pumpkin pine. We wade so gently and reverently, or we pull together so smoothly, that the fishes of thought are not scared from the stream, but come and go grandly, like yonder clouds that float peacefully through the western sky. When we walk it seems as if the heavens—whose mother-o'-pearl and rainbow tints come and go, form and dissolve—and the earth had met together, and righteousness and peace had kissed each other. I have an ally against the arch-enemy. A blue-robed man dwells under the blue concave. The blue sky is a distant reflection of the azure serenity that looks out from under a human brow.

May 10

He is the richest who has most use for nature as raw material of tropes and symbols with which to describe his life. If these gates of

[1] [A. Bronson Alcott, 1799–1888. For Thoreau's estimate of him see "Winter Visitors" in *Walden*.]

golden willows affect me, they correspond to the beauty and promise of some experience on which I am entering. If I am overflowing with life, am rich in experience for which I lack expression, then nature will be my language full of poetry—all nature will *fable*, and every natural phenomenon be a myth. The man of science, who is not seeking for expression but for a fact to be expressed merely, studies nature as a dead language. I pray for such inward experience as will make nature significant.

May 11

I hear the distant drumming of a partridge. Its beat, however distant and low, falls still with a remarkably forcible, almost painful, impulse on the ear, like veritable little drumsticks on our tympanum, as if it were a throbbing or fluttering in our veins or brows or the chambers of the ear, and belonging to ourselves—as if it were produced by some little insect which had made its way up into the passages of the ear, so penetrating is it. It is as palpable to the ear as the sharpest note of a fife. Of course, that bird can drum with its wings on a log which can go off with such a powerful whir, beating the air. I have seen a thoroughly frightened hen and cockerel fly almost as powerfully, but neither can sustain it long. Beginning slowly and deliberately, the partridge's beat sounds faster and faster from far away under the boughs and through the aisles of the wood until it becomes a regular roll, but is speedily concluded. How many things shall we not see and be and do, when we walk there where the partridge drums!

May 12

William Wheeler has raised a new staring house beyond the Corner Bridge, and so done irreparable injury to a large section of country for walkers. It obliges us to take still more steps after weary ones, to reach the secluded fields and woods. Channing proposes that we petition him to put his house out of sight; that we send it into him in the form of a round-robin with his name on one side and mine on the other— so to abate a nuisance.

May 15

The first cricket's chirrup which I have chanced to hear now falls on my ear and makes me forget all else; all else is a thin and movable crust down to that depth where he resides eternally. He already fore-tells autumn. Deep under the dry border of some rock in this hillside he sits, and makes the finest singing of birds outward and insignificant, his own song is so much deeper and more significant. His voice has set me thinking, philosophizing, moralizing at once. It is not so wildly melodious, but it is wiser and more mature than that of the wood thrush. With this elixir I see clear through the summer now to autumn, and any summer work seems frivolous. I am disposed to ask this humblebee that hurries humming past so busily if he knows what he is about. At one leap I go from the just opened buttercup to the life-everlasting. This singer has antedated autumn. His strain is superior (inferior?) [1] to seasons. It annihilates time and space; the summer is for time-servers.

May 22

When yesterday Sophia and I were rowing past Mr. Prichard's land, where the river is bordered by a row of elms and low willows, at 6 P.M., we heard a singular note of distress as it were from a catbird—a loud, vibrating, catbird sort of note, as if the catbird's mew were imitated by a smart vibrating spring. Blackbirds and others were flitting about, apparently attracted by it. At first, thinking it was merely some peevish catbird or red-wing, I was disregarding it, but on second thought turned the bows to the shore, looking into the trees as well as over the shore, thinking some bird might be in distress, caught by a snake or in a forked twig. The hovering birds dispersed at my approach; the note of distress sounded louder and nearer as I approached the shore covered with low osiers. The sound came from the ground, not from the trees. I saw a little black animal making haste to meet the boat under the osiers. A young muskrat? a mink? No, it was a little dot of a kitten. It was scarcely six inches long from the face to the base—or I might as well say the tip—of the tail, for the latter was a short, sharp pyramid, perfectly perpendicular but not swelled in the least. It was a very handsome and very precocious kitten, in perfectly good condition, its breadth being considerably more than one third of its length. Leaving its mewing, it came scrambling over the stones as fast as its weak legs would permit, straight to me. I took it up and dropped it into the boat, but while I was pushing off it ran the length of the boat to Sophia, who held it while we rowed homeward. Evidently it had not been weaned—was smaller than we remembered that kittens ever were—almost infinitely small; yet it had hailed a boat, its life being in danger, and saved itself. Its performance, considering its age and amount of experience, was more wonderful than that of any young mathematician or musician that I

---

[1] Exaltedly inferior. [Thoreau's note.]

have read of. Various were the conjectures as to how the kitten came there, a quarter of a mile from a house. The possible solutions were finally reduced to three: first, it must either have been born there, or, secondly, carried there by its mother, or, thirdly, by human hands. In the first case, it had possibly brothers and sisters, one or both, and its mother had left them to go a-hunting on her own account and might be expected back. In the second, she might equally be expected to return. At any rate, not having thought of all this till we got home, we found that we had got ourselves into a scrape; for this kitten, though exceedingly interesting, required one nurse to attend it constartly for the present, and, of course, another to spell the first; and, beside, we had already a cat well-nigh grown, who manifested such a disposition toward the young stranger that we had no doubt it would have torn it in pieces in a moment if left alone with it. As nobody made up his or her mind to have it drowned, and still less to drown it—having once looked into its innocent extremely pale blue eyes (as of milk thrice skimmed) and had his finger or his chin sucked by it, while, its eyes being shut, its little paws played a soothing tune—it was resolved to keep it till it could be suitably disposed of. It rested nowhere, in no lap, under no covert, but still faintly cried for its mother and its accustomed supper. It ran toward every sound or movement of a human being, and whoever crossed the room it was sure to follow at a rapid pace. It had all the ways of a cat of the maturest years; could purr divinely and raised its back to rub all boots and shoes. When it raised its foot to scratch its ear, which by the way it never hit, it was sure to fall over and roll on the floor. It climbed straight up the sitter, faintly mewing all the way, and sucked his chin. In vain, at first, its head was bent down into saucers of milk which its eyes did not see, and its chin was wetted. But soon it learned to suck a finger that had been dipped in it, and better still a rag; and then at last it slept and rested.

May 23

At Loring's Wood heard and saw a tanager. That contrast of a *red* bird with the green pines and the blue sky! Even when I have heard his note and look for him and find the bloody fellow, sitting on a dead twig of a pine, I am always startled. (They seem to love the darkest and thickest pines.) That incredible red, with the green and blue, as if these were the trinity we wanted. Yet with his hoarse note he pays for his color. I am transported; these are not the woods I ordinarily walk in. He sunk Concord in his thought. How he enhances the wildness and wealth of the woods! This and the emperor moth make the tropical phenomena of our zone. There is warmth in the pewee's strain, but this bird's colors and his note tell of Brazil.

May 24, P.M.

Talked, or tried to talk, with R.W.E. Lost my time—nay, almost my identity. He, assuming a false opposition where there was no difference of opinion, talked to the wind—told me what I knew—and I lost my time trying to imagine myself somebody else to oppose him.[1]

June 5, Sunday

For the most part we are inclined to doubt the prevalence of gross superstition among the civilized ancients—whether the Greeks, for instance, accepted literally the mythology which we accept as matchless poetry—but we have only to be reminded of the kind of respect paid to the Sabbath as a *holy* day here in New England, and the fears which haunt those who *break* it, to see that our neighbors are the creatures of an equally gross superstition with the ancients. I am convinced that there is no very important difference between a New-Englander's religion and a Roman's. We both worship in the shadow of our sins: they erect the temples for us. Jehovah has no superiority to Jupiter. The New-Englander is a pagan suckled in a creed outworn.[2] Superstition has always reigned. It is absurd to think that these farmers, dressed in their Sunday clothes, proceeding to church, differ essentially in this respect from the Roman peasantry. They have merely changed the names and number of their gods. Men were as good then as they are now, and loved one another as much—or little.

June 7

Visited my nighthawk on her nest. Could hardly believe my eyes when I stood within seven feet and beheld her sitting on her eggs, her head to me. She looked so Saturnian, so one with the earth, so sphinx-like, a relic of the reign of Saturn which Jupiter did not destroy, a riddle that might well cause a man to go dash his head against a stone. It was not an actual living creature, far less a winged creature of the air, but a figure in stone or bronze, a fanciful production of art, like the gryphon or phœnix. In fact, with its breast toward me, and owing to its color or size no bill perceptible, it looked like the end [of] a brand, such as are common in a clearing, its breast mottled or alternately waved with dark brown and gray, its flat, grayish, weather-beaten

---

1 [Compare the *Heart of Emerson's Journals* for June, undated, 1853.]
2 [Wordsworth's familiar line is here given a bolder meaning.]

crown, its eyes nearly closed, purposely, lest those bright beads should
betray it, with the stony cunning of the sphinx. A fanciful work in
bronze to ornament a mantel. It was enough to fill one with awe. The
sight of this creature sitting on its eggs impressed me with the venerableness of the globe. There was nothing novel about it. All the while, this
seemingly sleeping bronze sphinx, as motionless as the earth, was
watching me with intense anxiety through those narrow slits in its
eyelids. Another step, and it fluttered down the hill close to the ground,
with a wabbling motion, as if touching the ground now with the tip
of one wing, now with the other, so ten rods to the water, which [it]
skimmed close over a few rods, then rose and soared in the air above
me. Wonderful creature, which sits motionless on its eggs on the barest,
most exposed hills, through pelting storms of rain or hail, as if it were a
rock or a part of the earth itself, the outside of the globe, with its eyes
shut and its wings folded, and, after the two days' storm, when you
think it has become a fit symbol of the rheumatism, it suddenly rises
into the air a bird, one of the most aerial, supple, and graceful of
creatures, without stiffness in its wings or joints! I was a fit prelude to
meeting Prometheus bound to his rock on Caucasus.

June 14

The wood thrush [1] launches forth his evening strains from the midst
of the pines. I admire the moderation of this master. There is nothing
tumultuous in his song. He launches forth one strain with all his heart
and life and soul, of pure and unmatchable melody, and then he
pauses and gives the hearer and himself time to digest this, and then
another and another at suitable intervals. Men talk of the *rich* song of
other birds—the thrasher, mocking-bird, nightingale. But I doubt, I
doubt. They know not what they say! There is as great an interval
between the thrasher and the wood thrush as between Thomson's
Seasons and Homer. The sweetness of the day crystallizes in this
morning coolness.

June 17

Here have been three ultra-reformers, lecturers on Slavery, Temper-
ance, the Church, etc., in and about our house and Mrs. Brooks's the
last three or four days—A. D. Foss, once a Baptist minister in Hopkin-
ton, N.H.; Loring Moody, a sort of travelling pattern-working chap-
lain; and H. C. Wright, who shocks all the old women with his infidel
writings. Though Foss was a stranger to the others, you would have

---

[1] [Probably the hermit thrush is meant here.]

thought them old and familiar cronies. (They happened here together by accident.) They addressed each other constantly by their Christian names, and rubbed you continually with the greasy cheeks of their kindness. They would not keep their distance, but cuddle up and lie spoon-fashion with you, no matter how hot the weather or how narrow the bed—chiefly ——. I was awfully pestered with his benignity; feared I should get greased all over with it past restoration; tried to keep some starch in my clothes. He wrote a book called *A Kiss for a Blow*, and he behaved as if there were no alternative between these, or as if I had given him a blow. I would have preferred the blow, but he was bent on giving me the kiss, when there was neither quarrel nor agreement between us. I wanted that he should straighten his back, smooth out those ogling wrinkles of benignity about his eyes, and, with a healthy reserve, pronounce something in a downright manner. It was difficult to keep clear of his slimy benignity, with which he sought to cover you before he swallowed you and took you fairly into his bowels. It would have been far worse than the fate of Jonah. I do not wish to get any nearer to a man's bowels than usual. They lick you as a cow her calf. They would fain wrap you about with their bowels. —— addressed me as "Henry" within one minute from the time I first laid eyes on him, and when I spoke, he said with drawling, sultry sympathy, "Henry, I know all you would say; I understand you perfectly; you need not explain anything to me;" and to another, "I am going to dive into Henry's inmost depths." I said, "I trust you will not strike your head against the bottom." He could tell in a dark room, with his eyes blinded and in perfect stillness, if there was one there whom he loved. One of the most attractive things about the flowers is their beautiful reserve.

June 22

As I come over the hill, I hear the wood thrush singing his evening lay. This is the only bird whose note affects me like music, affects the flow and tenor of my thought, my fancy and imagination. It lifts and exhilarates me. It is inspiring. It is a medicative draught to my soul. It is an elixir to my eyes and a fountain of youth to all my senses. It changes all hours to an eternal morning. It banishes all trivialness. It reinstates me in my dominion, makes me the lord of creation, is chief musician of my court. This minstrel sings in a time, a heroic age, with which no event in the village can be contemporary. How can they be contemporary when only the latter is *temporary* at all? How can the infinite and eternal be contemporary with the finite and temporal?

So there is something in the music of the cow-bell, something sweeter and more nutritious, than in the milk which the farmers drink. This thrush's song is a *ranz des vaches*[1] to me. I long for wildness, a nature which I cannot put my foot through, woods where the wood thrush forever sings, where the hours are early morning ones, and there is dew on the grass, and the day is forever unproved, where I might have a fertile unknown for a soil about me. I would go after the cows, I would watch the flocks of Admetus there forever, only for my board and clothes. A New Hampshire everlasting and unfallen.

July 30

The wayfarer's tree![2] How good a name! Who bestowed it? How did it get adopted? The mass of men are very unpoetic, yet that Adam that names things is always a poet. The boor is ready to accept the name the poet gives. How nameless is the poet among us! He is abroad, but is not recognized. He does not get crowned with the laurel.

Aug. 7

Is it not as language that all natural objects affect the poet? He sees a flower or other object, and it is beautiful or affecting to him because it is a symbol of his thought, and what he indistinctly feels or perceives is matured in some other organization. The objects I behold correspond to my mood.

Aug. 10

Alcott spent the day with me yesterday. He spent the day before with Emerson. He observed that he had got his wine and now he had come after his venison. Such was the compliment he paid me. The question of a livelihood was troubling him. He knew of nothing which he could do for which men would pay him. He could not compete with the Irish in cradling grain. His early education had not fitted him for a clerkship. He had offered his services to the Abolition Society, to go about the country and speak for freedom as their agent, but they declined him. This is very much to their discredit: they should have been forward to secure him. Such a connection with him would confer unexpected dignity on their enterprise. But they cannot tolerate a man who stands by a head above them. They are as bad—Garrison

---

1 [A tune sung or played by Swiss herdsmen to call cattle.]

2 [In Europe a viburnum; in America, the hobble-bush. The name was invented by John Gerard, Elizabethan herbalist.]

and Phillips, etc.—as the overseers and faculty of Harvard College. They require a man who will train well *under* them. Consequently they have not in their employ any but small men—trainers.

Aug. 16

How earthy old people become—mouldy as the grave! Their wisdom smacks of the earth. There is no foretaste of immortality in it. They remind me of earthworms and mole crickets.

Aug. 23

Live in each season as it passes; breathe the air, drink the drink, taste the fruit, and resign yourself to the influences of each. Let them be your only diet drink and botanical medicines. In August live on berries, not dried meats and pemmican, as if you were on shipboard making your way through a waste ocean, or in a northern desert. Be blown on by all the winds. Open all your pores and bathe in all the tides of Nature, in all her streams and oceans, at all seasons. Miasma and infection are from within, not without. The invalid, brought to the brink of the grave by an unnatural life, instead of imbibing only the great influence that Nature is, drinks only the tea made of a particular herb, while he still continues his unnatural life—saves at the spile and wastes at the bung. He does not love Nature or his life, and so sickens and dies, and no doctor can cure him. Grow green with spring, yellow and ripe with autumn. Drink of each season's influence as a vial, a true panacea of all remedies mixed for your especial use. The vials of summer never made a man sick, but those which he stored in his cellar. Drink the wines, not of your bottling, but Nature's bottling; not kept in goat-skins or pig-skins, but the skins of a myriad fair berries. Let Nature do your bottling and your pickling and preserving. For all Nature is doing her best each moment to make us well. She exists for no other end. Do not resist her. With the least inclination to be well, we should not be sick. Men have discovered— or think they have discovered—the salutariness of a few wild things only, and not of all nature. Why, "nature" is but another name for health, and the seasons are but different states of health. Some men think that they are not well in spring, or summer, or autumn, or winter; it is only because they are not *well in* them.

Sept. 12

It occurred to me when I awoke this morning, feeling regret for intemperance of the day before in eating fruit, which had dulled my

sensibilities, that man was to be treated as a musical instrument, and
if any viol was to be made of sound timber and kept well tuned always,
it was he, so that when the bow of events is drawn across him he may
vibrate and resound in perfect harmony. A sensitive soul will be continually trying its strings to see if they are in tune. A man's body must
be rasped down exactly to a shaving. It is of far more importance than
the wood of a Cremona violin.

Oct. 12

Today I have had the experience of borrowing money for a poor
Irishman who wishes to get his family to this country. One will never
know his neighbors till he has carried a subscription paper among
them. Ah! it reveals many and sad facts to stand in this relation to
them. To hear the selfish and cowardly excuses some make—that *if*
they help any they must help the Irishman who lives with them—and
him they are sure never to help! Others, with whom public opinion
weighs, will think of it, trusting you never will raise the sum and so
they will not be called on again; who give stingily after all. What a
satire in the fact that you are much more inclined to call on a certain
slighted and so-called crazy woman in moderate circumstances rather
than on the president of the bank! But some are generous and save the
town from the distinction which threatened it, and *some* even who do
not lend, plainly would if they could.[1]

Oct. 20

How pleasant to walk over beds of these fresh, crisp, and rustling
fallen leaves—young hyson, green tea, clean, crisp, and wholesome!
How beautiful they go to their graves! how gently lay themselves down
and turn to mould!—painted of a thousand hues and fit to make the
beds of us living. So they troop to their graves, light and frisky. They
put on no weeds.[2] Merrily they go scampering over the earth, selecting
their graves, whispering all through the woods about it. They that
waved so loftily, how contentedly they return to dust again and are
laid low, resigned to lie and decay at the foot of the tree and afford
nourishment to new generations of their kind, as well as to flutter on
high! How they are mixed up, all species—oak and maple and chestnut and birch! They are about to add a leaf's breadth to the depth of
the soil. We are all the richer for their decay. Nature is not cluttered
with them. She is a perfect husbandman; she stores them all.

[1] [Compare Emerson's "Self-Reliance," eighth paragraph: "Are they *my* poor?"]
[2] [Mourning garments.]

Oct. 22

Yesterday, toward night, gave Sophia and mother a sail as far as the Battle-Ground. One-eyed John Goodwin, the fisherman, was loading into a hand-cart and conveying home the piles of driftwood which of late he had collected with his boat. It was a beautiful evening, and a clear amber sunset lit up all the eastern shores; and that man's employment, so simple and direct—though he is regarded by most as a vicious character—whose whole motive was so easy to fathom—thus to obtain his winter's wood—charmed me unspeakably. So much do we love actions that are simple. They are all poetic. We, too, would fain be so employed. So unlike the pursuits of most men, so artificial or complicated. Consider how the broker collects his winter's wood, what sport he makes of it, what is his boat and hand-cart! Postponing instant life, he makes haste to Boston in the cars, and there deals in stocks, not quite relishing his employment—and so earns the money with which he buys his fuel. And when, by chance, I meet him about this indirect and complicated business, I am not struck with the beauty of his employment. It does not harmonize with the sunset. How much more the former consults his genius, some genius at any rate! Now I should love to get my fuel so—I have got some so—but though I may be glad to have it, I do not love to get it in any other way less simple and direct. For if I buy one necessary of life, I cheat myself to some extent, I deprive myself of the pleasure, the inexpressible joy, which is the unfailing reward of satisfying any want of our nature simply and truly.[1]

No *trade* is simple, but artificial and complex. It postpones life and substitutes death. It goes against the grain. If the first generation does not die of it, the third or fourth does. In face of all statistics, I will never believe that it is the descendants of tradesmen who keep the state alive, but of simple yeomen or laborers. This, indeed, statistics say of the city reinforced by the country. The oldest, wisest politician grows not more human so, but is merely a gray wharf rat at last. He makes a habit of disregarding the moral right and wrong for the legal or political, commits a slow suicide, and thinks to recover by retiring on to a farm at last. This simplicity it is, and the vigor it imparts, that enables the simple vagabond, though he does get drunk and is sent to the house of correction so often, to hold up his head among men.

"If I go to Boston every day and sell tape from morning till night," says the merchant (which we will admit is not a beautiful action),

[1] [Compare the entry for October 20, 1855.]

"some time or other I shall be able to buy the best of fuel without stint." Yes, but not the pleasure of picking it up by the riverside, which, I may say, is of more value than the warmth it yields, for it but keeps the vital heat in us that we may repeat such pleasing exercises. It warms us twice, and the first warmth is the most wholesome and memorable, compared with which the other is mere coke. It is to give no account of my employment to say that I cut wood to keep me from freezing, or cultivate beans to keep me from starving. Oh, no, the greatest value of these labors is received before the wood is teamed home, or the beans are harvested (or winnowed from it). Goodwin stands on the solid earth. The earth looks solider under him, and for such as he no *political* economies, with *their* profit and loss, supply and demand, need ever be written, for they will need to use no policy. As for the complex ways of living, I love them not, however much I practice them. In as many places as possible, I will get my feet down to the earth. There is no secret in his trade, more than in the sun's. It is no mystery how he gets his living; no, not even when he steals it. But there is less double-dealing in his living than in your trade.

Goodwin is a most constant fisherman. He must well know the taste of pickerel by this time. He will fish, I would not venture to say how many days in succession. When I can remember to have seen him fishing almost daily for some time, if it rains, I am surprised on looking out to see him slowly wending his way to the river in his oilcloth coat, with his basket and pole. I saw him the other day fishing in the middle of the stream, the day after I had seen him fishing on the shore, while by a kind of magic I sailed by him; and he said he was catching minnow for bait in the winter. When I was twenty rods off, he held up a pickerel that weighed two and a half pounds, which he had forgot to show me before, and the next morning, as he afterward told me, he caught one that weighed three pounds. If it is ever necessary to appoint a committee on fish-ponds and pickerel, let him be one of them. Surely he is tenacious of life, hard to scale.[1]

Oct. 26

How watchful we must be to keep the crystal well that we were made, clear!—that it be not made turbid by our contact with the world, so that it will not reflect objects. What other liberty is there worth having, if we have not freedom and peace in our minds—if our inmost and most private man is but a sour and turbid pool? Often we are so jarred by chagrins in dealing with the world, that we cannot reflect.

---

[1] [As pickerel are also. Several submerged puns here.]

Everything beautiful impresses us as sufficient to itself. Many men who have had much intercourse with the world, and not borne the trial well affect me as all resistance, all bur and rind, without any gentleman, or tender and innocent core left. They have become hedgehogs.

Ah! the world is too much with us, and our whole soul is stained by what it works in, like the dyer's hand. A man had better starve at once than lose his innocence in the process of getting his bread. This is the pool of Bethsaida [*sic*] which must be stilled and become smooth before we can enter to be healed. If within the old man there is not a young man—within the sophisticated, one unsophisticated—then he is but one of the devil's angels.[1]

When, after feeling dissatisfied with my life, I aspire to something better, am more scrupulous, more reserved and continent, as if expecting somewhat, suddenly I find myself full of life as a nut of meat —am overflowing with a quiet, genial mirthfulness. I think to myself, I must attend to my diet; I must get up earlier and take a morning walk; I must have done with luxuries and devote myself to my muse. So I dam up my stream, and my waters gather to a head. I am freighted with thought.

Oct. 28

For a year or two past, my *publisher*, falsely so called, has been writing from time to time to ask what disposition should be made of the copies of *A Week on the Concord and Merrimack Rivers* still on hand, and at last suggesting that he had use for the room they occupied in his cellar. So I had them all sent to me here, and they have arrived today by express, filling the man's wagon—706 copies out of an edition of 1000 which I bought of Munroe four years ago and have been ever since paying for, and have not quite paid for yet. The wares are sent to me at last, and I have an opportunity to examine my purchase. They are something more substantial than fame, as my back knows, which has borne them up two flights of stairs to a place similar to that to which they trace their origin. Of the remaining two hundred and ninety and odd, seventy-five were given away, the rest sold. I have now a library of nearly nine hundred volumes, over seven hundred of which I wrote myself. Is it not well that the author should behold the fruits of his labor? My works are piled up on one side of my chamber half as high as my head, my *opera omnia*. This is authorship; these are the work of my brain. There was just one piece of good luck in the venture. The

1 [A confused and inaccurate rendering of the event at the Pool of Bethesda— usually so spelled—as narrated in the Gospel of St. John, V, 2–9.]

unbound were tied up by the printer four years ago in stout paper wrappers, and inscribed:

H. D. Thoreau's
Concord River
50 cops.

So Munroe had only to cross out "River" and write "Mass." and deliver them to the expressman at once. I can see now what I write for, the result of my labors.

Nevertheless, in spite of this result, sitting beside the inert mass of my works, I take up my pen tonight to record what thought or experience I may have had, with as much satisfaction as ever. Indeed, I believe that this result is more inspiring and better for me than if a thousand had bought my wares. It affects my privacy less and leaves me freer.

Nov. 1

About three weeks ago my indignation was roused by hearing that one of my townsmen, notorious for meanness, was endeavoring to get and keep a premium of four dollars which a poor Irish laborer whom he hired had gained by fifteen minutes' spading at our Agricultural Fair. Tonight a free colored woman is lodging at our house, whose errand to the North is to get money to buy her husband, who is a slave to one Moore in Norfolk, Virginia. She persuaded Moore, though not a kind master, to buy him that he might not be sold further South. Moore paid six hundred dollars for him, but asks her eight hundred. My most natural reflection was that he was even meaner than my townsman. As mean as a slaveholder!

Nov. 2

What is Nature unless there is an eventful human life passing within her? Many joys and many sorrows are the lights and shadows in which she shows most beautiful.

Nov. 12

I cannot but regard it as a kindness in those who have the steering of me that, by the want of pecuniary wealth, I have been nailed down to this my native region so long and steadily, and made to study and love this spot of earth more and more. What would signify in comparison a thin and diffused love and knowledge of the whole earth instead, got by wandering?

Dec. 2

The skeleton which at first sight excites only a shudder in all mortals
becomes at last not only a pure but suggestive and pleasing object to
science. The more we know of it, the less we associate it with any
goblin of our imaginations. The longer we keep it, the less likely it is
that any such will come to claim it. We discover that the only spirit
which haunts it is a universal intelligence which has created it in
harmony with all nature. Science never saw a ghost, nor does it look
for any, but it sees everywhere the traces, and it is itself the agent, of a
Universal Intelligence.

Dec. 22

Surveying the last three days. They have not yielded much that I
am aware of. All I find is old boundmarks, and the slowness and
dullness of farmers reconfirmed. They even complain that I walk too
fast for them. Their legs have become stiff from toil. This coarse and
hurried outdoor work compels me to live grossly or be inattentive to
my diet; that is the worst of it. Like work, like diet; that, I find, is the
rule. Left to my chosen pursuits, I should never drink tea nor coffee,
nor eat meat. The diet of any class or generation is the natural result
of its employment and locality. It is remarkable how unprofitable it is
for the most part to talk with farmers. They commonly stand on their
good behavior and attempt to moralize or philosophize in a serious
conversation. Sportsmen and loafers are better company. For society a
man must not be too *good* or well-disposed, to spoil his natural disposition. The bad are frequently good enough to let you see how bad
they are, but the good as frequently endeavor [to] get between you and
themselves.

I am reminded of Haydon[1] the painter's experience when he went
about painting the nobility. I go about to the houses of the farmers and
squires in like manner. This is my portrait-painting—when I would
fain be employed on higher subjects. I have offered myself much more
earnestly as a lecturer than a surveyor. Yet I do not get any employment as a lecturer; was not invited to lecture once last winter, and only
once (without pay) this winter. But I can get surveying enough, which
a hundred others in this county can do as well as I, though it is not
boasting much to say that a hundred others in New England cannot
lecture as well as I on my themes. But they who do not make the

---

[1] [Benjamin Robert Haydon (1786–1846), English painter and writer.]

highest demand on you shall rue it. It is because they make a low demand on themselves. All the while that they use only your humbler faculties, your higher unemployed faculties, like an invisible cimetar, are cutting them in twain. Woe be to the generation that lets any higher faculty in its midst go unemployed! That is to deny God and know him not, and he, accordingly, will know not of them.

Jan. 30, 1854

It is for man the seasons and all their fruits exist. The winter was made to concentrate and harden and mature the kernel of his brain, to give tone and firmness and consistency to his thought. Then is the great harvest of the year, the harvest of thought. All previous harvests are stubble to this, mere fodder and green crop. Now we burn with a purer flame like the stars; our oil is winter-strained. We are islanded in Atlantic and Pacific and Indian Oceans of thought, Bermudas, or Friendly or Spice Islands.

Feb. 5

Shall we not have sympathy with the muskrat which gnaws its third leg off,[1] not as pitying its sufferings, but, through our kindred mortality, appreciating its majestic pains and its heroic virtue? Are we not made its brothers by fate? For whom are psalms sung and mass said, if not for such worthies as these? When I hear the church organ peal, or feel the trembling tones of the bass viol, I see in imagination the musquash gnawing off his leg, I offer up a note that his affliction may be sanctified to each and all of us. Prayer and praise fitly follow such exploits. I look round for majestic pains and pleasures. They have our sympathy, both in their joys and in their pains. When I think of the tragedies which are constantly permitted in the course of all animal life, they make the plaintive strain of the universal harp which elevates us above the trivial. When I think of the muskrat gnawing off his leg, it is as the plectrum on the harp or the bow upon the viol, drawing forth a majestic strain or psalm, which immeasurably dignifies our common fate. Even as the worthies of mankind are said to recommend human life by having lived it, so I could not spare the example of the muskrat.

I fear only lest my expressions may not be extravagant enough— may not wander far enough beyond the narrow limits of our ordinary insight and faith, so as to be adequate to the truth of which I have been convinced. I desire to speak somewhere without bounds, in order that I may attain to an expression in some degree adequate to truth of

[1] [To free itself from a trap.]

which I have been convinced. From a man in a waking moment, to men in their waking moments. Wandering toward the more distant boundaries of a wider pasture. Nothing is so truly bounded and obedient to law as music, yet nothing so surely breaks all petty and narrow bonds. Whenever I hear any music I fear that I may have spoken tamely and within bounds. And I am convinced that I cannot exaggerate enough even to lay the foundation of a true expression. As for books and the adequateness of their statements to the truth, they are as the tower of Babel to the sky.[1]

Feb. 12

To make a perfect winter day like this, you must have a clear, sparkling air, with a sheen from the snow, sufficient cold, little or no wind; and the warmth must come directly from the sun. It must not be a thawing warmth. The tension of nature must not be relaxed. The earth must be resonant if bare, and you hear the lisping tinkle of chickadees from time to time and the unrelenting steel-cold scream of a jay, unmelted, that never flows into a song, a sort of wintry trumpet, screaming cold; hard, tense, frozen music, like the winter sky itself; in the blue livery of winter's band. It is like a flourish of trumpets to the winter sky. There is no hint of incubation in the jay's scream. Like the creak of a cart-wheel. There is no cushion for sounds now. They tear our ears.

Feb. 16

Every judgment and action of a man qualifies every other, i.e. corrects our estimate of every other, as, for instance, a man's idea of immortality who is a member of a church, or his praise of you coupled with his praise of those whom you do not esteem. For in this sense a man is awfully consistent, above his own consciousness. All a man's strength and all his weakness go to make up the authority of any particular opinion which he may utter. He is strong or weak with all his strength and weakness combined. If he is your friend, you may have to consider that he loves you, but perchance he also loves gingerbread.

March 12

My companion tempts me to certain licenses of speech, i.e. to reckless and sweeping expressions which I am wont to regret that I have used. That is, I find that I have used more harsh, extravagant, and

---

1 [Compare the entry for March 12 of this year.]

cynical expressions concerning mankind and individuals than I intended. I find it difficult to make to him a sufficiently moderate statement. I think it is because I have not his sympathy in my sober and constant view. He asks for a paradox, an eccentric statement, and too often I give it to him.

March 15

I am sorry to think that you do not get a man's most effective criticism until you provoke him. Severe truth is expressed with some bitterness.

April 8

Some poets mature early and die young. Their fruits have a delicious flavor like strawberries, but do not keep till fall or winter. Others are slower in coming to their growth. Their fruits may be less delicious, but are a more lasting food and are so hardened by the sun of summer and the coolness of autumn that they keep sound over winter. The first are June-eatings, early but soon withering; the last are russets, which last till June again.

April 16

When I meet one of my neighbors these days who is ridiculously stately, being offended, I say in my mind: "Farewell! I will wait till you get your manners off. Why make politeness of so much consequence, when you are ready to assassinate with a word? I do not like any better to be assassinated with a rapier than to be knocked down with a bludgeon. You are so grand that I cannot get within ten feet of you." Why will men so try to impose on one another? Why not be simple, and pass for what they are worth only? O such thin skins, such crockery, as I have to deal with! Do they not know that I can laugh? Some who have so much dignity that they cannot be contradicted! Perhaps somebody will introduce me one day, and then we may have some intercourse. I meet with several who cannot afford to be simple and true men, but personate, so to speak, their own ideal of themselves, trying to make the manners supply the place of the man. They are puffballs filled with dust and ashes.

April 19

A man came to me yesterday to offer me as a naturalist a two-headed calf which his cow had brought forth, but I felt nothing but disgust at the idea and began to ask myself what enormity I had committed to have such an offer made to me. I am not interested in mere phenomena, though it were the explosion of a planet, only as it may have lain in the experience of a human being.

April 21

How can a man be a wise man, if he doesn't know any better how to live than other men?—if he is only more cunning and intellectually subtle? Does Wisdom work in a treadmill? Does Wisdom fail? or does she teach how to succeed by her example? Is she merely the miller who grinds the finest logic? Did Plato get his *living* in a better way or more successfully than his contemporaries? Did he succumb to the difficulties of life like other men? Did he merely prevail over them by indifference, or by assuming grand airs? or find it easier to live because his aunt remembered him in her will?

April 27

It is only the irresolute and idle who have no leisure for their proper pursuit. Be preoccupied with this, devoted to it, and no accident can befall you, no idle engagements distract you. No man ever had the opportunity to postpone a high calling to a disagreeable *duty*. Misfortunes occur only when a man is false to his Genius. You cannot hear music and noise at the same time. We avoid all the calamities that may occur in a lower sphere by abiding perpetually in a higher. Most men are engaged in business the greater part of their lives, because the soul abhors a vacuum, and they have not discovered any continuous employment for man's nobler faculties. Accordingly they do not pine, because they are not greatly disappointed. A little relaxation in your exertion, a little idleness, will let in sickness and death into your own body, or your family and their attendant duties and distractions. Every human being is the artificer of his own fate in these respects. The well have no time to be sick. Events, circumstances, etc., have their origin in ourselves. They spring from seeds which we have sown. Though I may call it a European War, it is only a phase or trait in my biography that I wot of. The most foreign scrap of news which the journals report to me—from Turkey to Japan—is but a hue of my inmost thought.

May 6

There is no such thing as pure *objective* observation. Your observation, to be interesting, i.e. to be significant, must be *subjective*. The sum of what the writer of whatever class has to report is simply some human experience, whether he be poet or philosopher or man of science. The man of most science is the man most alive, whose life is the greatest event. Senses that take cognizance of outward things merely are of no avail. It matters not where or how far you travel—the farther commonly the worse—but how much alive you are. If it is possible to conceive of an event outside to humanity, it is not of the slightest significance, though it were the explosion of a planet. Every important worker will report what life there is in him. It makes no odds into what seeming deserts the poet is born. Though all his neighbors pronounce it a Sahara, it will be a paradise to him; for the desert which we see is the result of the barrenness of our experience. No mere willful activity whatever, whether in writing verses or collecting statistics, will produce true poetry or science. If you are really a sick man, it is indeed to be regretted, for you cannot accomplish so much as if you were well. All that a man has to say or do that can possibly concern mankind, is in some shape or other to tell the story of his love—to sing, and, if he is fortunate and keeps alive, he will be forever in love. This alone is to be alive to the extremities. It is a pity that this divine creature should ever suffer from cold feet; a still greater pity that the coldness so often reaches to his heart. I look over the report of the doings of a scientific association and am surprised that there is so little life to be reported; I am put off with a parcel of dry technical terms. Anything living is easily and naturally expressed in popular language. I cannot help suspecting that the life of these learned professors has been almost as inhuman and wooden as a rain-gauge or self-registering magnetic machine. They communicate no fact which rises to the temperature of blood-heat. It doesn't all amount to one rhyme.

May 11

The true poet will ever live aloof from society, wild to it, as the finest singer is the wood thrush, a forest bird.

May 22

First observe the creak of crickets. It is quite general amid these rocks. The song of only one is more interesting to me. It suggests lateness, but only as we come to a knowledge of eternity after some acquaintance with time. It is only late for all trivial and hurried pursuits. It suggests a wisdom mature, never late, being above all temporal considerations, which possesses the coolness and maturity of autumn amidst the aspiration of spring and the heats of summer. To the birds they say: "Ah! you speak like children from impulse; Nature speaks through you; but with us it is ripe knowledge. The seasons do not revolve for us; we sing their lullaby." So they chant, eternal, at the roots of the grass. It is heaven where they are, and their dwelling need not be *heaved* up. Forever the same, in May and in November (?). Serenely wise, their song has the security of prose. They have drunk no wine but the dew. It is no transient love-strain, hushed when the incubating season is past, but a glorifying of God and enjoying of him forever. They sit aside from the revolution of the seasons. Their strain is unvaried as Truth. Only in their saner moments do men hear the crickets. It is balm to the philosopher. It tempers his thoughts. They dwell forever in a temperate latitude. By listening to whom, all voices are tuned. In their song they ignore our accidents. They are not concerned about the news. A quire has begun which pauses not for any news, for it knows only the eternal.

May 23

We soon get through with Nature. She excites an expectation which she cannot satisfy. The merest child which has rambled into a copse-wood dreams of a wilderness so wild and strange and inexhaustible as Nature can never show him. The red-bird which I saw on my companion's string on election days I thought but the outmost sentinel of the wild, immortal camp—of the wild and dazzling infantry of the wilderness—that the deeper woods abounded with redder birds still; but, now that I have threaded all our woods and waded the swamps, I have never yet met with his compeer, still less his wilder kindred. The red-bird which is the last of Nature is but the first of God. The White Mountains, likewise, were smooth mole-hills to my expectation. We *condescend* to climb the crags of earth. It is our weary legs alone that praise them. That forest on whose skirts the red-bird flits is not of earth. I expected a fauna more infinite and various, birds of more dazzling colors and more celestial song. How many springs shall I continue to see the common sucker (*Catostomus Bostoniensis*) floating dead on our river! Will not Nature select her types from a new fount? The vignette of the year. This earth which is spread out like a map around me is but the lining of my inmost soul exposed. In me is the sucker that I see. No wholly extraneous object can compel me to recognize it. I am guilty of suckers. I go about to look at flowers and listen to the birds. There was a time when the beauty and the music were all within, and I sat and listened to my thoughts, and there was a song in them. I sat for hours on rocks and wrestled with the melody which possessed me. I sat and listened by the hour to a positive though faint and distant music, not sung by any bird, nor vibrating any earthly harp. When you walked with a joy which knew not its own origin. When you were an organ of which the world was but one poor broken pipe. I lay on the rocks, foundered like a harp on the seashore, that knows not how it is dealt with. You sat on the earth as on a raft, listening to music that was not of the earth, but which ruled and arranged it. Man *should be* the harp articulate.

June 16

The effect of a good government is to make life more valuable—of a bad government, to make it less valuable. We can afford that railroad and all merely material stock should depreciate, for that only compels us to live more simply and economically; but suppose the value of life itself should be depreciated. Every man in New England capable of the sentiment of patriotism must have lived the last three weeks with the sense of having suffered a vast, indefinite loss. I had never respected this government, but I had foolishly thought that I might manage to live here, attending to my private affairs, and forget it. For my part, my old and worthiest pursuits have lost I cannot say how much of their attraction, and I feel that my investment in life here is worth many per cent less since Massachusetts last deliberately and forcibly restored an innocent man, Anthony Burns, to slavery. I dwelt before in the illusion that my life passed somewhere only *between* heaven and hell, but now I cannot persuade myself that I do not dwell wholly within hell. The sight of that political organization called Massachusetts is to me morally covered with scoriæ and volcanic cinders, such as Milton imagined. If there is any hell more unprincipled than our rulers and our people, I feel curious to visit it. Life itself being worthless, all things with it, that feed it, are worthless. Suppose you have a small library, with pictures to adorn the walls—a garden laid out around—and contemplate scientific and literary pursuits, etc., etc., and discover suddenly that your villa, with all its contents, is located in hell, and that the justice of the peace is one of the devil's angels, has a cloven foot and a forked tail—do not these things suddenly lose their value in your eyes? Are you not disposed to sell at a great sacrifice?

I feel that, to some extent, the State has fatally interfered with my just and proper business. It has not merely interrupted me in my passage through Court Street on errands of trade, but it has, to some extent, interrupted me and every man on his onward and upward path, on which he had trusted soon to leave Court Street far behind. I have found that hollow which I had relied on for solid.

I am surprised to see men going about their business as if nothing had happened, and say to myself, "Unfortunates! they have not heard the news;" that the man whom I just met on horseback should be so earnest to overtake his newly bought cows running away—since all property is insecure, and if they do not run away again, they may be taken away from him when he gets them. Fool! does he not know that his seed-corn is worth less this year—that all beneficent harvests fail as he approaches the empire of hell? No prudent man will build a stone house under these circumstances, or engage in any peaceful enterprise which it requires a long time to accomplish. Art is as long as ever, but life is more interrupted and less available for a man's proper pursuits. It is time we had done referring to our ancestors. We have used up all our inherited freedom, like the young bird the albumen in the egg. It is not an era of repose. If we would save our lives, we must fight for them.

The discovery is what manner of men your countrymen are. They steadily worship mammon—and on the seventh day curse God with a tintamarre from one end of the *Union* to the other. I heard the other day of a meek and sleek devil of a Bishop Somebody, who commended the law and order with which Burns was given up. I would like before I sit down to a table to inquire if there is one in the company who styles himself or is styled Bishop, and he or I should go out of it. I would have such a man wear his bishop's hat and his clerical bib and tucker, that we may know him.

What signifies the beauty of nature when men are base? We walk to lakes to see our serenity reflected in them. When we are not serene, we go not to them. Who can be serene in a country where both rulers and ruled are without principle? The remembrance of the baseness of politicians spoils my walks. My thoughts are murder to the State; I endeavor in vain to observe nature; my thoughts involuntarily go plotting against the State. I trust that all just men will conspire.

June 18

My advice to the State is simply this: to dissolve her union with the slaveholder instantly. She can find no respectable law or precedent which sanctions its continuance. And to each inhabitant of Massachusetts, to dissolve his union with the State, as long as she hesitates to do her duty.[1]

1 [The foregoing passages were written in preparation for Thoreau's speech on "Slavery in Massachusetts" delivered at Framingham, July 4, 1854.]

My attic chamber has compelled me to sit below with the family at evening for a month. I feel the necessity of deepening the stream of my life; I must cultivate privacy. It is very dissipating to be with people too much. As C. says, it takes the edge off a man's thoughts to have been much in society. I cannot spare my moonlight and my mountains for the best of man I am likely to get in exchange.

Aug. 5

I find that we are now in the midst of the meadow-haying season, and almost every meadow or section of a meadow has its band of half a dozen mowers and rakers, either bending to their manly work with regular and graceful motion or resting in the shade, while the boys are turning the grass to the sun. I passed as many as sixty or a hundred men thus at work today. They stick up a twig with the leaves on, on the river's brink, as a guide for the mowers, that they may not exceed the owner's bounds. I hear their scythes cronching the coarse weeds by the river's brink as I row near. The horse or oxen stand near at hand in the shade on the firm land, waiting to draw home a load anon. I see a platoon of three or four mowers, one behind the other, diagonally advancing with regular sweeps across the broad meadow and ever and anon standing to whet their scythes. Or else, having made several bouts, they are resting in the shade on the edge of the firm land. In one place I see one sturdy mower stretched on the ground amid his oxen in the shade of an oak, trying to sleep; or I see one wending far inland with a jug to some well-known spring.

Aug. 7

Do you not feel the fruit of your spring and summer beginning to ripen, to harden its seed within you? Do not your thoughts begin to acquire consistency as well as flavor and ripeness? How can we expect a harvest of thought who have not had a seed-time of character? Already some of my small thoughts—fruit of my spring life—are ripe, like the berries which feed the first broods of birds; and other some are prematurely ripe and bright, like the lower leaves of the herbs which have felt the summer's drought.

Seasons when our mind is like the strings of a harp which is swept, and we stand and listen. A man may hear strains in his thought far surpassing any oratorio.

In mid-summer we are of the earth—confounded with it—and

covered with its dust. Now we begin to erect ourselves somewhat and walk upon its surface. I am not so much reminded of former years as of existence prior to years.

Aug. 9, Wednesday

To Boston.
Walden published. Elder-berries. Waxwork yellowing.

Aug. 13

I remember only with a pang the past spring and summer thus far. I have not been an early riser. Society seems to have invaded and overrun me. I have drank tea and coffee and made myself cheap and vulgar. My days have been all noontides, without sacred mornings and evenings. I desire to rise early henceforth, to associate with those whose influence is elevating, to have such dreams and waking thoughts that my diet may not be indifferent to me.

Aug. 14

Ah! I need solitude. I have come forth to this hill at sunset to see the forms of the mountains in the horizon—to behold and commune with something grander than man. Their mere distance and unprofanedness is an infinite encouragement. It is with infinite yearning and aspiration that I seek solitude, more and more resolved and strong; but with a certain genial weakness that I seek society ever.

Aug. 18

I have just been through the process of killing the cistudo[1] for the sake of science; but I cannot excuse myself for this murder, and see that such actions are inconsistent with the poetic perception, however they may serve science, and will affect the quality of my observations. I pray that I may walk more innocently and serenely through nature. No reasoning whatever reconciles me to this act. It affects my day injuriously. I have lost some self-respect. I have a murderer's experience in a degree.

Aug. 22

Walking may be a science, so far as the direction of a walk is concerned. I go again to the Great Meadows, to improve this remarkably dry season and walk where in ordinary times I cannot go. There is, no

---

[1] [A box-turtle, collected for Agassiz.]

doubt, a particular season of the year when each place may be visited with most profit and pleasure, and it may be worth the while to consider what that season is in each case.

Aug. 26

How much lies quietly buried in the ground that we wot not of! We unconsciously step over the eggs of snapping turtles slowly hatching the summer through. Not only was the surface perfectly dry and trackless there, but blackberry vines had run over the spot where these eggs were buried and weeds had sprung up above. If Iliads are not composed in our day, snapping turtles are hatched and arrive at maturity. It already thrusts forth its tremendous head—for the first time in this sphere—and slowly moves from side to side—opening its small glistening eyes for the first time to the light—expressive of dull rage, as if it had endured the trials of this world for a century. When I behold this monster thus steadily advancing toward maturity, all nature abetting, I am convinced that there must be an irresistible necessity for mud turtles. With what tenacity Nature sticks to her idea! These eggs, not warm to the touch, buried in the ground, so slow to hatch, are like the seeds of vegetable life.

Aug. 27

When I awake in the morning, I remember what I have seen and heard of snapping turtles, and am in doubt whether it was dream or reality. I slowly raise my head and, peeping over the bedside, see my great mud turtle shell lying bottom up under the table, showing its prominent ribs, and realize into what world I have awaked. Before I was in doubt how much prominence my good Genius would give to that fact. That the first object you see on awakening should be an empty mud turtle's shell!! Will it not make me of the earth earthy? Or does it not indicate that I am of the earth earthy? What life, what character, this has shielded, which is now at liberty to be turned bottom upward! I can put specimens of all our other turtles into this cavity. This too was once an infant in its egg. When I see this, then I am sure that I am not dreaming, but am awake to this world. I do not know any more terrene fact. It still carries the earth on its back. Its life is between the animal and vegetable; like a seed it is planted deep in the ground and is all summer germinating. Does it not possess as much the life of the vegetable as the animal?

Would it not be well to describe some of those rough all-day walks across lots?—as that of the 15th, picking our way over quaking meadows and swamps and occasionally slipping into the muddy batter midleg deep; jumping or fording ditches and brooks; forcing our way through dense blueberry swamps, where there is water beneath and bushes above; then brushing through extensive birch forests all covered with green lice, which cover our clothes and face; then, relieved, under larger wood, more open beneath, steering for some more conspicuous trunk; now along a rocky hillside where the sweet-fern grows for a mile, then over a recent cutting, finding our uncertain footing on the cracking tops and trimmings of trees left by the choppers; now taking a step or two of smooth walking across a highway; now through a dense pine wood, descending into rank, dry swamp, where the cinnamon fern rises above your head, with isles of poison-dogwood; now up a scraggy hill covered with shrub oak, stooping and winding one's way for half a mile, tearing one's clothes in many places and putting out one's eyes, and find[ing] at last that it has no bare brow, but another slope of the same character; now through a corn-field diagonally with the rows; now coming upon the hidden melon-patch; seeing the back side of familiar hills and not knowing them—the nearest house to home which you do not know seeming further off than the farthest which you do know—in the spring defiled with the froth on various bushes, etc., etc., etc.; now reaching on higher land some open pigeon-place,[1] a breathing-place for us.

Aug. 29

Early for several mornings I have heard the sound of a flail. It leads me to ask if I have spent as industrious a spring and summer as the farmer, and gathered as rich a crop of experience. If so, the sound of my flail will be heard by those who have ears to hear, separating the kernel from the chaff all the fall and winter, and a sound no less cheering it will be. If the drought has destroyed the corn, let not all harvests fail. Have you commenced to thresh your grain? The lecturer must commence his threshing as early as August, that his fine flour may be ready for his winter customers. The fall rains will make full springs and raise his streams sufficiently to grind his grist. We shall hear the sound of his flail all the fall, early and late. It is made of tougher material than hickory, and tied together with resolution stronger than an eel-skin. For him there is no husking-bee, but he does it all alone and by hand, at evening by lamplight, with the barn door shut and only the pile of husks behind him for warmth. For him, too, I

1 [A roosting place for passenger pigeons, plentiful in Thoreau's time but now extinct.]

fear there is no patent corn-sheller, but he does his work by hand, ear by ear, on the edge of a shovel over a bushel, on his hearth, and after he takes up a handful of the yellow grain and lets it fall again, while he blows out the chaff; and he goes to bed happy when his measure is full.

Sept. 2

My faults are:

Paradoxes—saying just the opposite—a style which may be imitated.

Ingenious.

Playing with words—getting the laugh—not always simple, strong, and broad.

Using current phrases and maxims, when I should speak for myself.

Not always earnest.

"In short," "in fact," "alas!" etc.

Want of conciseness.

Sept. 4

In the wood-paths I find a great many of the Castile-soap galls, more or less fresh. Some are saddled on the twigs. They are now dropping from the shrub oaks. Is not Art itself a gall? Nature is stung by God and the seed of man planted in her. The artist changes the direction of Nature and makes her grow according to his idea. If the gall was anticipated when the oak was made, so was the canoe when the birch was made. Genius stings Nature, and she grows according to its idea.

Sept. 19

Thinking this afternoon of the prospect of my writing lectures and going abroad to read them the next winter, I realized how incomparably great the advantages of obscurity and poverty which I have enjoyed so long (and may still perhaps enjoy). I thought with what more than princely, with what poetical, leisure I had spent my years hitherto, without care or engagement, fancy-free. I have given myself up to nature; I have lived so many springs and summers and autumns and winters as if I had nothing else to do but *live* them, and imbibe whatever nutriment they had for me; I have spent a couple of years, for instance, with the flowers chiefly, having none other so binding engagement as to observe when they opened; I could have afforded to spend a whole fall observing the changing tints of the foliage. Ah, how I have thriven on solitude and poverty! I cannot overstate this advantage. I do not see how I could have enjoyed it, if the public had been expecting as much of me as there is danger now that they will. If I go abroad lecturing, how shall I ever recover the lost winter?

It has been my vacation, my season of growth and expansion, a prolonged youth.

Sept. 21

I sometimes seem to myself to owe all my little success, all for which men commend me, to my vices. I am perhaps more willful than others and make enormous sacrifices, even of others' happiness, it may be, to gain my ends. It would seem even as if nothing good could be accomplished without some vice to aid in it.

Dec. 6

After lecturing twice this winter I feel that I am in danger of cheapening myself by trying to become a successful lecturer, i.e., to interest my audiences. I am disappointed to find that most that I am and value myself for is lost, or worse than lost, on my audience. I fail to get even the attention of the mass. I should suit them better if I suited myself less. I feel that the public demand an average man—average thoughts and manners—not originality, nor even absolute excellence. You cannot interest them except as you are like them and sympathize with them. I would rather that my audience come to me than that I should go to them, and so they be sifted; i.e., I would rather write books than lectures. That is fine, this coarse. To read to a promiscuous audience who are at your mercy the fine thoughts you solaced yourself with far away is as violent as to fatten geese by cramming, and in this case they do not get fatter.

Dec. 8

Winter has come unnoticed by me, I have been so busy writing. This is the life most lead in respect to Nature. How different from my habitual one! It is hasty, coarse, and trivial, as if you were a spindle in a factory. The other is leisurely, fine, and glorious, like a flower. In the first case you are merely getting your living; in the second you live as you go along. You travel only on roads of the proper grade without jar or running off the track, and sweep round the hills by beautiful curves.

1855-57

The last years of Thoreau's life were devoted primarily to preparations for a work which he sometimes called a "History of Concord." No definite plan for that work has survived, but Thoreau's journals and notebooks indicate that he meant it to deal with the total past of his township from the glacial epoch onward, and as much with the natural environment as with human beings and events. Something of the sort had been in his mind ever since, at twenty-four, he had envisaged "a poem to be called 'Concord.'" The project was really poetical in the sense that it involved a creative transformation of raw fact into stuff of the mind. Thoreau's intense local patriotism provided one motive, but equally strong was the autobiographical purpose which pervades all his writing. By this time he had come to feel that he was Concord in human form. From that belief it seemed to follow that studying Concord in its full sweep of time and place would amount to a close self-examination.

To the eye of common sense this looks fantastic, even morbid. Some would add that it becomes both ridiculous and pathetic when, for purposes of self-scrutiny Thoreau begins counting tree rings, measuring snowdrifts, dating plant growths, piling up notes on American Indians and polar expeditions, and blaming himself for the annual appearance of dead suckers in Concord River.

There was undoubtedly something feverish in Thoreau's preparations, due in part to his gradual loss of physical vigor and the realization that his time might be short. This shows in the rapid deterioration of his journals, where now he let his field notes stand as bare factual statements awaiting the time when their symbolic interpretation might be made. That time never came; but we are not to infer from the mass and miscellaneity of the notations he left "in disconnection dead and spiritless" that he ever valued factual knowledge for its own sake. The habit of metaphorical thinking was inveterate and dominant in him until the end. With regard to the "defeat" and "despair" which some readers think they find in the work of his later years the following excerpts speak for themselves.

Jan. 12, 1855

Perhaps what most moves us in winter is some reminiscence of far-off summer. How we leap by the side of the open brooks! What beauty in the running brooks! What life! What society! The cold is merely superficial; it is summer still at the core, far, far within. It is in the cawing of the crow, the crowing of the cock, the warmth of the sun on our backs. I hear faintly the cawing of a crow far, far away, echoing from some unseen wood-side, as if deadened by the springlike vapor which the sun is drawing from the ground. It mingles with the slight murmur of the village, the sound of children at play, as one stream empties gently into another, and the wild and tame are one. What a delicious sound! It is not merely crow calling to crow, for it speaks to me too. I am part of one great creature with him; if he has voice, I have ears. I can hear when he calls, and have engaged not to shoot nor stone him if he will caw to me each spring. On the one hand, it may be, is the sound of children at school saying their a, b, ab's, on the other, far in the wood-fringed horizon, the cawing of crows from their blessed eternal vacation, out at their long recess, children who have got dismissed! While the vaporous incense goes up from all the fields of the spring—if it were spring. Ah, bless the Lord, O my soul! bless him for wildness, for crows that will not alight within gunshot! and bless him for hens, too, that croak and cackle in the yard!

Feb. 19

Many will complain of my lectures that they are transcendental. "Can't understand them." "Would you have us return to the savage state?" etc., etc. A criticism true enough, it may be, from their point of view. But the fact is, the earnest lecturer can speak only to his like, and the adapting of himself to his audience is a mere compliment which he pays them. If you wish to know how I think, you must endeavor to put yourself in my place. If you wish me to speak as if I were you, that is another affair.

March 20

Trying the other day to imitate the honking of geese, I found myself flapping my sides with my elbows, as with wings, and uttering something like the syllables *mow-ack* with a nasal twang and twist in my head; and I produced their note so perfectly in the opinion of the hearers that I thought I might possibly draw a flock down.

March 24

Passing up the Assabet, by the Hemlocks, where there has been a slide and some rocks have slid down into the river, I think I see how rocks come to be found in the midst of rivers. Rivers are continually changing their channels—eating into one bank and adding their sediment to the other—so that frequently where there is a great bend you see a high and steep bank or hill on one side, which the river washes, and a broad meadow on the other. As the river eats into the hill, especially in freshets, it undermines the rocks, large and small, and they slide down, alone or with the sand and soil, to the water's edge. The river continues to eat into the hill, carrying away all the lighter parts [of] the sand and soil, to add to its meadows or islands somewhere, but leaves the rocks where they rested, and thus in course of time they occupy the middle of the stream and, later still, the middle of the meadow, perchance, though it may be buried under the mud. But this does not explain how so many rocks lying in streams have been split in the direction of the current. Again, rivers appear to have travelled back and worn into the meadows of their creating, and then they become more meandering then ever. Thus in the course of ages the rivers wriggle in their beds, till it feels comfortable under them. Time is cheap and rather insignificant. It matters not whether it is a river which changes from side to side in a geological period or an eel that wriggles past in an instant.

June 11

When I would go a-visiting I find that I go off the fashionable street—not being inclined to change my dress—to where man meets man and not polished shoe meets shoe.

What if we feel a yearning to which no breast answers? I walk alone. My heart is full. Feelings impede the current of my thoughts. I knock on the earth for my friend.[1] I expect to meet him at every turn; but no friend appears, and perhaps none is dreaming of me. I am tired of frivolous society, in which silence is forever the most natural and the best manners. I would fain walk on the deep waters, but my companions will only walk on shallows and puddles. I am naturally silent in the midst of twenty from day to day, from year to year. I am rarely reminded of their presence. Two yards of politeness do not make society for me. One complains that I do not take his jokes. I took them before he had done uttering them, and went my way. One talks to me of his apples and pears, and I depart with my secret untold. His are not the apples that tempt me.

June 18

At 3 P.M., as I walked up the bank by the Hemlocks, I saw a painted tortoise just beginning its hole; then another a dozen rods from the river on the bare barren field near some pitch pines, where the earth was covered with cladonias, cinquefoil, sorrel, etc. Its hole was about two thirds done. I stooped down over it, and, to my surprise, after a slight pause it proceeded in its work, directly under and within

---

[1] [Perhaps his brother John, dead for thirteen years.]

eighteen inches of my face. I retained a constrained position for three
quarters of an hour or more for fear of alarming it. It rested on its
fore legs, the front part of its shell about one inch higher than the rear,
and this position was not changed essentially to the last. The hole was
oval, broadest behind, about one inch wide and one and three quarters
long, and the dirt already removed was quite wet or moistened. It
made the hole and removed the dirt with its hind legs only, not using
its tail or shell, which last of course could not enter the hole, though
there was some dirt on it. It first scratched two or three times with
one hind foot; then took up a pinch of the loose sand and deposited
it directly behind that leg, pushing it backward to its full length and
then deliberately opening it and letting the dirt fall; then the same
with the other hind foot. This it did rapidly, using each leg alternately
with perfect regularity, standing on the other one the while, and thus
tilting up its shell each time, now to this side, then to that. There was
half a minute or a minute between each change. The hole was made as
deep as the feet could reach, or about two inches. It was very neat
about its work, not scattering the dirt about any more than was
necessary. The completing of the hole occupied perhaps five minutes.

It then without any pause drew its head completely into its shell,
raised the rear a little, and protruded and dropped a wet flesh-colored
egg into the hole, one end foremost, the red skin of its body being
considerably protruded with it. Then it put out its head again a little,
slowly, and placed the egg at one side with one hind foot. After a delay
of about two minutes it again drew in its head and dropped another,
and so on to the fifth—drawing in its head each time, and pausing
somewhat longer between the last. The eggs were placed in the hole
without any *particular* care—only well down flat and [each] out of the
way of the next—and I could plainly see them from above.

After these ten minutes or more, it without pause or turning began
to scrape the moist earth into the hole with its hind legs, and, when it
had half filled it, it carefully pressed it down with the edges of its hind
feet, dancing on them alternately, for some time, as on its knees, tilting
from side to side, pressing by the whole weight of the rear of its shell.
When it had drawn in thus all the earth that had been moistened, it
stretched its hind legs further back and to each side, and drew in the
dry and lichen-clad crust, and then danced upon and pressed that
down, still not moving the rear of its shell more than one inch to right
or left all the while, or changing the position of the forward part at all.
The thoroughness with which the covering was done was remarkable.
It persevered in drawing in and dancing on the dry surface which had
never been disturbed, long after you thought it had done its duty, but

it never moved its fore feet, nor once looked round, nor saw the eggs it had laid. There were frequent pauses throughout the whole, when it rested, or ran out its head and looked about circumspectly, at any noise or motion. These pauses were especially long during the covering of its eggs, which occupied more than half an hour. Perhaps it was hard work.

When it had done, it immediately started for the river at a pretty rapid rate (the suddenness with which it made these transitions was amusing), pausing from time to time, and I judged that it would reach it in fifteen minutes. It was not easy to detect that the ground had been disturbed there. An Indian could not have made his cache more skillfully. In a few minutes all traces of it would be lost to the eye.

The object of moistening the earth was perhaps to enable it to take it up in its hands (?), and also to prevent its falling back into the hole. Perhaps it also helped to make the ground more compact and harder when it was pressed down.

Sept. 14

It costs so much to publish, would it not be better for the author to put his manuscripts in a safe?

Oct. 19

Talking with Bellew[1] this evening about Fourierism and communities, I said that I suspected any enterprise in which two were engaged together. "But," said he, "it is difficult to make a stick stand unless you slant two or more against it." "Oh, no," answered I, "you may split its lower end into three, or drive it single into the ground, which is the best way; but most men, when they start on a new enterprise, not only figuratively, but really, *pull up stakes*. When the sticks prop one another, none, or only one, stands erect."

Oct. 20

I have collected and split up now quite a pile of driftwood—rails and riders and stems and stumps of trees—perhaps half or three quarters of a tree. It is more amusing, not only to collect this with my boat and bring [it] up from the river on my back, but to split it also, than it would be to speak to a farmer for a load of wood and to saw and split that. Each stick I deal with has a history, and I read it as I am handling it, and, last of all, I remember my adventures in getting it, while it is burning in the winter evening. That is the most interesting

1 [Frank H. T. Bellew (1828–88), a caricaturist.]

part of its history. It has made part of a fence or a bridge, perchance, or has been rooted out of a clearing and bears the marks of fire on it. When I am splitting it, I study the effects of water on it, and, if it is a stump, the curiously winding grain by which it separates into so many prongs—how to take advantage of its grain and split it most easily. I find that a dry oak stump will split pretty easily in the direction of its diameter, but not at right angles with it or along its circles of growth. I got out some good knees for a boat. Thus one half the value of my wood is enjoyed before it is housed, and the other half is equal to the whole value of an equal quantity of the wood which I buy.

Some of my acquaintances have been wondering why I took all this pains, bringing some nearly three miles by water, and have suggested various reasons for it. I tell them in my despair of making them understand me that it is a profound secret—which it has proved—yet I did hint to them that one reason was that I wanted to get it. I take some satisfaction in eating my food, as well as in being nourished by it. I feel well at dinner-time as well as after it. The world will never find out why you don't love to have your bed tucked up for you—why you will be so perverse. I enjoy more drinking water at a clear spring than out of a goblet at a gentleman's table. I like best the bread which I have baked, the garment which I have made, the shelter which I have constructed, the fuel which I have gathered.[1]

It is always a recommendation to me to know that a man has ever been poor, has been regularly born into this world, knows the language. I require to be assured of certain philosophers that they have once been barefooted, footsore, have eaten a crust because they had nothing better, and know what sweetness resides in it.[2]

Oct. 26

I sometimes think that I must go off to some wilderness where I can have a better opportunity to play life—can find more suitable materials to build my house with, and enjoy the pleasure of collecting my fuel in the forest. I have more taste for the wild sports of hunting, fishing, wigwam-building, making garments of skins, and collecting wood wherever you find it, than for butchering, farming, carpentry, working in a factory, or going to a wood market.

[1] [Compare the entry for October 22, 1853.]
[2] [In this praise of the "nobly poor" Thoreau rests not upon what was once the Christian ideal of "Holy Poverty"—an ideal unknown to the Puritans and completely lost in modern America—but upon what he knew about the spiritual and philosophic life of ancient India.]

Nov. 5

But what is the use of trying to live simply, raising what you eat, making what you wear, building what you inhabit, burning what you cut or dig, when those to whom you are allied insanely want and will have a thousand other things which neither you nor they can raise and nobody else, perchance, will pay for? The fellow-man to whom you are yoked is a steer that is ever bolting right the other way.

I was suggesting once to a man [1] who was wincing under some of the consequences of our loose and expensive way of living, "But you might raise all your own potatoes, etc., etc." We had often done it at our house and had some to sell. At which he demurring, I said, setting it high, "You could raise twenty bushels even." "But," said he, "I use thirty-five." "How large is your family?" "A wife and three infant children." This was the real family; I need not enumerate those who were hired to *help* eat the potatoes and waste them. So he had to hire a man to raise his potatoes.

Thus men invite the devil in at every angle and then prate about the garden of Eden and the fall of man.

I know many children to whom I would fain make a present on some one of their birthdays, but they are so far gone in the luxury of presents—have such perfect museums of costly ones—that it would absorb my entire earnings for a year to buy them something which would not be beneath their notice.

Nov. 7

I find it good to be out this still, dark, mizzling afternoon; my walk or voyage is more suggestive and profitable than in bright weather. The view is contracted by the misty rain, the water is perfectly smooth, and the stillness is favorable to reflection. I am more open to impressions, more sensitive (not calloused or indurated by sun and wind), as if in a chamber still. My thoughts are concentrated; I am all compact. The solitude is real, too, for the weather keeps other men at home. This mist is like a roof and walls over and around, and I walk with a domestic feeling. The sound of a wagon going over an unseen bridge is louder than ever, and so of other sounds. I am *compelled* to look at near objects. All things have a soothing effect; the very clouds and mists brood over me. My power of observation and contemplation is much increased. My attention does not wander. The world and my life are simplified. What now of Europe and Asia?

---

[1] [Probably Emerson.]

Nov. 9

I affect what would commonly be called a mean and miserable way of living. I thoroughly sympathize with all savages and gypsies in so far as they merely assert the original right of man to the productions of Nature and a place in her. The Irishman moves into the town, sets up a shanty on the railroad land, and then gleans the dead wood from the neighboring forest, which would never get to market. But the so-called owner forbids it and complains of him as a trespasser. The highest law gives a thing to him who can use it.

Nov. 17

It is interesting to me to talk with Rice,[1] he lives so thoroughly and satisfactorily to himself. He has learned that rare art of living, the every elements of which most professors do not know. His life has been not a failure but a success. Seeing me going to sharpen some plane-irons, and hearing me complain of the want of tools, he said that I ought to have a chest of tools. But I said it was not worth the while. I should not use them enough to pay for them. "You would use them more, if you had them," said he. "When I came to do a piece of work I used to find commonly that I wanted a certain tool, and I made it a rule first always to make that tool. I have spent as much as $3000 thus on my tools." Comparatively speaking, his life is a success; not such a failure as most men's. He gets more out of any enterprise than his neighbors, for he helps himself more and hires less. Whatever pleasure there is in it he enjoys. By good sense and calculation he has become rich and has invested his property well, yet practices a fair and neat economy, dwells not in untidy luxury. It costs him less to live, and he gets more out of life, than others. To get his living, or keep it, is not a hasty or disagreeable toil. He works slowly but surely, enjoying the sweet of it. He buys a piece of meadow at a profitable rate, works at it in pleasant weather, he and his son, when they are inclined, goes a-fishing or a-bee-hunting or a-rifle-shooting quite as often, and thus the meadow gets redeemed, and potatoes get planted, perchance, and he is very sure to have a good crop stored in his cellar in the fall, and some to sell. He always has the best of potatoes there. In the same spirit in which he and his son tackle up their Dobbin (he never keeps a fast horse) and go a-spearing or a-fishing through the ice, they also tackle up and go to their Sudbury farm to hoe or harvest a little, and when they return they bring home a load of stumps in their hay-rigging, which impeded their labors, but, perchance, supply them with their

---

[1] [Compare the entry for February 13, 1852.]

winter wood. All the woodchucks they shoot or trap in the bean-field are brought home also. And thus their life is a long sport and they know not what hard times are.

Dec. 3

Every larger tree which I knew and admired is being gradually culled out and carried to mill. I see one or two more large oaks in E. Hubbard's wood lying high on stumps, waiting for snow to be removed. I miss them as surely and with the same feeling that I do the old inhabitants out of the village street.

Dec. 11

When some rare northern bird like the pine grosbeak is seen thus far south in the winter, he does not suggest poverty, but dazzles us with his beauty. There is in them a warmth akin to the warmth that melts the icicle. Think of these brilliant, warm-colored, and richly warbling birds, birds of paradise, dainty-footed, downy-clad, in the midst of a New England, a Canadian winter. The woods and fields, now somewhat solitary, being deserted by their more tender summer residents, are now frequented by these rich but delicately tinted and hardy northern immigrants of the air. Here is no imperfection to be suggested. The winter, with its snow and ice, is not an evil to be corrected. It is as it was designed and made to be, for the artist has had leisure to add beauty to use. My acquaintances, angels from the north. I had a vision thus prospectively of these birds as I stood in the swamps. I saw this familiar—too *familiar*—fact at a different angle, and I was charmed and haunted by it. But I could only attain to be thrilled and enchanted, as by the sound of a strain of music dying away. I had seen into paradisaic regions, with their air and sky, and I was no longer wholly or merely a denizen of this vulgar earth. Yet had I hardly a foothold there. I was only sure that I was charmed, and no mistake. It is only necessary to behold thus the least fact or phenomenon, however familiar, from a point a hair's breadth aside from our habitual path or routine, to be overcome, enchanted by its beauty and significance. Only what we have touched and worn is trivial—our scurf, repetition, tradition, conformity. To perceive freshly, with fresh senses, is to be inspired. Great winter itself looked like a precious gem, reflecting rainbow colors from one angle.

My body is all sentient. As I go here or there, I am tickled by this or that I come in contact with, as if I touched the wires of a battery. I can generally recall—have fresh in my mind—several scratches last received. These I continually recall to mind, reimpress, and harp upon. The age of miracles is each moment thus returned. Now it is wild apples, now river reflections, now a flock of lesser redpolls. In winter, too, resides immortal youth and perennial summer. Its head is not silvered; its cheek is not blanched but has a ruby tinge to it.

If any part of nature excites our pity, it is for ourselves we grieve, for there is eternal health and beauty. We get only transient and partial glimpses of the beauty of the world. Standing at the right angle, we are dazzled by the colors of the rainbow in colorless ice. From the right point of view, every storm and every drop in it is a rainbow. Beauty and music are not mere traits and exceptions. They are the rule and character. It is the exception that we see and hear. Then I try to discover what it was in the vision that charmed and translated me. What if we could daguerreotype our thoughts and feelings! for I am surprised and enchanted often by some quality which I cannot detect. I have seen an attribute of another world and condition of things. It is a wonderful fact that I should be affected, and thus deeply and powerfully, more than by aught else in all my experience— that this fruit should be borne in me, sprung from a seed finer than the spores of fungi, floated from other atmospheres! finer than the dust caught in the sails of vessels a thousand miles from land! Here the invisible seeds settle, and spring, and bear flowers of immortal beauty.

Dec. 23

Think of the life of a kitten, ours for instance: last night her eyes set in a fit, doubtful if she will ever come out of it, and she is set away in a basket and submitted to the recuperative powers of nature; this morning running up the clothes-pole and erecting her back in frisky sport to every passer.

Jan. 5, 1856

The thin snow now driving from the north and lodging on my coat consists of those beautiful star crystals, not cottony and chubby spokes, as on the 13th December, but thin and partly transparent crystals. They are about a tenth of an inch in diameter, perfect little wheels with six spokes without a tire, or rather with six perfect little leaflets, fern-like, with a distinct straight and slender mid-rib, raying from the centre. . . . How full of the creative genius is the air in which these are generated! I should hardly admire more if real stars fell and lodged on my coat. Nature is full of genius, full of the divinity; so that not a snowflake escapes its fashioning hand.

A divinity must have stirred within them before the crystals did thus shoot and set. Wheels of the storm-chariots. The same law that shapes the earth-star shapes the snow-star. As surely as the petals of a flower are fixed, each of these countless snow-stars comes whirling to earth, pronouncing thus, with emphasis, the number six. Order, κόσμος.

On the Saskatchewan, when no man of science is there to behold, still down they come, and not the less fulfill their destiny, perchance melt at once on the Indian's face. What a world we live in! where myriads of these little disks, so beautiful to the most prying eye, are whirled down on every traveller's coat, the observant and the unobservant, and on the restless squirrel's fur, and on the far-stretching fields and forests, the wooded dells, and the mountain-tops. Far, far away from the haunts of man, they roll down some little slope, fall over and come to their bearings, and melt or lose their beauty in the mass, ready anon to swell some little rill with their contribution, and so, at last, the universal ocean from which they came. There they lie, like the wreck of chariot-wheels after a battle in the skies. Meanwhile the meadow mouse shoves them aside in his gallery, the schoolboy casts them in his snowball, or the woodman's sled glides smoothly over them, these glorious spangles, the sweeping of heaven's floor. And they all sing, melting as they sing of the mysteries of the number six— six, six, six. He takes up the water of the sea in his hand, leaving the salt; He disperses it in mist through the skies; He recollects and sprinkles it like grain in six-rayed snowy stars over the earth, there to lie till He dissolves its bonds again.

Jan. 10

I love to wade and flounder through the swamp now, these bitter cold days when the snow lies deep on the ground, and I need travel but little way from the town to get up to a Nova Zembla solitude—to wade through the swamps, all snowed up, untracked by man, into which the fine dry snow is still drifting till it is even with the tops of the water andromeda and halfway up the high blueberry bushes. I penetrate to islets inaccessible in summer, my feet slumping to the sphagnum far out of sight beneath, where the alder berry glows yet and the azalea buds, and perchance a single tree sparrow or a chickadee lisps by my side, where there are few tracks even of wild animals; perhaps only a mouse or two have burrowed up by the side of some twig, and hopped away in straight lines on the surface of the light, deep snow, as if too timid to delay, to another hole by the side of another bush; and a few rabbits have run in a path amid the blueberries and alders about the edge of the swamp. This is instead of a Polar Sea expedition and going after Franklin.[1]

1 [Sir John Franklin (1786–1847), a British explorer in the Arctic long sought for after he had perished with all his men.]

Jan. 20

In my experience I have found nothing so truly impoverishing as what is called wealth, i.e. the command of greater means than you had before possessed, though comparatively few and slight still, for you thus inevitably acquire a more expensive habit of living, and even the very same necessaries and comforts cost you more than they once did. Instead of gaining, you have lost some independence, and if your income should be suddenly lessened, you would find yourself poor, though possessed of the same means which once made you rich. Within the last five years I have had the command of a little more money than in the previous five years, for I have sold some books and some lectures;[1] yet I have not been a whit better fed or clothed or warmed or sheltered, not a whit richer, except that I have been less concerned about my living, but perhaps my life has been the less serious for it, and, to balance it, I feel now that there is a possibility of failure. Who knows but I *may* come upon the town, if, as is likely, the public want no more of my books, or lectures (which last is already the case)? Before, I was much likelier to take the town upon my shoulders. That is, I have lost some of my independence on them, when they would say that I had gained an independence. If you wish to give a man a sense of poverty, give him a thousand dollars. The next hundred dollars he gets will not be worth more than ten that he used to get. Have pity on him; withhold your gifts.

Jan. 22

Most were not aware of the size of the great elm till it was cut down. . . . I have attended the felling and, so to speak, the funeral of this old citizen of the town—I who commonly do not attend funerals—as it became me to do. I was the chief if not the only mourner there. I have taken the measure of his grandeur; have spoken a few words of eulogy at his grave, remembering the maxim *de mortuis nil nisi bonum* (in this case *magnum*). But there were only the choppers and the passers-by to hear me. Further the town was not represented; the fathers of the town, the selectmen, the clergy were not there. But I have not known a fitter occasion for a sermon of late. Travellers whose journey was for a short time delayed by its prostrate body were forced to pay it some attention and respect, but the axe-boys had climbed upon it like ants, and commenced chipping at it before it had fairly ceased groaning. There was a man already bargaining for some part. How have the

[1] [Chiefly the "pencil business," seldom mentioned in the journals, was bringing in money.]

mighty fallen! Its history extends back over more than half the whole
history of the town. . . . Methinks its fall marks an epoch in the history
of the town. It has passed away together with the clergy of the old
school and the stage-coach which used to rattle beneath it. Its virtue
was that it steadily grew and expanded from year to year to the very
last. How much of old Concord falls with it! . . . Our town has lost
some of its venerableness. No longer will our eyes rest on its massive
gray trunk, like a vast Corinthian column by the wayside; no longer
shall we walk in the shade of its lofty, spreading dome. It is as if you
had laid the axe at the feet of some venerable Buckley [*sic*] or Ripley.[1]
You have laid the axe, you have made fast your tackle, to one of the
king-posts of the town. I feel the whole building wracked by it. Is it
not sacrilege to cut down the tree which has so long looked over
Concord beneficently?

Jan. 24

I have seen many a collection of stately elms which better deserved
to be represented at the General Court than the manikins beneath—
than the barroom and victualling cellar and groceries they overshadowed. When I see their magnificent domes, miles away in the
horizon, over intervening valleys and forests, they suggest a village, a
community, there. But, after all, it is a secondary consideration
whether there are human dwellings beneath them; these may have long
since passed away. I find that into my idea of the village has entered
more of the elm than of the human being. They are worth many a
political borough. They constitute a borough. The poor human
representative of his party sent out from beneath their shade will not
suggest a tithe of the dignity, the true nobleness and comprehensive-
ness of view, the sturdiness and independence, and the serene bene-
ficence that they do. They look from township to township. . . . They
battle with the tempests of a century. See what scars they bear, what
limbs they lost before we were born! Yet they never adjourn; they
steadily vote for their principles, and send their roots further and
wider from the *same centre*. They die at their posts, and they leave a
tough butt for the choppers to exercise themselves about, and a stump
which serves for their monument. They attend no caucus, they make
no compromise, they use no policy. Their one principle is growth.
They combine a true radicalism with a true conservatism. Their
radicalism is not cutting away of roots, but an infinite multiplication

1 [Peter Bulkeley (the surname is misspelled by Thoreau) was Concord's first
minister. Ezra Ripley, who baptized Thoreau, served the same church for sixty
years.]

and extension of them under all surrounding institutions.[1] They take a firmer hold on the earth that they may rise higher into the heavens. Their conservative heart-wood, in which no sap longer flows, does not impoverish their growth, but is a firm column to support it; and when their expanding trunks no longer require it, it utterly decays. Their conservatism is a dead but solid heart-wood, which is the pivot and firm column of support to all this growth, appropriating nothing to itself, but forever by its support assisting to extend the area of their radicalism. Half a century after they are dead at the core, they are preserved by radical reforms. They do not, like men, from radicals turn conservative. Their conservative part dies out first; their radical and growing part survives.

Jan. 25

If you would be convinced how differently armed the squirrel is naturally for dealing with pitch pine cones, just try to get one off with your teeth. He who extracts the seeds from a single closed cone with the aid of a knife will be constrained to confess that the squirrel earns his dinner. It is a rugged customer, and will make your fingers bleed. But the squirrel has the key to this conical and spiny chest of many apartments. He sits on a post, vibrating his tail, and twirls it as a plaything.

But so is a man commonly a locked-up chest to us, to open whom, unless we have the key of sympathy, will make our hearts bleed.

Jan. 26

When I took the ether my consciousness amounted to this: I put my finger on myself in order to keep the place, otherwise I should never have returned to this world.

Men have been talking now for a week at the post-office about the age of the great elm, as a matter interesting but impossible to be determined. The very choppers and travellers have stood upon its prostrate trunk and speculated upon its age, as if it were a profound mystery. I stooped and read its years to them (127 at nine and a half feet), but they heard me as the wind that once sighed through its branches. They still surmised that it might be two hundred years old, but they never stooped to read the inscription. Truly they love darkness rather than light. One said it was probably one hundred and fifty, for he had heard somebody say that for fifty years the elm grew, for fifty it stood still, and for fifty it was dying. (Wonder what portion of

[1] [A learned pun on "radicalism," derived from Latin *radix*, a root.]

his career he stood still!) Truly all men are not men of science. They dwell within an integument of prejudice thicker than the bark of the cork-tree, but it is valuable chiefly to stop bottles with. Tied to their buoyant prejudices, they keep themselves afloat when honest swimmers sink.

Talking with Miss Mary Emerson this evening, she said, "It was not the fashion to be so original when I was young." She is readier to take my view—look through my eyes for the time—than any young person that I know in the town.

Feb. 1

Our kitten Min, two-thirds grown, was playing with Sophia's broom this morning, as she was sweeping the parlor, when she suddenly went into a fit, dashed round the room, and, the door being opened, rushed up two flights of stairs and leaped from the attic window to the ice and snow by the side of the doorstep—a descent of a little more than twenty feet—passed round the house and was lost. But she made her appearance again about noon, at the window, quite well and sound in every point, even playful and frisky.

Feb. 27

The papers are talking about the prospect of a war between England and America. Neither side sees how its country can avoid a long and fratricidal war without sacrificing its honor. Both nations are ready to take a desperate step, to forget the interests of civilization and Christianity and their commercial prosperity and fly at each other's throats. When I see an individual thus beside himself, thus desperate, ready to shoot or be shot, like a blackleg who has little to lose, no serene aims to accomplish, I think he is a candidate for bedlam. What asylum is there for nations to go to? Nations are thus ready to talk of wars and challenge one another, because they are made up to such an extent of poor, low-spirited, despairing men, in whose eyes the chance of shooting somebody else without being shot themselves exceeds their actual good fortune. Who, in fact, will be the first to enlist but the most desperate class, they who have lost all hope? And they may at last infect the rest.

Feb. 28

How various are the talents of men! From the brook in which one lover of nature has never during all his lifetime detected anything larger than a minnow, another extracts a trout that weighs three pounds, or an otter four feet long. How much more game he will see who carries a gun, i.e. who goes to see it! Though you roam the woods all your days, you never will see by chance what he sees who goes on purpose to see it. One gets his living by shooting woodcocks; most never see one in their lives.[1]

Our young maltese cat Min, which has been absent five cold nights, the ground covered deep with crusted snow—her first absence—and given up for dead, has at length returned at daylight, awakening the whole house with her mewing and afraid of the strange girl we have got in the meanwhile. She is a mere wrack of skin and bones, with a sharp nose and wiry tail. She is as one returned from the dead. There is as much rejoicing as at the return of the prodigal son, and if we had a fatted calf we should kill it. Various are the conjectures as to her adventures—whether she has had a fit, been shut up somewhere, or lost, torn in pieces by a certain terrier or frozen to death. In the meanwhile she is fed with the best that the house affords, minced meats and saucers of warmed milk, and, with the aid of unstinted sleep in all laps in succession, is fast picking up her crumbs. She has already found her old place under the stove, and is preparing to make a stew of her brains there.

March 4

I had two friends. The one offered me friendship on such terms that I could not accept it without a sense of degradation. He would not meet me on equal terms, but only be to some extent my patron. He would not come to see me, but was hurt if I did not visit him. He would not readily accept a favor, but would gladly confer one. He treated me with ceremony occasionally, though he could be simple and downright sometimes; and from time to time acted a part, treating me as if I were a distinguished stranger; was on stilts, using made words. Our relation was one long tragedy, yet I did not directly speak of it. I do not believe in complaint, nor in explanation. The whole is but too plain, alas, already. We grieve that we do not love each other, that we cannot confide in each other. I could not bring myself to speak, and so recognize an obstacle to our affection.

I had another friend, who, through a slight obtuseness, perchance, did not recognize a fact which the dignity of friendship would by no means allow me to descend so far as to speak of, and yet the inevitable effect of that ignorance was to hold us apart forever.

[1] [Apparently Thoreau himself never *heard* one.]

When it is proposed to me to go abroad, rub off some rust, and *better my condition* in a worldly sense, I fear lest my life will lose some of its homeliness. If these fields and streams and woods, the phenomena of nature here, and the simple occupations of the inhabitants should cease to interest and inspire me, no culture or wealth would atone for the loss. I fear the dissipation that travelling, going into society, even the best, the enjoyment of intellectual luxuries, imply. If Paris is much in your mind, if it is more and more to you, Concord is less and less, and yet it would be a wretched bargain to accept the proudest Paris in exchange for my native village. At best, Paris could only be a school in which to learn to live here, a stepping-stone to Concord, a school in which to fit for this university. I wish so to live ever as to derive my satisfactions and inspirations from the commonest events, every-day phenomena, so that what my senses hourly perceive, my daily walk, the conversation of my neighbors, may inspire me, and I may dream of no heaven but that which lies about me. A man may acquire a taste for wine or brandy, and so lose his love for water, but should we not pity him?

The sight of a marsh hawk in Concord meadows is worth more to me than the entry of the allies into Paris. In this sense I am not ambitious. I do not wish my native soil to become exhausted and run out through neglect. Only that travelling is good which reveals to me the value of home and enables me to enjoy it better. That man is the richest whose pleasures are the cheapest.

WHAT BEFELL AT MRS. BROOKS'S

On the morning of the 17th, Mrs. Brooks's Irish girl Joan fell down the cellar stairs, and was found by her mistress lying at the bottom, apparently lifeless. Mrs. Brooks ran to the street-door for aid to get her up, and asked a Miss Farmer, who was passing, to call the blacksmith near by. The latter lady turned instantly, and, making haste across the road on this errand, fell flat in a puddle of melted snow, and came back to Mrs. Brooks's, bruised and dripping and asking for opodeldoc. Mrs. Brooks again ran to the door and called to George Bigelow to complete the unfinished errand. He ran nimbly about it and fell flat in another puddle near the former, but, his joints being limber, got along without opodeldoc and raised the blacksmith. He also notified James Burke, who was passing, and he, rushing in to render aid, fell off one side of the cellar stairs in the dark. They no sooner got the girl upstairs than she came to and went raving, then had a fit.

Haste makes waste. It never rains but it pours. I have this from those who have heard Mrs. Brooks's story, seen the girl, the stairs, and the puddles.

March 23

I spend a considerable portion of my time observing the habits of the wild animals, my brute neighbors. By their various movements and migrations they fetch the year about to me. Very significant are the flight of geese and the migration of suckers, etc., etc. But when I consider that the nobler animals have been exterminated here—the cougar, panther, lynx, wolverene, wolf, bear, moose, deer, the beaver, the turkey, etc., etc.—I cannot but feel as if I lived in a tamed, and, as it were, emasculated country. Would not the motions of those larger and wilder animals have been more significant still? Is it not a maimed and imperfect nature that I am conversant with? As if I were to study a tribe of Indians that had lost all its warriors. Do not the forest and the meadow now lack expression, now that I never see nor think of the moose with a lesser forest on his head in the one, nor of the beaver in the other? When I think what were the various sounds and notes, the migrations and works, and changes of fur and plumage which ushered in the spring and marked the other seasons of the year, I am reminded that this my life in nature, this particular round of natural phenomena which I call a year, is lamentably incomplete. I listen to [a] concert in which so many parts are wanting. The whole civilized country is to some extent turned into a city, and I am that citizen whom I pity. Many of those animal migrations and other phenomena by which the Indians marked the season are no longer to be observed. I seek acquaintance with Nature—to know her moods and manners. Primitive Nature is the most interesting to me. I take infinite pains to know all the phenomena of the spring, for instance, thinking that I have here the entire poem, and then, to my chagrin, I hear that it is but an imperfect copy that I possess and have read, that my ancestors have torn out many of the first leaves and grandest passages, and mutilated it in many places. I should not like to think that some demigod had come before me and picked out some of the best of the stars. I wish to know an entire heaven and an entire earth. All the great trees and beasts, fishes and fowl are gone. The streams, perchance, are somewhat shrunk.

March 27

Farewell, my friends,[1] my path inclines to this side the mountain, yours to that. For a long time you have appeared further and further off to me. I see that you will at length disappear altogether. For a season my path seems lonely without you. The meadows are like barren ground. The memory of me is steadily passing away from you. My path grows narrower and steeper, and the night is approaching. Yet I have faith that, in the definite future, new suns will rise, and new plains expand before me, and I trust that I shall therein encounter pilgrims who bear that same virtue that I recognized in you, who will be that very virtue that was you. I accept the everlasting and salutary law, which was promulgated as much that spring that I first knew you, as this that I seem to lose you.

My former friends, I visit you as one walks amid the columns of a ruined temple. You belong to an era, a civilization and glory, long past. I recognize still your fair proportions, notwithstanding the convulsions which we have felt, and the weeds and jackals that have sprung up around. I come here to be reminded of the past, to read your inscriptions, the hieroglyphics, the sacred writings. We are no longer the representatives of our former selves.

Love is a thirst that is never slaked. Under the coarsest rind, the sweetest meat. If you would read a friend aright, you must be able to read through something thicker and opaquer than horn. If you can read a friend, all languages will be easy to you. Enemies publish themselves. They declare war. The friend never declares his love.

April 3

Hosmer is overhauling a vast heap of manure in the rear of his barn, turning the ice within it up to the light; yet he asks despairingly what life is for, and says he does not expect to stay here long. But I have just come from reading Columella,[2] who describes the same kind of spring work, in that to him new spring of the world, with hope, and I suggest to be brave and hopeful with nature. Human life may be transitory and full of trouble, but the perennial mind, whose survey extends from that spring to this, from Columella to Hosmer, is superior to change. I will identify myself with that which did not die with Columella and will not die with Hosmer.

---

1 [Perhaps Waldo and Lydian Emerson.]
2 [A Latin writer on agriculture of the first century A.D.]

April 19

Was awakened in the night to a strain of music dying away—passing travellers singing. My being was so expanded and infinitely and divinely related for a brief season that I saw how unexhausted, how almost wholly unimproved, was man's capacity for a divine life. When I remembered what a narrow and finite life I should anon awake to!

April 28

Again, as so many times, I [am] reminded of the advantage to the poet, and philosopher, and naturalist, and whomsoever, of pursuing from time to time some other business than his chosen one—seeing with the side of the eye. The poet will so get visions which no deliberate abandonment can secure. The philosopher is so forced to recognize principles which long study might not detect. And the naturalist even will stumble upon some new and unexpected flower or animal.

How promising a simple, unpretending, quiet, somewhat reserved man, whether among generals or scholars or farmers! How rare an equanimity and serenity which are an encouragement to all observers! Some youthfulness, some manliness, some goodness. Like Tarbell, a man apparently made a deacon on account of some goodness, and not on account of some hypocrisy and badness as usual.

May 19

As I sail up the reach of the Assabet above Dove Rock with a fair wind, a traveller riding along the highway is watching my sail while he hums a tune. How inspiring and elysian it is to hear when the traveller or the laborer from a call to his horse or the murmur of ordinary conversation rises into song! It paints the landscape suddenly as no agriculture, no flowery crop that can be raised. It is at once another land, the abode of poetry. I am always thus affected when I hear in the fields any singing or instrumental music at the end of the day. It implies a different life and pursuits than the ordinary. As he looked at my sail, I listened to his singing. Perchance they were equally poetic, and we repaid each other. Why will not men oftener advertise me of musical thoughts? The singer is in the attitude of one inviting the muse—aspiring.

Aug. 2, P.M.

To Hill.
A green bittern comes, noiselessly flapping, with stealthy and

inquisitive looking to this side the stream and then that, thirty feet above the water. This antediluvian bird, creature of the night, is a fit emblem of a dead stream like this Musketicook. This especially is the bird of the river. There is a sympathy between its sluggish flight and the sluggish flow of the stream—its slowly lapsing flight, even like the rills of Musketicook and my own pulse sometimes.

Aug. 8, 3.30 P.M.

When I came forth, thinking to empty my boat and go a-meditating along the river—for the full ditches and drenched grass forbade other routes, except the highway—and this is one advantage of a boat—I learned to my chagrin that Father's pig was gone. He had leaped out of the pen some time since his breakfast, but his dinner was untouched. Here was an ugly duty not to be shirked—a wild shoat that weighed but ninety to be tracked, caught, and penned—an afternoon's work, at least (if I were lucky enough to accomplish it so soon), prepared for me, quite different from what I had anticipated. I felt chagrined, it is true, but I could not ignore the fact nor shirk the duty that lay so near to me. Do the duty that lies nearest to thee. I proposed to Father to sell the pig as he was running (somewhere) to a neighbor who had talked of buying him, making a considerable reduction. But my suggestion was not acted on, and the responsibilities of the case all devolved on me, for I could run faster than Father. Father looked to me, and I ceased to look to the river. Well, let us see if we can track him. Yes, this is the corner where he got out, making a step of his trough. Thanks to the rain, his tracks are quite distinct. Here he went along the edge of the garden over the water and musk melons, then through the beans and potatoes, and even along the front-yard walk I detect the print of his divided hoof, his two sharp toes (*ungulæ*). It's a wonder we did not see him. And here he passed out under the gate, across the road—how naked he must have felt!—into a grassy ditch, and whither next? Is it of any use to go hunting him up unless you have devised some mode of catching him when you have found? Of what avail to know where he has been, even where he is? He was so shy the little while we had him, of course he will never come back; he cannot be tempted by a swill-pail. Who knows how many miles off he is! Perhaps he has taken the back track and gone to Brighton, or Ohio! At most, probably we shall only have the satisfaction of glimpsing the nimble beast at a distance, from time to time, as he trots swiftly through the green meadows and corn-fields. But, now I speak, what is that I see pacing deliberately up the middle of the street forty rods off? It is *he*. As if to tantalize, to tempt us to waste

our afternoon without further hesitation, he thus offers himself. He
roots a foot or two and then lies down on his belly in the middle of the
street. But think not to catch him a-napping. He has his eyes about,
and his ears too. He has already been chased. He gives that wagon a
wide berth, and now, seeing me, he turns and trots back down the
street. He turns into a front yard. Now if I can only close that gate
upon him ninety-nine hundredths of the work is done, but ah! he
hears me coming afar off, he foresees the danger, and, with swinish
cunning and speed, he scampers out. My neighbor in the street tries
to head him; he jumps to this side the road, then to that, before him;
but the third time the pig was there first and went by. "Whose is it?"
he shouts. "It's ours." He bolts into that neighbor's yard and so
across his premises. He has been twice there before, it seems; he knows
the road; see what work he has made in his flower-garden! He must be
fond of bulbs. Our neighbor picks up one tall flower with its bulb
attached, holds it out at arm's length. He is excited about the pig; it
is a subject he is interested in. But where is [he] gone now? The last
glimpse I had of him was as he went through the cow-yard; here are
his tracks again in this corn-field, but they are lost in the grass. We lose
him; we beat the bushes in vain; he may be far away. But hark! I
heard a grunt. Nevertheless for half an hour I do not see him that
grunted. At last I find fresh tracks along the river, and again lose them.
Each neighbor whose garden I traverse tells me some anecdote of
losing pigs, or the attempt to drive them, by which I am not en-
couraged. Once more he crosses our first neighbor's garden and is
said to be in the road. But I am not there yet; it is a good way off. At
length my eyes rest on him again, after three quarters of an hour's
separation. There he trots with the whole road to himself, and now
again drops on his belly in a puddle. Now he starts again, seeing me
twenty rods [off], deliberates, considers which way I want him to go,
and goes the other. There was some chance of driving him along the
sidewalk, or letting him go rather, till he slipped under our gate again,
but of what avail would that be? How corner and catch him who keeps
twenty rods off? He never lets the open side of the triangle be less than
half a dozen rods wide. There was one place where a narrower street
turned off at right angles with the main one, just this side our yard, but
I could not drive him past that. Twice he ran up the narrow street, for
he knew I did not wish it, but though the main street was broad and
open and no traveller in sight, when I tried to drive him past this
opening he invariably turned his piggish head toward me, dodged
from side to side, and finally ran up the narrow street or down the
main one, as if there were a high barrier erected before him. But really

he is no more obstinate than I. I cannot but respect his tactics and his independence. He will be he, and I may be I. He is not unreasonable because he thwarts me, but only the more reasonable. He has a strong will. He stands upon his idea. There is a wall across the path not where a man bars the way, but where he is resolved not to travel. Is he not superior to man therein? Once more he glides down the narrow street, deliberates at a corner, chooses wisely for him, and disappears through an openwork fence eastward. He has gone to fresh gardens and pastures new. Other neighbors stand in the doorways but half sympathizing, only observing, "Ugly thing to catch." "You have a job on your hands." I lose sight of him, but hear that he is far ahead in a large field. And there we try to let him alone a while, giving him a wide berth.

At this stage an Irishman was engaged to assist. "I can catch him," says he, with Buonapartean confidence. He thinks him a family Irish pig. His wife is with him, bare-headed, and his little flibbertigibbet of a boy, seven years old. "Here, Johnny, do you run right off there" (at the broadest possible angle with his own course). "Oh, but he can't do anything." "Oh, but I only want him to tell me where he is—to keep sight of him." Michael soon discovers that he is not an Irish pig, and his wife and Johnny's occupation are soon gone. Ten minutes afterward I am patiently tracking him step by step through a corn-field, a near-sighted man helping me, and then into garden after garden far eastward, and finally into the highway, at the graveyard; but hear and see nothing. One suggests a dog to track him. Father is meanwhile selling him to the blacksmith, who also is trying to get sight of him. After fifteen minutes since he disappeared eastward, I hear that he has been to the river twice far on [?] the north, through the first neighbor's premises. I wend that way. He crosses the street far ahead, Michael behind; he dodges up an avenue. I stand in the gap there, Michael at the other end, and now he tries to corner him. But it is a vain hope to corner him in a yard. I see a carriage-manufactury door open. "Let him go in there, Flannery." For once the pig and I are of one mind; he bolts in, and the door is closed. Now for a rope. It is a large barn, crowded with carriages. The rope is at length obtained; the windows are barred with carriages lest he bolt through. He is resting quietly on his belly in the further corner, thinking unutterable things.

Now the course recommences within narrower limits. Bump, bump, bump he goes, against wheels and shafts. We get no hold yet. He is all ear and eye. Small boys are sent under the carriages to drive him out. He froths at the mouth and deters them. At length he is stuck for an instant between the spokes of a wheel, and I am securely attached to his hind leg. He squeals deafeningly, and is silent. The rope is attached to a hind leg. The door is opened, and the *driving* commences. Roll an egg as well. You may drag him, but you cannot drive him. But he is in the road, and now another thunder-shower greets us. I leave Michael with the rope in one hand and a switch in the other and go home. He seems to be gaining a little westward. But, after long delay, I look out and find that he makes but doubtful progress. A boy is made to face him with a stick, and it is only when the pig springs at him savagely that progress is made homeward. He will be killed before he is driven home. I get a wheelbarrow and go to the rescue. Michael is alarmed. The pig is rabid, snaps at him. We drag him across the barrow, hold him down, and so, at last, get him home.

If a wild shoat like this gets loose, first track him if you can, or otherwise discover where he is. Do not scare him more than you can help. Think of some yard or building or other inclosure that will hold him and, by showing your forces—yet as if uninterested parties—fifteen or twenty rods off, let him of his own accord enter it. Then slightly shut the gate. Now corner and tie him and put him into a cart or barrow.

All progress in driving at last was made by facing and endeavoring to switch him from home. He rushed upon you and made a few feet in the desired direction. When I approached with the barrow he advanced to meet it with determination.

So I get home at dark, wet through and supperless, covered with mud and wheel-grease, without any rare flowers.

Aug. 12

Labor Lost.—For one of this generation to talk with a man of the old school. You might have done a solid work the meanwhile with a contemporary. I thought of this when I saw Neighbor B., the worthy man! and thought of my interviews with him. If I could only get the parish clerk to read what I have to say to him!

Aug. 28

June, July, and August, the tortoise eggs are hatching a few inches beneath the surface in sandy fields. You tell of active labors, of works of art, and wars the past summer; meanwhile the tortoise eggs underlie this turmoil. What events have transpired on the lit and airy surface three inches above them! Sumner knocked down; Kansas living an age of suspense.[1] Think what is a summer to them! How many worthy

---

[1] [Senator Charles Sumner of Massachusetts, after denouncing the Kansas-Nebraska Bill, was physically attacked in the Senate chamber on May 22, 1856.]

men have died and had their funeral sermons preached since I saw the
mother turtle bury her eggs here! They contained an undeveloped
liquid then, they are now turtles. June, July, and August—the livelong
summer—what are they with their heats and fevers but sufficient to
hatch a tortoise in? Be not in haste; mind your private affairs. Consider the turtle. A whole summer—June, July, and August—is not too
good nor too much to hatch a turtle in. Perchance you have worried
yourself, despaired of the world, meditated the end of life, and all
things seemed rushing to destruction; but nature has steadily and
serenely advanced with a turtle's pace. The young turtle spends its
infancy within its shell. It gets experience and learns the ways of the
world through that wall. While it rests warily on the edge of its hole,
rash schemes are undertaken by men and fail. Has not the tortoise also
learned the true value of time? You go to India and back, and the
turtle eggs in your field are still unhatched. French empires rise or fall,
but the turtle is developed only so fast. What's a summer? Time for a
turtle's eggs to hatch. So is the turtle developed, fitted to endure, for
he outlives twenty French dynasties. One turtle[1] knows several
Napoleons. They have seen no berries, had no cares, yet has not the
great world existed for them as much as for you?

Aug. 30

If you would really take a position outside the street and daily life
of men, you must have deliberately planned your course, you must
have business which is not your neighbors' business, which they cannot
understand. For only absorbing employment prevails, succeeds, takes
up space, occupies territory, determines the future of individuals and
states, drives Kansas out of your head, and actually and permanently
occupies the only desirable and free Kansas against all border ruffians.
The attitude of resistance is one of weakness, inasmuch as it only faces
an enemy; it has its back to all that is truly attractive. You shall have
your affairs, I will have mine. You will spend this afternoon in setting
up your neighbor's stove, and be paid for it; I will spend it in gathering
the few berries of the *Vaccinium Oxycoccus*[2] which Nature produces here,
before it is too late, and *be paid for it also* after another fashion.

It is in vain to dream of a wildness distant from ourselves. There is
none such. . . . I shall never find in the wilds of Labrador any greater
wildness than in some recess in Concord, i.e. than I import into it. A
little more manhood or virtue will make the surface of the globe anywhere thrillingly novel and wild.

[1] [The turtle that knew Napoleon is said to be still living on the island of St. Helena.]
[2] [Cranberry.]

Aug. 31, Sunday, P.M.

To Hubbard Bath Swamp by boat.

There sits one by the shore who wishes to go with me, but I cannot think of it. I must be fancy-free. There is no such mote in the sky as a man who is not perfectly transparent to you—who has any opacity. I would rather attend to him earnestly for half an hour, on shore or elsewhere, and then dismiss him. He thinks I could merely take him into my boat and then not mind him. He does not realize that I should by the same act take him into my mind, where there is no room for him, and my bark would surely founder in such a voyage as I was contemplating. I know very well that I should never reach that expansion of the river I have in my mind, with him aboard with his broad terrene qualities. He would sink my bark (not to another sea) and never know it. I could better carry a heaped load of meadow mud and sit on the tholepins. There would be more room for me, and I should reach that expansion of the river nevertheless.

Sept. 2

My father asked John Legross if he took an interest in politics and did his duty to his country at this crisis. He said he did. He went into the wood-shed and read the newspaper Sundays. Such is the dawn of the literary taste, the first seed of literature that is planted in the new country.

I feel this difference between great poetry and small: that in the one, the sense outruns and overflows the words; in the other, the words the sense.

Oct. 5

It is well to find your employment and amusement in simple and homely things. These wear best and yield most. I think I would rather watch the motions of these cows in their pasture for a day, which I now see all headed one way and slowly advancing—watch them and project their course carefully on a chart, and report all their behavior faithfully—than wander to Europe or Asia and watch other motions there; for it is only ourselves that we report in either case, and per-chance we shall report a more restless and worthless self in the latter case than in the first.

Oct. 18

Men commonly exaggerate the theme. Some themes they think are significant and others insignificant. I feel that my life is very homely, my pleasures very cheap. Joy and sorrow, success and failure, grandeur and meanness, and indeed most words in the English language do not mean for me what they do for my neighbors. I see that my neighbors look with compassion on me, that they think it is a mean and unfortunate destiny which makes me to walk in these fields and woods so much and sail on this river alone. But so long as I find here the only real elysium, I cannot hesitate in my choice. My work is writing, and I do not hesitate, though I know that no subject is too trivial for me, tried by ordinary standards; for, ye fools, the theme is nothing, the life is everything. All that interests the reader is the depth and intensity of the life excited. We touch our subject but by a point which has no breadth, but the pyramid of our experience, or our interest in it, rests on us by a broader or narrower base. That is, man is all in all, Nature nothing, but as she draws him out and reflects him. Give me simple, cheap, and homely themes.[1]

Dec. 1

I see the old pale-faced farmer out again on his sled now for the five-thousandth time—Cyrus Hubbard, a man of a certain New England probity and worth, immortal and natural, like a natural product, like the sweetness of a nut, like the toughness of hickory. He, too, is a redeemer for me. How superior actually to the faith he professes! He is not an office-seeker. What an institution, what a revelation is a man! We are wont foolishly to think that the creed which a man professes is more significant than the fact he is. It matters not how hard the conditions seemed, how mean the world, for a man is a prevalent force and a new law himself. He is a system whose law is to be observed. The old farmer condescends to countenance still this nature and order of things. It is a great encouragement that an honest man makes this world his abode. . . . Moderate, natural, true, as if he were made of earth, stone, wood, snow. I thus meet in this universe kindred of mine, composed of these elements. I see men like frogs; their peeping I partially understand.

The dear wholesome color of shrub oak leaves, so clean and firm, not decaying, but which have put on a kind of immortality, not wrinkled and thin like the white oak leaves, but full-veined and plump, as nearer earth. Well-tanned leather on the one side, sun-tanned, color of colors, color of the cow and the deer, silver-downy beneath, turned toward the late bleached and russet fields. What are acanthus leaves and the rest

---

[1] [Examples of such themes are given in the following entries.]

to this? Emblem of my winter condition. I love and could embrace the shrub oak with its scanty garment of leaves rising above the snow, lowly whispering to me, akin to winter thoughts, and sunsets, and to all virtue. Covert which the hare and the partridge seek, and I too seek. What cousin of mine is the shrub oak? How can any man suffer long? For a sense of want is a prayer, and all prayers are answered. Rigid as iron, clean as the atmosphere, hardy as virtue, innocent and sweet as a maiden is the shrub oak. In proportion as I know and love it, I am natural and sound as a partridge. I felt a positive yearning toward one bush this afternoon. There was a match found for me at last. I fell in love with a shrub oak.

No, I am a stranger in your towns. I am not at home at French's, or Lovejoy's, or Savery's. I can winter more to my mind amid the shrub oaks. I have made arrangements to stay with them.

Dec. 2, P.M.

Saw Melvin's lank bluish-white black-spotted hound, and Melvin with his gun near, going home at eve. He follows hunting, praise be to him, as regularly in our tame fields as the farmers follow farming. Persistent Genius! How I respect him and thank him for him! [*sic*] I trust the Lord will provide us with another Melvin when he is gone. How good in him to follow his own bent, and not continue at the Sabbath-school all his days! What a wealth he thus becomes in the neighborhood! Few know how to take the census. I thank my stars for Melvin. I think of him with gratitude when I am going to sleep, grateful that he exists—that Melvin who is such a trial to his mother. Yet he is agreeable to me as a tinge of russet on the hillside. I would fain give thanks morning and evening for my blessings. Awkward, gawky, loose-hung, dragging his legs after him. He is my contemporary and neighbor. He is one tribe, I am another, and we are not at war.

As for the sensuality in Whitman's *Leaves of Grass*, I do not so much wish that it was not written, as that men and women were so pure that they could read it without harm.

Dec. 3

How I love the simple, reserved countrymen, my neighbors, who mind their own business and let me alone, who never waylaid nor shot at me, to my knowledge, when I crossed their fields, though each one has a gun in his house! For nearly twoscore years I have known, at a distance, these long-suffering men, whom I never spoke to, who never spoke to me, and now feel a certain tenderness for them, as if this long probation were but the prelude to an eternal friendship. What a long trial we have withstood, and how much more admirable we are to each other, perchance, than if we had been bedfellows! I am not only grateful because Veias, and Homer, and Christ, and Shakespeare have lived, but I am grateful for Minott, and Rice, and Melvin, and Goodwin, and Puffer even. I see Melvin all alone filling his sphere, in russet suit, which no other could fill or suggest. He takes up as much room in nature as the most famous.

Dec. 5

My themes shall not be far-fetched. I will tell of homely every-day phenomena and adventures. Friends! Society! It seems to me that I have an abundance of it, there is so much that I rejoice and sympathize with, and men, too, that I never speak to but only know and think of. What you call bareness and poverty is to me simplicity. God could not be unkind to me if he should try. I love the winter, with its imprisonment and its cold, for it compels the prisoner to try new fields and resources. I love to have the river closed up for a season and a pause put to my boating, to be obliged to get my boat in. I shall launch it again in the spring with so much more pleasure. This is an advantage in point of abstinence and moderation compared with the seaside boating, where the boat ever lies on the shore. I love best to have each thing in its season only, and enjoy doing without it at all other times. It is the greatest of all advantages to enjoy no advantage at all. I find it invariably true, the poorer I am, the richer I am. What you consider my disadvantage, I consider my advantage. While you are pleased to get knowledge and culture in many ways, I am delighted to think that I am getting rid of them. I have never got over my surprise that I should have been born into the most estimable place in all the world, and in the very nick of time, too.

Dec. 7

The winters come now as fast as snowflakes. It is wonderful that old men do not lose their reckoning. It was summer, and now again it is winter. Nature loves this rhyme so well that she never tires of repeating it. So sweet and wholesome is the winter, so simple and moderate, so satisfactory and perfect, that her children will never weary of it. What a poem! an epic in blank verse, enriched with a million tinkling rhymes. It is solid beauty. It has been subjected to the vicissitudes of millions of years of the gods, and not a single superfluous ornament remains. The severest and coldest of the immortal critics have shot their arrows at and pruned it till it cannot be amended.

Dec. 9

Such is a winter eve. Now for a merry fire, some old poet's pages, or else serene philosophy, or even a healthy book of travels to last far into the night, eked out perhaps with the walnuts which we gathered in November.

Dec. 18

At my lecture, the audience attended to me closely, and I was satisfied; that is all I ask or expect generally. Not one spoke to me afterward, nor needed they. I have no doubt that they liked it, in the main, though few of them would have dared say so, provided they were conscious of it. Generally, if I can only get the ears of an audience, I do not care whether they say they like my lecture or not. I think I know as well as they can tell. At any rate, it is none of my business, and it would be impertinent for me to inquire. The stupidity of most of these country towns, not to include the cities, is in its innocence infantile. Lectured in basement (vestry) of the orthodox church,[1] and I trust helped to undermine it.

Dec. 28

I thrive best on solitude. If I have had a companion only one day in a week, unless it were one or two I could name, I find that the value of the week to me has been seriously affected. It dissipates my days, and often it takes another week to get over it. As the Esquimaux of Smith's Strait in North Greenland laughed when Kane warned them of their utter extermination, cut off as they were by ice on all sides from their race, unless they attempted in season to cross the glacier southward, so do I laugh when you tell me of the danger of impoverishing myself by isolation. It is here that the walrus and the seal, and the white bear, and the eider ducks and auks on which I batten, most abound.

Jan. 4, 1857

It does look sometimes as if the world were on its last legs. How many there are whose principal employment it is nowadays to eat their meals and go to the post-office!

---

[1] [At Amherst, New Hampshire. The church still stands.]

Jan. 7

The man I meet with is not often so instructive as the silence he breaks. This stillness, solitude, wildness of nature is a kind of thorough-wort, or boneset, to my intellect. This is what I go out to seek. It is as if I always met in those places some grand, serene, immortal, infinitely encouraging, though invisible, companion, and walked with him.

Jan. 11

For some years past I have partially offered myself as a lecturer; have been advertised as such several years. Yet I have had but two or three invitations to lecture in a year, and some years none at all. I congratulate myself on having been permitted to stay at home thus, I am so much richer for it. I do not see what I should have got of much value, but money, by going about, but I do see what I should have lost. It seems to me that I have a longer and more liberal lease of life thus. I cannot afford to be telling my experience, especially to those who perhaps will take no interest in it. I wish to be getting experience. You might as well recommend to a bear to leave his hollow tree and run about all winter scratching at all the hollow trees in the woods. He would be leaner in the spring than if he had stayed at home and sucked his claws. As for the lecture-goers, it is none of their business what I think. I perceive that most make a great account of their relations, more or less personal and direct, to many men, coming before them as lecturers, writers, or public men. But all this is impertinent and unprofitable to me. I never yet recognized, nor was recognized by, a crowd of men.

Jan. 13

I hear one thrumming a guitar below stairs. It reminds me of moments that I have lived. What a comment on our life is the least strain of music! It lifts me up above all the dust and mire of the universe. I soar or hover with clean skirts over the field of my life. It is ever life within life, in concentric spheres. The field wherein I toil or rust at any time is at the same time the field for such different kinds of life! The farmer's boy or hired man has an instinct which tells him as much indistinctly, and hence his dreams and his restlessness; hence, even, it is that he wants money to realize his dreams with. The identical field where I am leading my humdrum life, let but a strain of music be heard there, is seen to be the field of some unrecorded crusade or tournament the thought of which excites in us an ecstasy of joy. The way in which I am affected by this faint thrumming advertises me that there is still some health and immortality in the springs of me. What an elixir is this sound! I, who but lately came and went and lived under *a dish cover*, live now under the heavens. It releases me; it bursts my bonds. Almost all, perhaps all, our life is, speaking comparatively, a stereotyped despair; i.e., we never at any time realize the full grandeur of our destiny. We forever and ever and habitually underrate our fate. Talk of infidels! Why, all the race of men, except in the rarest moments when they are lifted above themselves by an ecstasy, are infidels. With the very best disposition, what does my belief amount to? This poor, timid, unenlightened, thick-skinned creature, what *can* it believe? I am, of course, hopelessly ignorant and unbelieving until some divinity stirs within me. Ninety-nine one-hundredths of our lives we are mere hedgers and ditchers, but from time to time we meet with reminders of our destiny.

We hear the kindred vibrations, music! and we put out our dormant feelers unto the limits of the universe. We attain to a wisdom that passeth understanding. The stable continents undulate. The hard and fixed becomes fluid.

> Unless above himself he can
> Erect himself, how poor a thing is man![1]

When I *hear* music I fear no danger, I am invulnerable, I see no foe. I am related to the earliest times and to the latest.

There are infinite degrees of life, from that which is next to sleep and death, to that which is forever awake and immortal. We must not confound man with man. We cannot conceive of a greater difference than between the life of one man and that of another. I am constrained to believe that the mass of men are never so lifted above themselves that their destiny is seen to be transcendently beautiful and grand.

Jan. 15

Suppose I try to describe faithfully the prospect which a strain of music exhibits to me. The field of my life becomes a boundless plain, glorious to tread, with no death nor disappointment at the end of it. All meanness and trivialness disappear. I become adequate to any deed. No particulars survive this expansion; persons do not survive it. In the light of this strain there is no thou nor I. We are actually lifted above ourselves.

[1] [From Samuel Daniel's "Epistle to the Lady Margaret, Countess of Cumberland."]

Feb. 4

I sometimes hear a prominent but dull-witted worthy man say, or hear that he has said, rarely, that if it were not for his firm belief in "an overruling power," or a "perfect Being," etc., etc. But such poverty-stricken expressions only convince me of his habitual doubt and that he is surprised into a transient belief. Such a man's expression of faith, moving solemnly in the traditional furrow, and casting out all free-thinking and living souls with the rusty mould-board of his compassion or contempt, thinking that he has Moses and all the prophets in his wake, discourages and saddens me as an expression of his narrow and barren want of faith. I see that the infidels and skeptics have formed themselves into churches and weekly gather together at the ringing of a bell.

Sometimes when, in conversation or a lecture, I have been grasping at, or even standing and reclining upon, the serene and everlasting truths that underlie and support our vacillating life, I have seen my auditors standing on their *terra firma*, the quaking earth, crowded together on their Lisbon Quay, and compassionately or timidly watching my motions as if they were the antics of a rope-dancer or mountebank pretending to walk on air.

Feb. 8

Again and again I congratulate myself on my so-called poverty. I was almost disappointed yesterday to find thirty dollars in my desk which I did not know that I possessed, though now I should be sorry to lose it. The week that I go away to lecture, however much I may get for it, is unspeakably cheapened. The preceding and succeeding days are a mere sloping down and up from it.

In the society of many men, or in the midst of what is called success, I find my life of no account, and my spirits rapidly fall. I would rather be the barrenest pasture lying fallow than cursed with the compliments of kings, than be the sulphurous and accursed desert where Babylon once stood. But when I have only a rustling oak leaf, or the faint metallic cheep of a tree sparrow, for variety in my winter walk, my life becomes continent and sweet as the kernel of a nut. I would rather hear a single shrub oak leaf at the end of a wintry glade rustle of its own accord at my approach, than receive a shipload of stars and garters from the strange kings and people of the earth.

By poverty, i.e. simplicity of life and fewness of incidents, I am solidified and crystallized, as a vapor or liquid by cold. It is a singular concentration of strength and energy and flavor. Chastity is perpetual acquaintance with the All. My diffuse and vaporous life becomes as the frost leaves and spiculæ radiant as gems on the weeds and stubble in a winter morning. You think that I am impoverishing myself by withdrawing from men, but in my solitude I have woven for myself a silken web or *chrysalis*, and, nymph-like, shall ere long burst forth a more perfect creature, fitted for a higher society. By simplicity, commonly called poverty, my life is concentrated and so becomes organized, or a κόσμος, which before was inorganic and lumpish.

And now another friendship is ended. I do not know what has made my friend doubt me, but I know that in love there is no mistake, and that every estrangement is well founded. But my destiny is not narrowed, but if possible the broader for it. The heavens withdraw and arch themselves higher. I am sensible not only of a moral, but even a grand physical pain, such as gods may feel, about my head and breast, a certain ache and fullness. This rending of a tie, it is not my work nor thine. It is no accident that we mind; it is only the awards of fate that are affecting. I know of no æons, or periods, no life and death, but these meetings and separations. My life is like a stream that is suddenly dammed and has no outlet; but it rises the higher up the hills that shut it in, and will become a deep and silent lake. Certainly there is no event comparable for grandeur with the eternal separation—if we may conceive it so—from a being that we have known. I become in a degree sensible of the meaning of finite and infinite. What a grand significance the word "never" acquires! With one with whom we have walked on high ground we cannot deal on any lower ground ever after. We have tried for so many years to put each other to this immortal use, and have failed. Undoubtedly our good genii have mutually found the material unsuitable. We have hitherto paid each other the highest possible compliment; we have recognized each other constantly as divine, have afforded each other that opportunity to live that no other wealth or kindness can afford. And now, for some reason inappreciable by us, it has become necessary for us to withhold this mutual aid. Perchance there is none beside who knows us for a god, and none whom we know for such. Each man and woman is a veritable god or goddess, but to the mass of their fellows disguised. There is only one in each case who sees through the disguise. That one who does not stand so near to any man as to see the divinity in him is truly alone. I am perfectly sad at parting from you. I could better have the earth taken away from under my feet, than the thought of you from my mind.[1]

[1] [It is not known to what particular friend Thoreau is saying farewell in this impressive utterance.]

Feb. 18

I am excited by this wonderful air and go listening for the note of the bluebird or other comer. The very grain of the air seems to have undergone a change and is ready to split into the form of the bluebird's warble. Methinks if it were visible, or I could cast up some fine dust which would betray it, it would take a corresponding shape. The bluebird does not come till the air consents and his wedge will enter easily. The air over these fields is a foundry full of moulds for casting bluebirds' warbles. Any sound uttered now would take that form, not of the harsh, vibrating, rending scream of the jay, but a softer, flowing, curling warble, like a purling stream or the lobes of flowing sand and clay. Here is the soft air and the moist expectant apple trees, but not yet the bluebird. They do not quite attain to song.

Feb. 19

A man cannot be said to succeed in this life who does not satisfy one friend.

Feb. 20

What is the relation between a bird and the ear that appreciates its melody, to whom, perchance, it is more charming and significant than to any else? Certainly they are intimately related, and the one was made for the other. It is a natural fact. If I were to discover that a certain kind of stone by the pond-shore was affected, say partially disintegrated, by a particular natural sound, as of a bird or insect, I see that one could not be completely described without describing the other. I am that rock by the pond-side.

Feb. 23

I say in my thought to my neighbor, who was once my friend, "It is of no use to speak the truth to you, you will not hear it. What, then, shall I say to you?" At the instant that I seem to be saying farewell forever to one who has been my friend, I find myself unexpectedly near to him, and it is our very nearness and dearness to each other that gives depth and significance to that forever. Thus I am a helpless prisoner, and these chains I have no skill to break. While I think I have broken one link, I have been forging another.

I have not yet known a friendship to cease, I think. I fear I have experienced its decaying. Morning, noon, and night, I suffer a physical pain, an aching of the breast which unfits me for my tasks. It is perhaps most intense at evening. With respect to Friendship I feel like a wreck that is driving before the gale, with a crew suffering from hunger and thirst, not knowing what shore, if any, they may reach, so long have I *breasted* the conflicting waves of this sentiment, my seams open, my timbers laid bare. I float on Friendship's sea simply because my specific gravity is less than its, but no longer that stanch and graceful vessel that careered so buoyantly over it. My planks and timbers are scattered. At most I hope to make a sort of raft of Friendship, on which, with a few of our treasures, we may float to some firm land.

That aching of the breast, the grandest pain that man endures, which no ether can assuage.

Feb. 24

If I should make the least concession, my friend would spurn me. I am obeying his law as well as my own.

Where is the actual friend you love? Ask from what hill the rainbow's arch springs! It adorns and crowns the earth.

Our friends are our kindred, of our species. There are very few of our species on the globe.

Between me and my friend what unfathomable distance! All mankind, like motes and insects, are between us.

If my friend says in his mind, I will *never* see you again, I translate it of necessity into *ever*. That is its definition in Love's lexicon.

Those whom we can love, we can hate; to others we are indifferent.

March 28

When I witness the first plowing and planting, I acquire a long-lost confidence in the earth—that it will nourish the seed that is committed to its bosom. I am surprised to be reminded that there is warmth in it. We have not only warmer skies, then, but a warmer earth. The frost is out of it, and we may safely commit these seeds to it in some places. Yesterday I walked with Farmer beside his team and saw one furrow turned quite round his field. What noble work is plowing, with the broad and solid earth for material, the ox for fellow-laborer, and the simple but efficient plow for tool! Work that is not done in any shop, in a cramped position, work that tells, that concerns all men, which the sun shines and the rain falls on, and the birds sing over! You turn over the whole vegetable mould, expose how many grubs, and put a new aspect on the face of the earth. It comes pretty near to making a world. Redeeming a swamp does, at any rate. A good plowman is a *terræ filius*. The plowman, we all know, whistles as he drives his team afield.

April 16

About a month ago, at the post-office, Abel Brooks, who is pretty deaf, sidling up to me, observed in a loud voice which all could hear, "Let me see, your society is pretty large, ain't it?" "Oh, yes, large enough," said I, not knowing what he meant. "There's Stewart belongs to it, and Collier, he's one of them, and Emerson, and my boarder" (Pulsifer), "and Channing, I believe, I think he goes there." "You mean the *walkers*; don't you?" "Ye-es, I call you the Society. All go to the woods; don't you?" "Do you miss any of your wood?" I asked. "No, I hain't worried any yet. I believe you're a pretty clever set, as good as the average," etc., etc.

Telling Sanborn of this, he said that, when he first came to town and boarded at Holbrook's, he asked H. how many religious societies there were in town. H. said that there were three—the Unitarian, the Orthodox, and the Walden Pond Society.

April 23

How rarely a man's love for nature becomes a ruling principle with him, like a youth's affection for a maiden, but more enduring! All nature is my bride.

May 1

It is foolish for a man to accumulate material wealth chiefly, houses and land. Our stock in life, our real estate, is that amount of thought which we have had, which we have thought out. The ground we have thus created is forever pasturage for our thoughts. I fall back on to visions which I have had. What else adds to my possessions and makes me rich in all lands? If you have ever done any work with these finest tools, the imagination and fancy and reason, it is a new creation, independent on the world, and a possession forever. You have laid up something against a rainy day. You have to that extent cleared the wilderness.

May 3, Sunday

Up and down the town, men and boys that are under subjection are polishing their shoes and brushing their go-to-meeting clothes. I, a descendant of Northmen[1] who worshipped Thor, spend my time worshipping neither Thor nor Christ; a descendant of Northmen who

[1] [There is no evidence for this in what we know about Thoreau's ancestry, and his surname can have no such significance as he implies here.]

sacrificed men and horses, sacrifice neither men nor horses. I care not
for Thor nor for the Jews. I sympathize not today with those who go
to church in newest clothes and sit quietly in straight-backed pews. I
sympathize rather with the boy who has none to look after him, who
borrows a boat and paddle and in common clothes sets out to explore
these temporary vernal lakes. I meet such a boy paddling along under
a sunny bank, with bare feet and his pants rolled up above his knees,
ready to leap into the water at a moment's warning. Better for him to
read *Robinson Crusoe* than Baxter's *Saints' Rest*.

May 12

How rarely I meet with a man who can be free, even in thought!
We live according to rule. Some men are bed-ridden; all, world-ridden.
I take my neighbor, an intellectual man, out into the woods and invite
him to take a new and absolute view of things, to empty clean out of his
thoughts all institutions of men and start again; but he can't do it, he
sticks to his traditions and his crotchets. He thinks that governments,
colleges, newspapers, etc., are from everlasting to everlasting.

As the bay-wing[1] sang many a thousand years ago, so sang he
tonight. In the beginning God heard his song and pronounced it good,
and hence it has endured. It reminded me of many a summer sunset,
of many miles of gray rails, of many a rambling pasture, of the farm-
house far in the fields, its milk-pans and well-sweep, and the cows
coming home from pasture.

I would thus from time to time take advice of the birds, correct my
human views by listening to their volucral (?). He is a brother poet,
this small gray bird (or bard), whose muse inspires mine. His lay is an
idyl or pastoral, older and sweeter than any that is classic. He sits on
some gray perch like himself, on a stake, perchance, in the midst of
the field, and you can hardly see him against the plowed ground. You
advance step by step as the twilight deepens, and lo! he is gone, and in
vain you strain your eyes to see whither, but anon his tinkling strain is
heard from some other quarter. One with the rocks and with
us.

Methinks I hear these sounds, have these reminiscences, only when
well employed, at any rate only when I have no reason to be ashamed
of my employment. I am often aware of a certain compensation of this
kind for doing something from a sense of duty, even unconsciously.
Our past experience is a never-failing capital which can never be

---

[1] [The vesper sparrow.]

alienated, of which each kindred future event reminds us. If you would have the song of the sparrow inspire you a thousand years hence, let your life be in harmony with its strain today.

I ordinarily plod along a sort of whitewashed prison entry, subject to some indifferent or even grovelling mood. I do not distinctly realize my destiny. I have turned down my light to the merest glimmer and am doing some task which I have set myself. I take incredibly narrow views, live on the limits, and have no recollection of absolute truth. Mushroom institutions hedge me in. But suddenly, in some fortunate moment, the voice of eternal wisdom reaches me, even in the strain of the sparrow, and liberates me, whets and clarifies my senses, makes me a competent witness.

May 26

My mother was telling tonight of the sounds which she used to hear summer nights when she was young and lived on the Virginia Road[1]— the lowing of cows, or cackling of geese, or the beating of a drum as far off as Hildreth's, but above all Joe Merriam whistling to his team, for he was an admirable whistler. Says she used to get up at midnight and go and sit on the door-step when all in the house were asleep, and she could hear nothing in the world but the ticking of the clock in the house behind her.

May 27, P.M.

To Hill.

I hear the sound of fife and drum the other side of the village, and am reminded that it is May Training. Some thirty young men are marching in the streets in two straight sections, with each a very heavy and warm cap for the season on his head and a bright red stripe down the legs of his pantaloons, and at their head march two with white stripes down their pants, one beating a drum, the other blowing a fife. I see them all standing in a row by the side of the street in front of their captain's residence, with a dozen or more ragged boys looking on, but presently they all remove to the opposite side, as it were with one consent, not being satisfied with their former position, which probably had its disadvantages. Thus they march and strut the better part of the day, going into the tavern two or three times, to abandon themselves to unconstrained positions out of sight, and at night they may be seen going home singly with swelling breasts.

[1] [The road in Concord where Thoreau's birthplace stood.]

June 1

I hear the note of a bobolink concealed in the top of an apple tree behind me. Though this bird's full strain is ordinarily somewhat trivial, this one appears to be meditating a strain as yet unheard in meadow or orchard. *Paulo majora canamus.* He is just touching the strings of his theorbo, his glassichord, his water organ, and one or two notes globe themselves and fall in liquid bubbles from his teeming throat. It is as if he touched his harp within a vase of liquid melody, and when he lifted it out, the notes fell like bubbles from the trembling strings. Methinks they are the most *liquidly* sweet and melodious sounds I ever heard. They are refreshing to my ear as the first distant tinkling and gurgling of a rill to a thirsty man. Oh, never advance farther in your art, never let us hear your full strain, sir. But away he launches, and the meadow is all bespattered with melody. His notes fall with the apple blossoms, in the orchard. The very divinest part of his strain dropping from his overflowing breast *singultim*, in globes of melody. It is the foretaste of such strains as never fell on mortal ears, to hear which we should rush to our doors and contribute all that we possess and are. Or it seemed as if in that vase full of melody some notes sphered themselves, and from time to time bubbled up to the surface and were with difficulty repressed.

June 3

I have several friends and acquaintances who are very good companions in the house or for an afternoon walk, but whom I cannot make up my mind to make a longer excursion with; for I discover, all at once, that they are too gentlemanly in manners, dress, and all their habits. I see in my mind's eye that they wear black coats, considerable starched linen, glossy hats and shoes, and it is out of the question. It is a great disadvantage for a traveller to be a gentleman of this kind; he is so ill-treated, only a prey to landlords. It would be too much of a circumstance to enter a strange town or house with such a companion. You could not travel incognito; you might get into the papers. You should travel as a common man. If such a one were to set out to make a walking-journey, he would betray himself at every step. Every one would see that he was trying an experiment, as plainly as they see that a lame man is lame by his limping. The natives would bow to him, other gentlemen would invite him to ride, conductors would warn him that this was the second-class car, and many would take him for a clergyman; and so he would be continually pestered and balked and run upon. You would not see the natives at all. Instead of going in quietly at the back door and sitting by the kitchen fire, you would be shown into a cold parlor, there to confront a fireboard, and excite a commotion in a whole family. The women would scatter at your approach, and their husbands and sons would go right up to hunt up their black coats. . . . No, you must be a common man, or at least travel as one, and then nobody will know that you are there or have been there.

June 6

Each season is but an infinitesimal point. It no sooner comes than it is gone. It has no duration. It simply gives a tone and hue to my thought. Each annual phenomenon is a reminiscence and prompting. Our thoughts and sentiments answer to the revolutions of the seasons, as two cog-wheels fit into each other. We are conversant with only one point of contact at a time, from which we receive a prompting and impulse and instantly pass to a new season or point of contact. A year is made up of a certain series and number of sensations and thoughts which have their language in nature. Now I am ice, now I am sorrel. Each experience reduces itself to a mood of the mind.

July 30

To a philosopher there is in a sense no great and no small, and I do not often submit to the criticism which objects to comparing so-called great things with small. It is often a question which is most dignified by the comparison, and, beside, it is pleasant to be reminded that ancient worthies who dealt with affairs of state recognized small and familiar objects known to ourselves.

Aug. 10

I hear the neighbors complain sometimes about the peddlers selling their help *false* jewelry, as if they themselves wore *true* jewelry; but if their help pay as much for it as they did for theirs, then it is just as *true* jewelry as theirs, just as becoming to them and no more; for unfortunately it is the cost of the article and not the merits of the wearer that is considered. The money is just as well spent, and perhaps better earned. I don't care how much false jewelry the peddlers sell, nor how many of the eggs which you steal are rotten. What, pray, is *true* jewelry? The hardened tear of a diseased clam, murdered in its old age. Is that fair play? If not, it is no jewel. The mistress wears this in her ear, while her help has one made of paste which you cannot tell from it. False jewelry! Do you know of any shop where *true* jewelry can be bought?

I always look askance at a jeweller and wonder what *church* he can belong to.

I heard some ladies the other day laughing about some one of their *help* who had *helped* herself to a real hoop from off a hogshead for her gown. I laughed too, but which party do you think I laughed at? Isn't hogshead as good a word as crinoline?

Sept. 27

How out of all proportion to the *value* of an idea, when you come to one—in Hindoo literature, for instance—is the historical fact about it—the when, where, etc., it was actually expressed, and what precisely it might signify to a sect of worshippers! Anything that is called history of India—or of the world—is impertinent beside any real poetry or inspired thought which is dateless.

A small red maple has grown, perchance, far away on some moist hillside, a mile from any road, unobserved. It has faithfully discharged the duties of a maple there, all winter and summer, neglected none of its economies, added to its stature in the virtue which belongs to a maple, by a steady growth all summer, and is nearer heaven than in the spring, never having gone gadding abroad; and now, in this month of September, when men are turned travellers, hastening to the seaside, or the mountains, or the lakes—in this month of travelling—this modest maple, having ripened its seeds, still without budging an inch, travels on its reputation, runs up its scarlet flag on that hillside, to show that it has finished its summer work before all other trees, and withdraws from the contest. Thus that modest worth which no scrutiny could have detected when it was most industrious, is, by the very tint of its maturity, by its very blushes, revealed at last to the most careless and distant observer. It rejoices in its existence; its reflections are unalloyed. It is the day of thinksgiving with it. At last, its labors for the year being consummated and every leaf ripened to its full, it flashes out conspicuous to the eye of the most casual observer, with all the virtue and beauty of a maple—*Acer rubrum*. In its hue is no regret nor pining. Its leaves have been asking their parent from time to time in a whisper, "When shall we redden?" It has faithfully husbanded its sap, and builded without babbling [1] nearer and nearer to heaven. Long since it committed its seeds to the winds and has the satisfaction of knowing perhaps that a thousand little well-behaved and promising maples of its stock are already established in business somewhere. It deserves well of Mapledom. It has afforded a shelter to the wandering

---

[1] [A pun, referring to the Tower of Babel.]

bird. Its autumnal tint shows how it has spent its summer; it is the hue
of its virtue.

Sept. 28

I see that E. Wood has sent a couple of Irishmen, with axe and bush-
whack, to cut off the natural hedges of sumach, Roxbury waxwork,
grapes, etc., which have sprung up by the walls on this hill farm, in
order that his cows may get a little more green. And they have cut
down two or three of the very rare celtis[1] trees, not found anywhere
else in the town. The Lord deliver us from these vandalic proprietors!
The botanist and lover of nature has, perchance, discovered some rare
tree which has sprung up by a farmer's wall-side to adorn and bless it,
sole representative of its kind in these parts. Strangers send for a seed
or a sprig from a distance, but, walking there again, he finds that the
farmer has sent a raw Irishman, a hireling just arrived on these shores,
who was never there before—and, we trust, will never be let loose there
again—who knows not whether he is hacking at the upas tree or the
Tree of Knowledge, with axe and stub-scythe to exterminate it, and he
will know it no more forever. What is trespassing? This Hessian, the
day after he was landed, was whirled twenty miles into the interior to
do this deed of vandalism on our favorite hedge. I would as soon admit
a living mud turtle into my herbarium. If some are prosecuted for
abusing children, others deserve to be prosecuted for maltreating the
face of nature committed to their care.

Oct. 4

While I lived in the woods I did various jobs about the town—some
fence-building, painting, gardening, carpentering, etc., etc. One day a
man came from the east edge of the town and said that he wanted to
get me to brick up a fireplace, etc., etc., for him. I told him that I
was not a mason, but he knew that I had built my own house entirely
and would not take no for an answer. So I went.

It was three miles off, and I walked back and forth each day,
arriving early and working as late as if I were living there. The man
was gone away most of the time, but had left some sand dug up in his
cow-yard for me to make mortar with. I bricked up a fireplace, papered
a chamber, but my principal work was whitewashing ceilings. Some
were so dirty that many coats would not conceal the dirt. In the kitchen
I finally resorted to yellow-wash to cover the dirt. I took my meals
there, sitting down with my employer (when he got home) and his hired

[1] [The hackberry.]

men. I remember the awful condition of the sink, at which I washed one day, and when I came to look at what was called the towel I passed it by and wiped my hands on the air, and thereafter I resorted to the pump. I worked there hard three days, charging only a dollar a day.

Oct. 6

I have just read Ruskin's *Modern Painters*. I am disappointed in not finding it a more out-of-door book, for I had heard that such was its character, but its title might have warned me. He does not describe Nature as Nature, but as Turner painted her, and though the work betrays that he has given a close attention to Nature, it appears to have been with an artist's and critic's design. How much is written about Nature as somebody has portrayed her, how little about Nature as she is, and chiefly concerns us, i.e. how much prose, how little poetry!

Oct. 7

One wonders that the tithing-men and fathers of the town are not out to see what the trees mean by their high colors and exuberance of spirits, fearing that some mischief is brewing. I do not see what the Puritans did at that season when the maples blazed out in scarlet. They certainly could not have worshipped in groves then. Perhaps that is what they built meeting-houses and surrounded them with horse-sheds for.

I do not know how to entertain one who can't take long walks. The first thing that suggests itself is to get a horse to draw them, and that brings us at once into contact with stablers and dirty harness, and I do not get over my ride for a long time. I give up my forenoon to them and get along pretty well, the very elasticity of the air and promise of the day abetting me, but they are as heavy as dumplings by mid-afternoon. If they can't walk, why won't they take an honest nap and let me go in the afternoon? But, come two o'clock, they alarm me by an evident disposition to sit. In the midst of the most glorious Indian-summer afternoon, there they sit, breaking your chairs and wearing out the house, with their backs to the light, taking no note of the lapse of time.

Oct. 9

The elms are now at the height of their change. As I look down our street, which is lined with them, now clothed in their very rich brownish-yellow dress, they remind me of yellowing sheaves of grain, as if the harvest had come to the village itself, and we might expect to find some maturity and *flavor* in the thoughts of the villagers at last. Under those light-rustling yellow piles, just ready to fall on the heads of the walker, how can any crudity or greenness of thought or act prevail? The street is a great harvest-home. It would be worth the while to set out these trees, if only for their autumnal value. Think of these great yellow canopies or parasols held over our heads and houses by the mile together, making the village all one and compact, an *ulmarium*. And then how gently and unobserved they drop their burdens and let in the sun when it is wanted, their leaves not heard when they fall on our roofs and in our streets!

Oct. 20

I had gone but little way on the old Carlisle road when I saw Brooks Clark, who is now about eighty and bent like a bow, hastening along the road, barefooted, as usual, with an axe in his hand; was in haste perhaps on account of the cold wind on his bare feet. . . . When he got up to me, I saw that besides the axe in one hand, he had his shoes in the other, filled with knurly apples and a dead robin. He stopped and talked with me a few moments; said that we had had a noble autumn and might now expect some cold weather. I asked if he had found the robin dead. No, he said, he found it with its wing broken and killed it. He also added that he found some apples in the wood, and as he hadn't anything to carry them in, he put 'em in his shoes. They were queer-looking trays to carry fruit in. How many he got in along toward the toes, I don't know. I noticed, too, that his pockets were stuffed with them. His old tattered frock coat was hanging about his naked feet. He appeared to have been out on a scout this gusty afternoon, to see what he could find, as the youngest boy might. It pleased me to see this cheery old man, with such a feeble hold on life, bent almost double, thus enjoying the evening of his days. Far be it from me to call it avarice or penury, this childlike delight in finding something in the woods or fields and carrying it home in the October evening, as a trophy to be added to his winter's store. Oh, no; he was happy to be Nature's pensioner still and birdlike to pick up his living. Better his robin than your turkey, his shoes full of apples than your barrels full; they will be sweeter and suggest a better tale. He can afford to tell how he got them, and we to listen. There is an old wife, too, at home, to share them and hear how they were obtained. Like an old squirrel shuffling to his hole with a nut. Far less pleasing to me the loaded wain, more suggestive of avarice and of spiritual penury.

This old man's cheeriness was worth a thousand of the church's sacraments and *memento mori's*. It was better than a prayerful mood. It proves to me old age as tolerable, as happy, as infancy. I was glad of an occasion to suspect that this afternoon he had not been at "work" but living somewhat after my own fashion (though he did not explain the axe)—had been out to see what nature had for him, and now was hastening home to a burrow he knew, where he could warm his old feet. If he had been a young man, he would probably have thrown away his apples and put on his shoes when he saw me coming, for shame. But old age is manlier; it has learned to live, makes fewer apologies, like infancy. This seems a very manly man.

Oct. 21

Is not the poet bound to write his own biography? Is there any other work for him but a good journal? We do not wish to know how his imaginary hero, but how he, the actual hero, lived from day to day.

Oct. 22

There is scarcely a square rod of sand exposed, in this neighborhood, but you may find on it the stone arrowheads of an extinct race. Far back as that time seems when men went armed with bows and pointed stones here, yet so numerous are the signs of it. The finer particles of sand are blown away and the arrow-points remain. The race is as clean gone—from here—as this sand is clean swept by the wind. Such are our antiquities. These were our predecessors. Why, then, make so great ado about the Roman and the Greek, and neglect the Indian? We [need] not wander off with boys in our imaginations to Juan Fernandez, to wonder at footprints in the sand there. Here is a print still more significant at our doors, the print of a race that has preceded us, and this the little symbol that Nature has transmitted to us. Yes, *this* arrow-headed character is probably more ancient than any other, and to my mind it has not been deciphered. Men should not go to New Zealand to write or think of Greece and Rome, nor more to New England. New earths, new themes expect us. Celebrate not the Garden of Eden, but your own.

Oct. 26

These regular phenomena of the seasons get at last to be—they were *at first*, of course—simply and plainly phenomena or phases of my life. The seasons and all their changes are in me. I see not a dead eel or floating snake, or a gull, but it rounds my life and is like a line or accent in its poem. Almost I believe the Concord would not rise and overflow its banks again, were I not here.[1] After a while I learn what my moods and seasons are. I would have nothing subtracted. I can imagine nothing added. My moods are thus periodical, not two days in my year alike. The perfect correspondence of Nature to man, so that he is at home in her!

Those sparrows, too, are thoughts I have. They come and go; they flit by quickly on their migrations, uttering only a faint *chip*, I know not whither or why exactly. One will not rest upon its twig for me to scrutinize it. The whole copse will be alive with my rambling thoughts, bewildering me by their very multitude, but they will be all gone directly without leaving me a feather. My loftiest thought is somewhat like an eagle that suddenly comes into the field of view, suggesting great things and thrilling the beholder, as if it were bound hitherward with a message for me; but it comes no nearer, but circles and soars away, growing dimmer, disappointing me, till it is lost behind a cliff or a cloud.

Oct. 29

Forever in my dream and in my morning thought,
    Eastward a mount ascends;
But when in the sunbeam its hard outline is sought,
    It all dissolves and ends.
The woods that way are gates; the pastures too slope up
    To an unearthly ground;
But when I ask my mates to take the staff and cup,
    It can no more be found.
Perhaps I have no shoes fit for the lofty soil
    Where my thoughts graze,
No properly spun clues, nor well-strained mid-day oil,
    Or must I mend my ways?
It is a promised land which I have not yet earned.
    I have not made beginning
With consecrated hand, nor have I ever learned
    To lay the underpinning.
The mountain sinks by day, as do my lofty thoughts,
    Because I'm not high-minded.
If I could think alway above these hills and warts,
    I should see it, though blinded.
It is a spiral path within the pilgrim's soul
    Leads to this mountain's brow;
Commencing at his hearth he climbs up to this goal
    He knows not when nor how.

[1] [An extreme example of Thoreau's transcendental idealism.]

We see mankind generally either (from ignorance or avarice) toiling too hard and becoming mere machines in order to acquire wealth, or perhaps inheriting it or getting it by other accident, having recourse, for relaxation after excessive toil or as a mere relief to their idle ennui, to artificial amusements, rarely elevating and often debasing. I think that men generally are mistaken with regard to amusements. Every one who deserves to be regarded as higher than the brute may be supposed to have an earnest purpose, to accomplish which is the object of his existence, and this is at once his work and his supremest pleasure; and for diversion and relaxation, for suggestion and education and strength, there is offered the never-failing amusement of getting a living—never-failing, I mean, when temperately indulged in. I know of no such amusement—so wholesome and in every sense profitable—for instance, as to spend an hour or two in a day picking some berries or other fruits which will be food for the winter, or collecting driftwood from the river for fuel, or cultivating the few beans or potatoes which I want. Theatres and operas, which intoxicate for a season, are as nothing compared to these pursuits. And so it is with all the true arts of life. Farming and building and manufacturing and sailing are the greatest and wholesomest amusements that were ever invented (for God invented them), and I suppose that the farmers and mechanics know it, only I think they indulge to excess generally, and so what was meant for a joy becomes the sweat of the brow. Gambling, horse-racing, loafing, and rowdyism generally, after all tempt but few. The mass are tempted by those other amusements, of farming, etc. It is a great amusement, and more profitable than I could have invented, to go and spend an afternoon hour picking cranberries. By these various pursuits your experience becomes singularly complete and rounded. The novelty and significance of such pursuits are remarkable. Such is the path by which we climb to the heights of our being; and compare the poetry which such simple pursuits have inspired with the unreadable volumes which have been written about art.

Who is the most profitable companion? He who has been picking cranberries and chopping wood, or he who has been attending the opera all his days? I find when I have been building a fence or surveying a farm, or even collecting simples, that these were the true paths to perception and enjoyment. My being seems to have put forth new roots and to be more strongly planted. This is the true way to crack the nut of happiness. If, as a poet or naturalist, you wish to explore a given neighborhood, go and live in it, i.e. get your living in it. Fish in its streams, hunt in its forests, gather fuel from its water, its woods, cultivate the ground, and pluck the wild fruits, etc., etc.

This will be the surest and speediest way to those perceptions you covet. No amusement has worn better than farming. It tempts men just as strongly today as in the day of Cincinnatus. Healthily and properly pursued, it is not a whit more grave than huckleberrying, and if it takes any airs on itself as superior there's something wrong about it.

I have aspired to practice in succession all the honest arts of life, that I may gather all their fruits. But then, if you are intemperate, if you toil to raise an unnecessary amount of corn, even the large crop of wheat becomes as a small crop of chaff.

If our living were once honestly got, then it would be time to invent other amusements.

After reading Ruskin on the love of Nature, I think, "Drink deep, or taste not the Pierian spring." He there, to my surprise, expresses the common infidelity of his age and race. He has not implicitly surrendered himself to her. And what does he substitute for that Nature? I do not know, unless it be the Church of England. Questioning whether that relation to Nature was of so much value, after all! It is sour grapes! He does not speak to the condition of foxes that have more spring in their legs. The love of Nature and fullest perception of the revelation which she is to man is not compatible with the belief in the peculiar revelation of the Bible which Ruskin entertains.

Oct. 31

If you are afflicted with melancholy at this season, go to the swamp and see the brave spears of skunk-cabbage buds already advanced toward a new year. Their gravestones are not bespoken yet. Who shall be sexton to them? Is it the winter of their discontent? Do they seem to have lain down to die, despairing of skunk-cabbagedom? "Up and at 'em," "Give it to 'em," "Excelsior," "Put it through"—these are their mottoes. Mortal human creatures must take a little respite in this fall of the year; their spirits do flag a little. There is a little questioning of destiny, and thinking to go like cowards to where the "weary shall be at rest." But not so with the skunk-cabbage. Its withered leaves fall and are transfixed by a rising bud. Winter and death are ignored; the circle of life is complete. Are these false prophets? Is it a lie or a vain boast underneath the skunk-cabbage bud, pushing it upward and lifting the dead leaves with it? They rest with spears advanced; they rest to shoot!

Nov. 1

A higher truth, though only dimly hinted at, thrills us more than a lower expressed.

Nov. 5

For a man to pride himself on this kind of wealth, as if it enriched him, is as ridiculous as if one struggling in the ocean with a bag of gold on his back should gasp out, "I am worth a hundred thousand dollars!" I see his ineffectual struggles just as plainly, and what it is that sinks him.

Nov. 7

Minott adorns whatever part of nature he touches; whichever way he walks he transfigures the earth for me. If a common man speaks of Walden Pond to me, I see only a shallow, dull-colored body of water without reflections or peculiar color, but if Minott speaks of it, I see the green water and reflected hills at once, for he *has been* there. I hear the rustle of the leaves from woods which he goes through.

Nov. 8

About 10 A.M. a long flock of geese are going over from northeast to southwest, or parallel with the general direction of the coast and great mountain-ranges. The sonorous, quavering sounds of the geese are the voice of this cloudy air—a sound that comes from directly between us and the sky, an aerial sound, and yet so distinct, heavy, and sonorous, a clanking chain drawn through the heavy air.

Ah, my friends, I know you better than you think, and love you better, too. The day after never, we will have an explanation.

Nov. 20

In books, that which is most generally interesting is what comes home to the most cherished private experience of the greatest number. It is not the book of him who has travelled the farthest over the surface of the globe, but of him who has lived the deepest and been the most at home. If an equal emotion is excited by a familiar homely phenomenon as by the Pyramids, there is no advantage in seeing the Pyramids. It is on the whole better, as it is simpler, to use the common language. We require that the reporter be very permanently planted before the facts which he observes, not a mere passer-by; hence the facts cannot be too homely. A man is worth most to himself and to others, whether as an observer, or poet, or neighbor, or friend, where he is most himself, most contented and at home. There his life is the most intense and he loses the fewest moments. Familiar and surrounding objects are the best symbols and illustrations of his life. If a man who has had deep experiences should endeavor to describe them in a book of travels, it would be to use the language of a wandering tribe instead of a universal language. The poet has made the best roots in his native soil of any man, and is the hardest to transplant. The man who is often thinking that it is better to be somewhere else than where he is excommunicates himself. If a man is rich and strong anywhere, it must be on his native soil. Here I have been these forty years learning the language of these fields that I may the better express myself. If I should travel to the prairies, I should much less understand them, and my past life would serve me but ill to describe them. Many a weed here stands for more of life to me than the big trees of California would if I should go there. We only need travel enough to give our intellects an airing. In spite of Malthus and the rest, there will be plenty of room in this world, if every man will mind his own business. I have not heard of any planet running against another yet.

Dec. 8

Staples says he came to Concord some twenty-four years ago a poor boy with a dollar and three cents in his pocket, and he spent the three cents for drink at Bigelow's tavern, and how he's worth "twenty hundred dollars clear." He remembers many who inherited wealth whom he can buy out today. I told him that he had done better than I in a pecuniary respect, for I had only earned my living. "Well," said he, "that's all I've done, and I don't know as I've got much better clothes than you." I was particularly poorly clad then, in the woods; my hat, pants, boots, rubbers, and gloves would not have brought fourpence, and I told the Irishman that it wasn't everybody could afford to have a fringe round his legs, as I had, my corduroys not preserving a selvage.

1858-61

For the reasons previously suggested, Thoreau fills hundreds of pages in his last journals with minute notations of things measured and counted, mostly written in the lifeless style of professional scientists against which he had so often railed. No attempt is here made to represent these deserts of writing. One prefers to remember only the oases.

The last enthusiasm of Thoreau's life was for Captain John Brown, a man entirely after his own heart. His three speeches in defense of Brown's deed and reputation were compiled from his journals, but this material is slightly represented here because it is readily available elsewhere.

In May, 1861, Thoreau set out for Minnesota in hope of regaining his health. He returned to Concord in July, unimproved. The last entry in his journals was written four months later. Six months later still he died.

Jan. 1, 1858

I have lately been surveying the Walden woods so extensively and minutely that I now see it mapped in my mind's eye—as, indeed, on paper—as so many men's wood-lots, and am aware when I walk there that I am at a given moment passing from such a one's wood-lot to such another's. I fear this particular dry knowledge may affect my imagination and fancy, that it will not be easy to see so much wildness and native vigor there as formerly.

Jan. 6

Very little evidence of God or man did I see just then, and life not as rich and inviting an enterprise as it should be, when my attention was caught by a snowflake on my coat-sleeve. It was one of those perfect, crystalline, star-shaped ones, six-rayed, like a flat wheel with six spokes, only the spokes were perfect little pine trees in shape, arranged around a central spangle. This little object, which, with many of its fellows, rested unmelting on my coat, so perfect and beautiful, reminded me that Nature had not lost her pristine vigor yet, and why should man lose heart? . . . I may say that the maker of the world exhausts his skill with each snowflake and dewdrop that he sends down. We think that the one mechanically coheres and that the other simply flows together and falls, but in truth they are the product of *enthusiasm*, the children of an ecstasy, finished with the artist's utmost skill.

Jan. 25

You must love the crust of the earth on which you dwell more than the sweet crust of any bread or cake. You must be able to extract nutriment out of a sandheap. You must have so good an appetite as this, else you will live in vain.

Jan. 26

Some men have a peculiar taste for bad words, mouthing and licking them into lumpish shapes like the bear her cubs—words like "tribal" and "ornamentation," which drag a dead tail after them. They will pick you out of a thousand the still-born words, the falsettos, the wing-clipped and lame words, as if only the false notes caught their ears. They cry encore to all the discords.

March 2

The last new journal[1] thinks that it is very liberal, nay, bold, but it dares not publish a child's thought on important subjects, such as life and death and good books. It requires the sanction of the divines just as surely as the tamest journal does. If it had been published at the time of the famous dispute between Christ and the doctors, it would have published only the opinions of the doctors and suppressed Christ's. There is no need of a law to check the license of the press. It is law enough, and more than enough, to itself. Virtually, the community have come together and agreed what things shall be uttered, have agreed on a platform and to excommunicate him who departs from it, and not one in a thousand dares utter anything else. There are plenty of journals brave enough to say what they think about the government, this being a free one; but I know of none, widely circulated or well conducted, that dares say what it thinks about the Sunday or the Bible. They have been bribed to keep dark. They are in the service of hypocrisy.

March 5

How little I know of that *arbor-vitæ* when I have learned only what science can tell me! It is but a word. It is not a *tree* of *life*. But there are twenty words for the tree and its different parts which the Indian gave, which are not in our botanies, which imply a more practical and vital science. He used it every day. He was well acquainted with its wood, and its bark, and its leaves. No science does more than arrange what

[1] [The first edition of *The Atlantic Monthly* appeared in November, 1857.]

knowledge we have of any class of objects. But, generally speaking, how much more conversant was the Indian with any wild animal or plant than we are, and in his language is implied all that intimacy, as much as ours is expressed in our language. How many words in his language about a moose, or birch bark, and the like! The Indian stood nearer to wild nature than we. The wildest and noblest quadrupeds, even the largest fresh-water fishes, some of the wildest and noblest birds and the fairest flowers have actually receded as *we* advanced, and we have but the most distant knowledge of them. A rumor has come down to us that the skin of a lion was seen and his roar heard here by an early settler. But there was a race here that slept on his skin. It was a new light when my guide gave me Indian names for things for which I had only scientific ones before. In proportion as I understood the language, I saw them from a new point of view.

A dictionary of the Indian language reveals another and wholly new life to us. Look at the word "canoe," and see what a story it tells of outdoor life, with the names of all its parts and modes of using it, as our words describing the different parts and seats of a coach—with the difference in practical knowledge between him who rides and him who walks; or at the word "wigwam," and see how close it brings you to the ground; or "Indian corn," and see which race was most familiar with it. It reveals to me a life within a life, or rather a life without a life, as it were threading the woods between our towns still, and yet we can never tread in its trail. The Indian's earthly life was as far off from us as heaven is.

March 17

Ah! there is the note of the first flicker, a prolonged, monotonous *wick-wick-wick-wick-wick-wick*, etc., or, if you please, *quick-quick*, heard far over and through the dry leaves. But how that single sound peoples and enriches all the woods and fields! They are no longer the same woods and fields that they were. This note really *quickens* what was dead. It seems to put a life into withered grass and leaves and bare twigs, and henceforth the days shall not be as they have been. It is as when a family, your neighbors, return to an empty house after a long absence, and you hear the cheerful hum of voices and the laughter of children, and see the smoke from the kitchen fire. The doors are thrown open, and children go screaming through the hall. So the flicker dashes through the aisles of the grove, throws up a window here and cackles out it, and then there, airing the house. It makes its voice ring up-stairs and down-stairs, and so, as it were, fits it for its habitation and ours, and takes possession.

March 18

Each new year is a surprise to us. We find that we had virtually forgotten the note of each bird, and when we hear it again it is remembered like a dream, reminding us of a previous state of existence. How happens it that the associations it awakens are always pleasing, never saddening; reminiscences of our sanest hours? The voice of nature is always encouraging.

I sit on the Cliff, and look toward Sudbury. I see its meeting-houses and its common, and its fields lie but little beyond my ordinary walk, but I never played on its common nor read the epitaphs in its graveyard, and many strangers to me dwell there. How distant in all important senses may be the town which yet is within sight! We see beyond our ordinary walks and thoughts. With a glass I might perchance read the time on its clock. How circumscribed are our walks, after all! With the utmost industry we cannot expect to know well an area more than six miles square, and yet we pretend to be travellers, to be acquainted with Siberia and Africa!

March 19

It is pardonable when we spurn the proprieties, even the sanctities, making them stepping-stones to something higher.

March 20

The fishes are going up the brooks as they open. They are dispersing themselves through the fields and woods, imparting new life into them. They are taking their places under the shelving banks and in the dark swamps. The water running down meets the fishes running up. They hear the latest news. Spring-aroused fishes are running up our veins too. Little fishes are seeking the sources of the brooks, seeking to disseminate their principles. Talk about a revival of religion! and business men's prayer-meetings! with which all the country goes mad now! What if it were as true and wholesome a *revival* as the little fishes feel which come out of the sluggish waters and run up the brooks toward their sources?

In order that a house and grounds may be picturesque and interesting in the highest degree, they must suggest the idea of necessity, proving the devotion of the builder, not of luxury. We need to see the honest and naked life here and there protruding. What is a fort without any foe before it, that is not now sustaining and never has sustained a siege? The gentleman whose purse is always full, who can meet all demands, though he employs the most famous artists, can never make a very interesting seat. He does not carve from near enough to the bone. No man is rich enough to keep a poet in his pay.

April 3

The gregariousness of men is their most contemptible and discouraging aspect. See how they follow each other like sheep, not knowing why. Day & Martin's blacking was preferred by the last generation, and also is by this. They have not so good a reason for preferring this or that religion as in this case even. Apparently in ancient times several parties were nearly equally matched. They appointed a committee and made a compromise, agreeing to vote or believe so and so, and they still helplessly abide by that. Men are the inveterate foes of all improvement. Generally speaking, they think more of their hen-houses than of any desirable heaven. If you aspire to anything better than politics, expect no coöperation from men. They will not further anything good. You must prevail of your own force, as a plant springs and grows by its own vitality.

May 1

When I am behind Cheney's this warm and still afternoon, I hear a voice calling to oxen three quarters of a mile distant, and I know it to be Elijah Wood's. It is wonderful how far the *individual* proclaims himself. Out of the thousand millions of human beings on this globe, I know that this sound was made by the lungs and larynx and lips of E. Wood, am as sure of it as if he nudged me with his elbow and shouted in my ear. He can impress himself on the very atmosphere, then, can launch himself a mile on the wind, through trees and rustling sedge and over rippling water, associating with a myriad sounds, and yet arrive distinct at my ear; and yet this creature that is felt so far, that was so noticeable, lives but a short time, quietly dies and makes no more noise that I know of. I can tell him, too, with my eyes by the very gait and motion of him half a mile distant. Far more wonderful his purely spiritual influence—that after the lapse of thousands of years you may still detect the individual in the turn of a sentence or the tone of a thought!

May 6

The thinker, he who is serene and self-possessed, is the brave, not the desperate soldier. He who can deal with his thoughts as a material, building them into poems in which future generations will delight, he is the man of the greatest and rarest vigor, not sturdy diggers and lusty polygamists. He is the man of energy, in whom subtle and poetic thoughts are bred. Common men can enjoy partially; they can go a-fishing rainy days; they can *read* poems perchance, but they have not the vigor to beget poems. They can enjoy feebly, but they cannot create.

July 2

There is something in the scenery of a broad river equivalent to culture and civilization. Its channel conducts our thoughts as well as bodies to classic and famous ports, and allies us to all that is fair and great. I like to remember that at the end of half a day's walk I can stand on the bank of the Merrimack. It is just wide enough to interrupt the land and lead my eye and thoughts down its channel to the sea. A river is superior to a lake in its liberating influence. It has motion and indefinite length. A river touching the back of a town is like a wing, it may be unused as yet, but ready to waft it over the world. With its rapid current it is a slightly fluttering wing. River towns are winged towns.

Aug. 5

The kingbird, by his activity and lively note and his white breast, keeps the air sweet. He sits now on a dead willow twig, akin to the flecks of mackerel sky, or its reflection in the water, or the white clamshell, wrong side out, opened by a musquash, or the fine particles of white quartz that may be found in the muddy river's sand. He is here to give a voice to all these.

Aug. 6

Emerson is gone to the Adirondack country with a hunting party. Eddy says he has carried a double-barrelled gun, one side for shot, the other for ball, for Lowell killed a bear there last year. But the story on the Mill Dam is that he has taken a gun which throws shot from one end and ball from the other!

I hear of pickers ordered out of the huckleberry-fields, and I see stakes set up with written notices forbidding any to pick there. Some let their fields, or allow so much for the picking. *Sic transit gloria ruris.* We are not grateful enough that we have lived part of our lives before these evil days came. What becomes of the true value of country life? What if you must go to market for it? Shall things come to such a pass that the butcher commonly brings round huckleberries in his cart? It is as if the hangman were to perform the marriage ceremony, or were to preside at the communion table. Such is the inevitable tendency of *our* civilization—to reduce huckleberries to a level with beef-steak. The butcher's item on the door is now "calf's head and huckleberries." I suspect that the inhabitants of England and of the Continent of Europe have thus lost their natural rights with the increase of population and of monopolies. The wild fruits of the earth disappear before civilization, or are only to be found in large markets. The whole country becomes, as it were, a town or beaten common, and the fruits left are a few hips and haws.

Aug. 9

The editors of newspapers, the popular clergy, politicians and orators of the day and office-holders, though they may be thought to be of very different politics and religion, are essentially one and homogeneous, inasmuch as they are only the various ingredients of the froth which ever floats on the surface of society.

Aug. 15

Wars are not yet over. I hear one in the outskirts learning to drum every night; and think you there will be no field for him? He relies on his instincts. He is instinctively meeting a demand.

Aug. 16

In my boating of late I have several times scared up a couple of summer ducks of this year, bred in our meadows. They allowed me to come quite near, and helped to people the river. I have not seen them for some days. Would you know the end of our intercourse? Goodwin shot them, and Mrs. ——, who never sailed on the river, ate them. Of course, she knows not what she did. What if I should eat her canary? Thus we share each other's sins as well as burdens. The lady who watches admiringly the matador shares his deed. They belonged to me, as much as to any one, when they were alive, but it was considered of more importance that Mrs. —— should taste the flavor of them dead than that I should enjoy the beauty of them alive.

Talked with Minott, who sits in his wood-shed, having, as I notice, several seats there for visitors—one a block on the sawhorse, another a patchwork mat on a wheelbarrow, etc., etc. His half-grown chickens, which roost overhead, perch on his shoulder or knee. According to him, the Holt is at the "diving ash," where is some of the deepest water in the river. He tells me some of his hunting stories again. He always lays a good deal of stress on the kind of gun he used, as if he had bought a new one every year, when probably he never had more than two or three in his life. In this case it was a "half-stocked" one, a little "cocking-piece," and whenever he finished his game he used the word "gavel," I think in this way, "gave him gavel," i.e. made him bite the dust, or settled him. Speaking of foxes, he said: "As soon as the nights get to be cool, if you step outdoors at nine or ten o'clock when all is still, you'll hear them bark out on the flat behind the houses, half a mile off, or sometimes *whistle* through their noses. I can tell 'em. I know what that means. I know all about that. They are out after something to eat, I suppose." He used to love to hear the goldfinches sing on the hemp which grew near his gate.

Aug. 18

Having left my note-book at home, I strip off a piece of birch bark for paper. It begins at once to curl up, yellow side out, but I hold that side to the sun, and as soon as it is dry it gives me no more trouble.

Aug. 18

Last evening one of our neighbors, who has just completed a costly house and front yard, the most showy in the village, illuminated in honor of the Atlantic telegraph. I read in great letters before the house the sentence "Glory to God in the highest." But it seemed to me that that was not a sentiment to be illuminated, but to keep dark about. A simple and genuine sentiment of reverence would not emblazon these words as on a signboard in the streets. They were exploding countless crackers beneath it, and gay company, passing in and out, made it a kind of housewarming. I felt a kind of shame for [it], and was inclined to pass quickly by, the ideas of indecent exposure and cant being suggested. What is religion? That which is never spoken.

Aug. 22, P.M.

I have spliced my old sail to a new one, and now go out to try it in a sail to Baker Farm. It is a "square sail," some five feet by six. I like it much. It pulls like an ox, and makes me think there's more wind abroad than there is. The yard goes about with a pleasant force, almost enough, I would fain imagine, to knock me overboard. How sturdily it pulls, shooting us along, catching more wind than I knew to be wandering in this river valley! It suggests a new power in the sail, like a Grecian god. I can even worship it, after a heathen fashion. And then, how it becomes my boat and the river—a simple homely square sail, all for use not show, so low and broad! *Ajacean.* The boat is like a plow drawn by a winged bull. If I had had this a dozen years ago, my voyages would have been performed more quickly and easily. But then probably I should have lived less in them. I land on a remote shore at an unexpectedly early hour, and have time for a long walk there. Before, my sail was so small that I was wont to raise the mast with the sail on it ready set, but now I have had to rig some tackling with which to haul up the sail.

Aug. 23

Emerson says that he and Agassiz and Company broke some dozens of ale bottles, one after another, with their bullets, in the Adirondack country, using them for marks! It sounds rather Cockneyish. He says that he shot a peetweet for Agassiz, and this, I think he said, was the first game he ever bagged. He carried a double-barrelled gun—rifle and shotgun—which he bought for the purpose, which he says received much commendation—all parties thought it a very pretty piece. Think of Emerson shooting a peetweet (with shot) for Agassiz, and cracking an ale bottle (after emptying it) with his rifle at six rods! They cut several pounds of lead out of the tree. It is just what Mike Saunders, the merchant's clerk, did when he was there.

Oct. 1

Let a full-grown but young cock stand near you. How full of life he is, from the tip of his bill through his trembling wattles and comb and his bright eye to the extremity of his clean toes! How alert and restless, listening to every sound and watching ever motion! How various his notes, from the finest and shrillest alarum as a hawk sails over, surpassing the most accomplished violinist on the short strings, to a hoarse and terrene voice or cluck! He has a word for every occasion; for the dog that rushes past, and partlet cackling in the barn. And then how, elevating himself and flapping his wings, he gathers impetus and air and launches forth that world-renowned ear-piercing strain! not a vulgar note of defiance, but the mere effervescence of life, like the bursting of a bubble in a wine-cup. Is any gem so bright as his eye?

Oct. 10

The simplest and most lumpish fungus has a peculiar interest to us, compared with a mere mass of earth, because it is so obviously organic and related to ourselves, however mute. It is the expression of an idea; growth according to a law; matter not dormant, not raw, but inspired, appropriated by spirit. If I take up a handful of earth, however separately interesting the particles may be, their relation to one another appears to be that of mere juxtaposition generally. I might have thrown them together thus. But the humblest fungus betrays a life akin to my own. It is a successful poem in its kind. There is suggested something superior to any particle of matter, in the idea or mind which uses and arranges the particles.

Oct. 18

An avenue of elms as large as our largest, and three miles long, would seem to lead to some admirable place, though only Concord were at the end of it. Such a street as I have described would be to the traveller, especially in October, an every-changing panorama.

A village needs these innocent stimulants of bright and cheery prospects to keep off melancholy and superstition. Show me two villages, one embowered in trees and blazing with all the glories of October, the other a merely trivial and treeless waste, and I shall be sure that in the latter will be found the most desperate and hardest drinkers.

Oct. 19

You come away from the great factory saddened, as if the chief end of man were to make pails; but, in the case of the countryman who makes a few by hand, rainy days, the relative importance of human life and of pails is preserved, and you come away thinking of the simple and helpful life of the man—you do not turn pale at the thought— and would fain go to making pails yourself.

Oct. 24

The brilliant autumnal colors are red and yellow and the various tints, hues, and shades of these. Blue is reserved to be the color of the sky, but yellow and red are the colors of the earth flower. Every fruit, on ripening, and just before its fall, acquires a bright tint. So do the leaves; so the sky before the end of the day, and the year near its setting. October is the red sunset sky, November the later twilight. Color stands for all ripeness and success. We have dreamed that the hero should carry his color aloft, as a symbol of the ripeness of his virtue. The noblest feature, the eye, is the fairest-colored, the jewel of the body. The warrior's flag is the flower which precedes his fruit. He unfurls his flag to the breeze with such confidence and brag as the flower its petals. Now we shall see what kind of fruit will succeed.

The very forest and herbage, the pellicle of the earth as it were, must acquire a bright color, an evidence of its ripeness, as if the globe itself were a fruit on its stem, with ever one cheek toward the sun.

Our appetites have commonly confined our views of ripeness and its phenomena—color and mellowness and perfectness—to the fruits which we eat, and we are wont to forget that an immense harvest which we do not eat, hardly use at all, is annually ripened by nature. At our annual cattle-shows and horticultural exhibitions we make, as we think, a great show of fair fruits, destined, however, to a rather ignoble fate, fruits not worshipped for this chiefly; but round about and within our towns there is annually another show of fruits, on an infinitely grander scale, fruits which address our taste for beauty alone.

Oct. 27

It is remarkable that the autumnal change of our woods has left no deeper impression on our literature yet. There is no record of it in English poetry, apparently because, according to all accounts, the trees acquire but few bright colors there. Neither do I know any adequate notice of it in our own youthful literature, nor in the traditions of the Indians. One would say it was the very phenomenon to have caught a savage eye, so devoted to bright colors. In our poetry and science there are many references to this phenomenon, but it has received no such particular attention as it deserves. High-colored as are most political speeches, I do not detect any reflection, even, from the autumnal tints in them. They are as colorless and lifeless as the herbage in November.

The year, with these dazzling colors on its margin, lies spread open like an illustrated volume. The preacher does not utter the essence of its teaching.

Nov. 1

Give me the old familiar walk, post-office and all, with this ever new self, with this infinite expectation and faith, which does not know when it is beaten. We'll go nutting once more. We'll pluck the nut of the world, and crack it in the winter evenings. Theatres and all other sight-seeing are puppet-shows in comparison. I will take another walk to the Cliff, another row on the river, another skate on the meadow, be out in the first snow, and associate with the winter birds. Here I am at home. In the bare and bleached crust of the earth I recognize my friend.

Nov. 8

Each phase of nature, while not invisible, is yet not too distinct and obtrusive. It is there to be found when we look for it, but not demanding our attention. It is like a silent but sympathizing companion in whose company we retain most of the advantages of solitude, with whom we can walk and talk, or be silent, naturally, without the necessity of talking in a strain foreign to the place.

Nov. 9

It is a great art in the writer to improve from day to day just that soil and fertility which he has, to harvest that crop which his life yields, whatever it may be, not be straining as if to reach apples or oranges when he yields only ground-nuts.

Nov. 16

Preaching? Lecturing? Who are ye that ask for these things? What do ye want to hear, ye puling infants? A trumpet-sound that would train you up to mankind, or a nurse's lullaby? The preachers and lecturers deal with men of straw, as they are men of straw themselves. Why, a free-spoken man, of sound lungs, cannot draw a long breath without causing your rotten institutions to come toppling down by the vacuum he makes. Your church is a baby-house made of blocks, and so of the state. It would be a relief to breathe one's self occasionally among men. If there were any magnanimity in us, any grandeur of soul, anything but sects and parties undertaking to patronize God and keep the mind within bounds, how often we might encourage and provoke one another by a free expression! I will not consent to walk with my mouth muzzled, not till I am rabid, until there is danger that I shall bite the unoffending and that my bite will produce hydrophobia.

Freedom of speech! It hath not entered into your hearts to conceive what those words mean. It is not leave given me by your sect to say this or that; it is when leave is given to your sect to withdraw. The church, the state, the school, the magazine, think they are liberal and free! It is the freedom of a prison-yard. I ask only that one fourth part of my honest thoughts be spoken aloud. What is it you tolerate, you church today? Not truth, but a lifelong hypocrisy. Let us have institu-

tions framed not out of our rottenness, but out of our soundness. This
factitious piety is like stale gingerbread. I would like to suggest what a
pack of fools and cowards we mankind are. They want me to agree
not to breathe too hard in the neighborhood of their paper castles. If I
should draw a long breath in the neighborhood of these institutions,
their weak and flabby sides would fall out, for my own inspiration
would exhaust the air about them. The church! it is eminently the
timid institution, and the heads and pillars of it are constitutionally
and by principle the greatest cowards in the community. The voice
that goes up from the monthly concerts is not so brave and so cheering
as that which rises from the frog-ponds of the land. The best "preachers," so called, are an effeminate class; their bravest thoughts wear
petticoats. If they have any manhood they are sure to forsake the
ministry, though they were to turn their attention to baseball. Look
at your editors of popular magazines. I have dealt with two or three
the most liberal of them. They are afraid to print a whole sentence, a
round sentence, a free-spoken sentence.[1] They want to get thirty
thousand subscribers, and they will do anything to get them. They
consult the D.D.'s and all the letters of the alphabet before printing a
sentence. I have been into many of these cowardly New England
towns where they *profess* Christianity—invited to speak, perchance—
where they were trembling in their shoes at the thought of the things
you might say, as if they knew their weak side—that they were weak
on all sides. The devil they have covenanted with is a timid devil. If
they would let their sores alone they might heal, and they could to the
wars again like men; but instead of that they get together in meeting-
house cellars, rip off the bandages and poultice them with sermons.

It is no compliment to be invited to lecture before the rich Institutes
and Lyceums. The settled lecturers are as tame as the settled ministers.
The audiences do not want to hear any prophets; they do not wish to be
stimulated and instructed, but entertained. They, their wives and
daughters, go to the Lyceum to suck a sugar-plum. The little of
medicine they get is disguised with sugar. It is never the reformer they
hear there, but a faint and timid echo of him only. They seek a pastime
merely. Their greatest guns and sons of thunder are only wooden guns
and great-grandsons of thunder, who give them smooth words well
pronounced from manuscripts well punctuated—they who have stolen
the little fire they have from prophets whom the audience would quake
to hear. They ask for orators that will entertain them and leave them
where they found them.

[1] [In May of this year James Russell Lowell had silently deleted a sentence from
an essay submitted by Thoreau to *The Atlantic Monthly*.]

They want all of a man but his truth and independence and manhood.

Nov. 30

Neither England nor America have [*sic*] any right to laugh at that
sentence in the rare book called *The Blazon of Gentry*, written by a
zealous student of heraldry, which says after due investigation that
"Christ was a gentleman, as to the flesh, by the part of his mother, . . .
and might have borne coat-armor. The apostles also were gentlemen
of blood, and many of them descended from that worthy conqueror
Judas Machabeus; but, through the tract of time, and persecution of
wars, poverty oppressed the kindred and they were constrayned to
servile workes." Whatever texts we may quote or commentaries we may
write, when we consider the laws and customs of these two countries
we cannot fail to perceive that the above sentence is perfectly of a
piece with our practical commentary on the New Testament. The
above is really a pertinent reason offered why Christianity should be
embraced in England and America. Indeed, it is, accordingly, only
what may be called "respectable Christianity" that is at all generally
embraced in the two countries.

Dec. 27

All the community may scream because one man is born who will
not do as it does, who will not conform because conformity to him is
death—he is so constituted. They know nothing about his case; they
are fools when they presume to advise him. The man of genius knows
what he is aiming at; nobody else knows. And he alone knows when
something comes between him and his object. In the course of generations, however, men will excuse you for not doing as they do, if you will
bring enough to pass in your own way.

Jan. 2, 1859

When I hear the hypercritical quarrelling about grammar and style,
the position of the particles, etc., etc., stretching or contracting every
speaker to certain rules of theirs—Mr. Webster, perhaps, not having
spoken according to Mr. Kirkham's rule—I see that they forget that
the first requisite and rule is that expression shall be vital and natural,
as much as the voice of a brute or an interjection: first of all, mother
tongue; and last of all, artificial or father tongue. Essentially your
truest poetic sentence is as free and lawless as a lamb's bleat. The
grammarian is often one who can neither cry nor laugh, yet thinks that

he can express human emotions. So the posture-masters tell you how you shall walk—turning your toes out, perhaps, excessively—but so the beautiful walkers are not made.

Jan. 22

There are poets of all kinds and degrees, little known to each other. The Lake School is not the only or the principal one. They love various things. Some love beauty, and some love rum. Some go to Rome, and some go a-fishing, and are sent to the house of correction once a month. They keep up their fires by means unknown to me. I know not their comings and goings. How can I tell what violets they watch for? I know them wild and ready to risk all when their muse invites. The most sluggish will be up early enough then, and face any amount of wet and cold. I meet these gods of the river and woods with sparkling faces (like Apollo's) late from the house of correction, it may be, carrying whatever mystic and forbidden bottles or other vessels concealed, while the dull regular priests are steering their parish rafts in a prose mood.

Feb. 3

One tells you with more contempt than pity that the Indian had no religion, holding up both hands, and this to all the shallow-brained and bigoted seems to mean something important, but it is commonly a distinction without a difference. Pray, how much more religion has the historian? If Henry Ward Beecher knows so much more about God than another, if he has made some discovery of truth in this direction, I would thank him to publish it in *Silliman's Journal*,[1] with as few flourishes as possible.

It is the spirit of humanity, that which animates both so-called savages and civilized nations, working through a man, and not the man expressing himself, that interests us most. The thought of a so-called savage tribe is generally far more just than that of a single civilized man.

Feb. 25

Measure your health by your sympathy with morning and spring. If there is no response in you to the awakening of nature—if the prospect of an early morning walk does not banish sleep, if the warble of

---

[1] [*The American Journal of Science and Arts*, founded in 1818 by Benjamin Silliman, Sr.]

the first bluebird does not thrill you—know that the morning and spring of your life are past. Thus may you feel your pulse.

March 2

The bluebird which some woodchopper or inspired walker is said to have seen in that sunny interval between the snow-storms is like a speck of clear blue sky seen near the end of a storm, reminding us of an ethereal region and a heaven which we had forgotten. Princes and magistrates are often styled serene, but what is their turbid serenity to that ethereal serenity which the bluebird embodies? His Most Serene Birdship! His soft warble melts in the ear, as the snow is melting in the valleys around. The bluebird comes and with his warble drills the ice and sets free the rivers and ponds and frozen ground. As the sand flows down the slopes a little way, assuming the forms of foliage where the frost comes out of the ground, so this little rill of melody flows a short way down the concave of the sky. The sharp whistle of the blackbird, too, is heard like single sparks or a shower of them shot up from the swamps and seen against the dark winter in the rear.

March 3

Talk about reading!—a good reader! It depends on how he is heard. There may be elocution and pronunciation (recitation, say) to satiety, but there can be no good reading unless there is good hearing also. It takes two at least for this game, as for love, and they must coöperate. The lecturer will read best those parts of his lecture which are best heard. . . . I saw some men unloading molasses-hogsheads from a truck at a depot the other day, rolling them up an inclined plane. The truck-man stood behind and shoved, after putting a couple of ropes one round each end of the hogshead, while two men standing in the depot steadily pulled at the ropes. The first man was the lecturer, the last was the audience. It is the duty of the lecturer to team his hogshead of sweets to the depot, or Lyceum, place the horse, arrange the ropes, and shove; and it is the duty of the audience to take hold of the ropes and pull with all their might. The lecturer who tries to read his essay without being abetted by a good hearing is in the predicament of a teamster who is engaged in the Sisyphean labor of rolling a molasses-hogshead up an inclined plane alone, while the freight-master and his men stand indifferent with their hands in their pockets.

March 10

I feel it to be a greater success as a lecturer to affect uncultivated natures than to affect the most refined, for all cultivation is necessarily superficial, and its roots may not even be *directed toward* the centre of the being.

The bluebird on the apple tree, warbling so innocently to inquire if any of its mates are within call—the angel of the spring! Fair and innocent, yet the offspring of the earth. The color of the sky above and of the subsoil beneath. Suggesting what sweet and innocent melody (terrestrial melody) may have its birthplace between the sky and the ground.

March 11

Find out as soon as possible what are the best things in your composition, and then shape the rest to fit them. The former will be the mid-rib and veins of the leaf.

There is always some accident in the best things, whether thoughts or expressions or deeds. The memorable thought, the happy expression, the admirable deed are only partly ours. The thought came to us because we were in a fit mood; also we were unconscious and did not know that we had said or done a good thing. We must walk consciously only part way toward our goal, and then leap in the dark to our success. What we do best or most perfectly is what we have most thoroughly learned by the longest practice, and at length it falls from us without our notice, as a leaf from a tree. It is the *last* time we shall do it—our unconscious leavings.

March 28

Time will soon destroy the works of famous painters and sculptors, but the Indian arrowhead will balk his efforts and Eternity will have to come to his aid. They are not fossil bones, but, as it were, fossil thoughts, forever reminding me of the mind that shaped them. I would fain know that I am treading in the tracks of human game—that I am on the trail of mind—and these little reminders never fail to set me right. When I see these signs I know that the subtle spirits that made them are not far off, into whatever form transmuted. What if you do plow and hoe amid them, and swear that not one stone shall be left upon another? They are only the less like to break in that case. When you turn up one layer you bury another so much the more securely. They are at peace with rust. This arrow-headed character promises to outlast all others. The larger pestles and axes may, per-chance, grow scarce and be broken, but the arrowhead shall, perhaps, never cease to wing its way through the ages to eternity. It was originally winged for but a short flight, but it still, to my mind's eye, wings its way through the ages, bearing a message from the hand that shot it. Myriads of arrow-points lie sleeping in the skin of the revolving earth, while meteors revolve in space. The footprint, the mind-print of the oldest men. When some Vandal chieftain has razed to the earth the British Museum, and, perchance, the winged bulls from Nineveh shall have lost most if not all of their features, the arrowheads which the museum contains will, perhaps, find themselves at home again in familiar dust, and resume their shining in new springs upon the bared surface of the earth then, to be picked up for the thousandth time by the shepherd or savage that may be wandering there, and once more suggest their story to him.

As we were paddling over the Great Meadows, I saw at a distance, high in the air above the middle of the meadow, a very compact flock of blackbirds advancing against the sun. Though there were more than a hundred, they did not appear to occupy more than six feet in breadth, but the whole flock was dashing first to the right and then to the left. When advancing straight toward me and the sun, they made but little impression on the eye—so many fine dark points merely, seen against the sky—but as often as they wheeled to the right or left, displaying their wings flatwise and the whole length of their bodies, they were a very conspicuous black mass. This fluctuation in the amount of dark surface was a very pleasing phenomenon. It reminded me [of] those blinds whose sashes [*sic*] are made to move all together by a stick, now admitted nearly all the light and now entirely excluding it; so the flock of blackbirds opened and shut. But at length they suddenly spread out and dispersed, some flying off this way, and others that, as, when a wave strikes against a cliff, it is dashed upward and lost in fine spray. So they lost their compactness and impetus and broke up suddenly in mid-air.

May 1

We accuse savages of worshipping only the bad spirit, or devil, though they may distinguish both a good and a bad; but they regard only that one which they fear and worship the devil only. We too are savages in this, doing precisely the same thing. This occurred to me yesterday as I sat in the woods admiring the beauty of the blue butterfly. We are not chiefly interested in birds and insects, for example, as they are ornamental to the earth and cheering to man, but we spare the lives of the former only on condition that they eat more grubs than they do cherries, and the only account of the insects which the State

encourages is of the "Insects *Injurious* to Vegetation." We too admit
both a good and a bad spirit, but we worship chiefly the bad spirit,
whom we fear. We do not think first of the good but of the harm things
will do us.

The catechism says that the chief end of man is to glorify God and
enjoy him forever, which of course is applicable mainly to God as
seen in his works. Yet the only account of its beautiful insects—butterflies, etc.—which God has made and set before us which the State
ever thinks of spending any money on is the account of those which are
injurious to vegetation! This is the way we glorify God and enjoy him
forever. Come out here and behold a thousand painted butterflies
and other beautiful insects which people the air, then go to the
libraries and see what kind of prayer and glorification of God is there
recorded. Massachusetts has published her report on "Insects Injurious
to Vegetation," and our neighbor the "Noxious Insects of New York."
We have attended to the evil and said nothing about the good. This is
looking a gift horse in the mouth with a vengeance. Children are
attracted by the beauty of butterflies, but their parents and legislators
deem it an idle pursuit. The parents remind me of the devil, but the
children of God. Though God may have pronounced his work good,
we ask, "Is it not poisonous?"

May 2

I feel no desire to go to California or Pike's Peak, but I often think
at night with inexpressible satisfaction and yearning of the *arrow-
headiferous* sands of Concord.

Oct. 3

Consider the infinite promise of a man, so that the sight of his roof
at a distance suggests an idyll or pastoral, or of his grave an "Elegy in
a Country Churchyard." How all poets have idealized the farmer's
life! What graceful figures and unworldly characters they have
assigned to them! Serene as the sky, emulating nature with their
calm and peaceful lives. As I come by a farmer's today, the house of
one who died some two years ago, I see the decrepit form of one whom
he had engaged to "carry through," taking his property at a venture,
feebly tying up a bundle of fagots with his knee on it, though time is
fast loosening the bundle that he is. When I look down on that roof I
am not reminded of the mortgage which the village bank has on that
property—that that family long since sold itself to the devil and wrote
the dead with their blood. I am not reminded that the old man I see

in the yard is one who has lived beyond his calculated time, whom the young one is merely "carrying through" in fulfillment of his contract; that the man at the pump is watering the milk. I am not reminded of the idiot that sits by the kitchen fire.

Oct. 4

It is only when we forget all our learning that we begin to know. I do not get nearer by a hair's breadth to any natural object so long as I presume that I have an introduction to it from some learned man. To conceive of it with a total apprehension I must for the thousandth time approach it as something totally strange. If you would make acquaintance with the ferns you must forget your botany. You must get rid of what is commonly called *knowledge* of them. Not a single scientific term or distinction is the least to the purpose, for you would fain perceive something, and you must approach the object totally unprejudiced. You must be aware that *no thing* is what you have taken it to be. In what book is this world and its beauty described? Who has plotted the steps toward the discovery of beauty? You have got to be in a different state from common. Your greatest success will be simply to perceive that such things are, and you will have no communication to make to the Royal Society.

Oct. 16

Talk about learning our *letters* and being *literate*! Why, the roots of *letters* are *things*. Natural objects and phenomena are the original symbols or types which express our thoughts and feelings, and yet American scholars, having little or no root in the soil, commonly strive with all their might to confine themselves to the imported symbols alone. All the true growth and experience, the living speech, they would fain reject as "Americanisms." It is the old error, which the church, the state, the school ever commit, choosing darkness rather than light, holding fast to the old and to tradition. A more intimate knowledge, a deeper experience, will surely originate a word. When I really know that our river pursues a serpentine course to the Merrimack, shall I continue to describe it by referring to some other river no older than itself which is like it, and call it a *meander*? It is no more *meandering* than the Meander is *musketaquidding*. As well sing of the nightingale here as the Meander. What if there were a tariff on words, on language, for the encouragement of home manufactures? Have we not the genius to coin our own?

Nov. 12

There was a remarkable sunset, I think the 25th of October. The sunset sky reached quite from west to east, and it was the most varied in its forms and colors of any that I remember to have seen. At one time the clouds were most softly and delicately rippled, like the ripple-marks on sand. But it was hard for me to see its beauty then, when my mind was filled with Captain Brown. So great a wrong as his fate implied overshadowed all beauty in the world.

Dec. 8

The expression "a *liberal* education" originally meant one worthy of freemen. Such is education simply in a true and broad sense. But education ordinarily so called—the learning of trades and professions which is designed to enable men to earn their living, or to fit them for a particular station in life—is *servile*.

How is it that what is actually present and transpiring is commonly perceived by the common sense and understanding only, is bare and bald, without halo or the blue enamel of intervening air? But let it be past or to come, and it is at once idealized. As the man dead is spiritual-ized, so the fact remembered is idealized. It is a deed ripe and with the bloom on it. It is not simply the understanding now, but the imagina-tion, that takes cognizance of it. The imagination requires a long range. It is the faculty of the poet to see present things as if, in this sense, also past and future, as if distant or universally significant.

Dec. 12

If labor mainly, or to any considerable degree, serves the purpose of a police, to keep men out of mischief, it indicates a rottenness at the foundation of our community.

Dec. 19

When a man is young and his constitution and body have not acquired firmness, i.e., before he has arrived at middle age, he is not an assured inhabitant of the earth, and his compensation is that he is not quite earthy, there is something peculiarly tender and divine about him. His sentiments and his weakness, nay, his very sickness and the greater uncertainty of his fate, seem to ally him to a noble race of beings, to whom he in part belongs, or with whom he is in communica-tion. The young man is a demigod; the grown man, alas! is commonly a mere mortal. He is but half here, he knows not the men of this world, the powers that be. They know him not. Prompted by the reminiscence of that other sphere from which he so lately arrived, his actions are unintelligible to his seniors. He bathes in light. He is interesting as a stranger from another sphere. He really thinks and talks about a larger sphere of existence than this world. It takes him forty years to accommodate himself to the carapax of this world. This is the age of poetry. Afterward he may be the president of a bank, and go the way of all flesh. But a man of settled views, whose thoughts are few and hardened like his bones, is truly mortal, and his only resource is to say his prayers.

Dec. 31

How vain to try to teach youth, or anybody, truths! They can only learn them after their own fashion, and when they get ready. I do not mean by this to condemn our system of education, but to show what it amounts to. A hundred boys at college are drilled in physics and metaphysics, languages, etc. There *may* be one or two in each hundred, prematurely old perchance, who approaches the subject from a similar point of view to his teachers, but as for the rest, and the most promising, it is like agricultural chemistry to so many Indians. They get a valuable drilling, it *may* be, but they do not learn what you profess to teach. They at most only learn where the arsenal is, in case they should ever want to use any of its weapons. The young men, being young, necessarily listen to the lecturer in history, just as they do to the singing of a bird. They expect to be affected by something he may say. It is a kind of poetic pabulum and imagery that they get. Nothing comes quite amiss to their mill.

A man thinks as well through his legs and arms as his brain. We exaggerate the importance and exclusiveness of the headquarters. Do you suppose they were a race of consumptives and dyspeptics who invented Grecian mythology and poetry? The poet's words are, "You would almost say the body thought!" I quite say it. I trust we have a good body then.[1]

Jan. 5, 1860

A man receives only what he is ready to receive, whether physically or intellectually or morally, as animals conceive at certain seasons their kind only. We hear and apprehend only what we already half know. If there is something which does not concern me, which is out of my line, which by experience or by genius my attention is not drawn to, however novel and remarkable it may be, if it is spoken, we hear it not, if it

[1] [Thoreau's health was at this time failing.]

is written, we read it not, or if we read it, it does not detain us. Every man thus *tracks himself* through life, in all his hearing and reading and observation and travelling. His observations make a chain.

Feb. 3

When I read some of the rules for speaking and writing the English language correctly—as that a sentence must never end with a particle—and perceive how implicitly even the learned obey it, I think:

> Any fool can make a rule
> And every fool will mind it.

Feb. 12

It excites me to see early in the spring that black artery[1] leaping once more through the snow-clad town. All is tumult and life there, not to mention the rails and cranberries that are drifting in it. Where this artery is shallowest, i.e., comes nearest to the surface and runs swiftest, there it shows itself soonest and you may see its pulse beat. These are the wrists, temples, of the earth, where I feel its pulse with my eye. The living waters, not the dead earth. It is as if the dormant earth opened its dark and liquid eye upon us.

Feb. 13

Always you have to contend with the stupidity of men. It is like a stiff soil, a hard-pan. If you go deeper than usual, you are sure to meet with a pan made harder even by the superficial cultivation. The stupid you have always with you. Men are more obedient at first to words than ideas. They mind names more than things. Read to them a lecture on "Education," naming that subject, and they will think that they have heard something important, but call it "Transcendental-ism," and they will think it moonshine. Or halve your lecture, and put a psalm at the beginning and a prayer at the end of it and read it from a pulpit, and they will pronounce it good without thinking.

The Scripture rule, "Unto him that hath shall be given," is true of composition. The more you have thought and written on a given theme, the more you can still write. Thought breeds thought. It grows under your hands.

Feb. 23

A fact stated barely is dry. It must be the vehicle of some humanity in order to interest us. It is like giving a man a stone when he asks you

[1] [Concord River.]

for bread. Ultimately the moral is all in all, and we do not mind it if
inferior truth is sacrificed to superior, as when the moralist fables and
makes animals speak and act like men. It must be warm, moist, in-
carnated—have been breathed on at least. A man has not seen a thing
who has not felt it.

March 5

The old naturalists were so sensitive and sympathetic to nature that
they could be surprised by the ordinary events of life. It was an incessant miracle to them, and therefore gorgons and flying dragons were
not incredible to them. The greatest and saddest defect is not credulity,
but our habitual forgetfulness that our science is ignorance.

March 15

A hen-hawk sails away from the wood southward. I get a very fair
sight of it sailing overhead. What a perfectly regular and neat outline
it presents! an easily recognized figure anywhere. Yet I never see it
represented in any books. The exact correspondence of the marks on
one side to those on the other, as the black or dark tip of one wing to
the other, and the dark line midway the wing. I have no idea that one
can get as correct an idea of the form and color of the under sides of a
hen-hawk's wings by spreading those of a dead specimen in his study as
by looking up at a free and living hawk soaring above him in the
fields. The penalty for obtaining a petty knowledge thus dishonestly
is that it is less interesting to men generally, as it is less significant.
Some, seeing and admiring the neat figure of the hawk sailing two or
three hundred feet above their heads, wish to get nearer and hold it in
their hands, perchance, not realizing that they can see it best at this
distance, better now, perhaps, than ever they will again. What is an
eagle in captivity!—screaming in a courtyard! I am not the wiser
respecting eagles for having seen one there. I do not wish to know the
length of its entrails.

April 1

The fruit a thinker bears is *sentences*[1]—statements or opinions. He
seeks to affirm something as true. I am surprised that my affirmations
or utterances come to me ready-made—not fore-thought—so that I
occasionally awake in the night simply to let fall ripe a statement
which I had never consciously considered before, and as surprising and
novel and agreeable to me as anything can be. As if we only thought

1 [Equivalent to the Latin *sententiae.*]

by sympathy with the universal mind, which thought while we were asleep. There is such a necessity [to] make a definite statement that our minds at length do it without our consciousness, just as we carry our food to our mouths. This occurred to me last night, but I was so surprised by the fact which I have just endeavored to report that I have entirely forgotten what the particular observation was.

Oct. 17

While the man that killed my lynx (and many others) thinks it came out of a menagerie, and the naturalists call it the Canada lynx, and at the White Mountains they call it the Siberian lynx—in each case forgetting, or ignoring, that it belongs here—I call it the Concord lynx.

Nov. 29

You would say that some men had been tempted to live in this world at all only by the offer of a bounty by the general government—a bounty on living—to any one who will consent to be *out* at this era of the world, the object of the governors being to create a nursery for their navy. I told such a man the other day that I had got a Canada lynx here in Concord, and his instant question was, "Have you got the reward for him?" What reward? Why, the ten dollars which the State offers. As long as I saw him he neither said nor thought anything about the lynx, but only about this reward. "Yes," said he, "this State offers ten dollars reward." You might have inferred that ten dollars was something rarer in his neighborhood than a lynx even, and he was anxious to see it on that account. I have thought that a lynx was a bright-eyed, four-legged, furry beast of the cat kind, very *current*, indeed, though its natural gait is by leaps. But he knew it to be a draught drawn by the cashier of the wildcat bank on the State treasury, payable at sight.

Yet, though money can buy no fine fruit whatever, and we are never made truly rich by the possession of it, the value of things generally is commonly estimated by the amount of money they will fetch. A thing is not valuable—e.g. a fine situation for a house—until it is convertible into so much money, that is, can cease to be what it is and become something else which you prefer. So you will see that all prosaic people who possess only the commonest sense, who believe strictly in this kind of wealth, are speculators in fancy stocks and continually cheat themselves, but poets and all discerning people, who have an object in life and know what they want, speculate in real values.

We hear a good deal said about moonshine by so-called practical people, and the next day, perchance, we hear of their failure, they having been dealing in fancy stock; but there really never is any moonshine of this kind in the practice of poets and philosophers; there never are any hard times or failures with them, for they deal with permanent values.

Dec. 3

Talking with Walcott and Staples today, they declared that John Brown did wrong. When I said that I thought he was right, they agreed in asserting that he did wrong because he threw his life away, and that no man had a right to undertake anything which he knew would cost him his life. I inquired if Christ did not foresee that he would be crucified if he preached such doctrines as he did, but they both, though as if it was their only escape, asserted that they did not believe that he did. Upon which a third party threw in, "You do not think that he had so much foresight as Brown." Of course, they as good as said that, if Christ *had* foreseen that he would be crucified, he would have "backed out." Such are the principles and the logic of the mass of men.

Dec. 4

Talk about slavery! It is not the peculiar institution of the South. It exists wherever men are bought and sold, wherever a man allows himself to be made a mere thing or a tool, and surrenders his inalienable rights of reason and conscience. Indeed, this slavery is more complete than that which enslaves the body alone. It exists in the Northern States, and I am reminded by what I find in the newspapers that it exists in Canada. I never yet met with, or heard of, a judge who was not a slave of this kind, and so the finest and most unfailing weapon of injustice. He fetches a slightly higher price than the black men only because he is a more valuable slave.

It appears that a colored man killed his would-be kidnapper in Missouri and fled to Canada. The bloodhounds have tracked him to Toronto and now demand him of her judges. From all that I can learn, they are playing their parts like judges. They are servile, while the poor fugitive in their jail is free in spirit at least.

Dec. 26

To such a pass our civilization and vision of labor has come that A, a professional huckleberry-picker, has hired B's field and, we will suppose, is now gathering the crop, perhaps with the aid of a patented machine; C, a professed cook, is superintending the cooking of a pudding made of some of the berries; while Professor D, for whom the pudding is intended, sits in his library writing a book—a work on the Vacciniæ[1], of course. And now the result of this downward course will be seen in that book, which should be the ultimate fruit of the huckleberry-field and account for the existence of the two professors who come between D and A. It will be worthless. There will be none of the spirit of the huckleberry in it. The reading of it will be a weariness to the flesh. To use a homely illustration, this is to save at the spile but waste at the bung. I believe in a different kind of division of labor, and that Professor D should divide himself between the library and the huckleberry-field.

Dec. 30

As in old times they who dwelt on the heath remote from towns were backward to adopt the doctrines which prevailed there, and were therefore called heathen in a bad sense, so we dwellers in the huckleberry pastures, which are our heath lands, are slow to adopt the notions of large towns and cities and may perchance be nicknamed huckleberry people.

Jan. 3, 1861

It is true we as yet take liberties and go across lots, and steal, or "hook," a good many things, but we naturally take fewer and fewer liberties every year, as we meet with more resistance. In old countries, as England, going across lots is out of the question. You must walk in some beaten path or other, though it may [be] a narrow one. We are tending to the same state of things here, when practically a few will have grounds of their own, but most will have none to walk over but what the few allow them.

But most men, it seems to me, do not care for Nature and would sell their share in all her beauty, as long as they may live, for a stated sum—many for a glass of rum. Thank God, men cannot as yet fly, and lay waste the sky as well as the earth! We are safe on that side for the present. It is for the very reason that some do not care for those things that we need to continue to protect all from the vandalism of a few.

Feb. 15

A kitten is so flexible that she is almost double; the hind parts are equivalent to another kitten with which the fore part plays. She does not discover that her tail belongs to her till you tread upon it.

[1] [Blueberries.]

How eloquent she can be with her tail! Its sudden swellings and vibrations! She jumps into a chair and then stands on her hind legs to look out the window; looks steadily at objects far and near, first turning her gaze to this side then to that, for she loves to look out a window as much as any gossip. Ever and anon she bends back her ears to hear what is going on within the room, and all the while her eloquent tail is reporting the progress and success of her survey by speaking gestures which betray her interest in what she sees.

Then what a delicate hint she can give with her tail! passing perhaps underneath, as you sit at table, and letting the tip of her tail just touch your legs, as much as to say, I am here and ready for that milk or meat, though she may not be so forward as to look round at you when she emerges.

Feb. 21

This plucking and stripping a pine cone is a business which he[1] and his family understand perfectly. That is their *forte*. I doubt if you could suggest any improvement. After ages of experiment their instinct has settled on the same method that our reason would finally, if we had to open a pine cone with our teeth; and they were thus accomplished before our race knew that a pine cone contained any seed.

He does not prick his fingers, nor pitch his whiskers, nor gnaw the solid core any more than is necessary. Having sheared off the twigs and needles that may be in his way—for like a skillful woodchopper he first secures room and verge enough—he neatly cuts off the stout stem of the cone with a few strokes of his chisels, and it is his. To be sure, he may let it fall to the ground and look down at it for a moment curiously, as if it were not his; but he is taking note where it lies and adding it to a heap of a hundred more like it in his mind, and it now is only so much the more his for his seeming carelessness. And, when the hour comes to open it, observe how he proceeds. He holds it in his hands—a solid embossed cone, so hard it almost rings at the touch of his teeth. He pauses for a moment perhaps—but not because he does not know how to begin—he only listens to hear what is in the wind, not being in a hurry. He knows better than try to cut off the tip and work his way downward against a *chevaux-de-frise* of advanced scales and prickles, or to gnaw into the side for three quarters of an inch in the face of many armed shields. But he does not have to think of what he knows, having heard the latest æolian rumor. If there ever was an age of the world when the squirrels opened their cones wrong end foremost, it was not

1 [A squirrel.]

the golden age at any rate. He whirls the cone bottom upward in a twinkling, where the scales are smallest and the prickles slight or none and the short stem is cut so close as not to be in his way, and then he proceeds to cut through the thin and tender bases of the scales, and each stroke tells, laying bare at once a couple of seeds. And then he strips it as easily as if its scales were chaff, and so rapidly, twirling it as he advances, that you cannot tell how he does it till you drive him off and inspect his unfinished work.

March 18

A feeble writer and without genius must have what he thinks a great theme, which we are already interested in through the accounts of others, but a genius—a Shakespeare, for instance—would make the history of his parish more interesting than another's history of the world.

Wherever men have lived there is a story to be told, and it depends chiefly on the storyteller or historian whether that is interesting or not. You are simply a witness on the stand to tell what you know about your neighbors and neighborhood.

All this is perfectly distinct to an observant eye, and yet could easily pass unnoticed by most.[1]

---

[1] [This sentence, the next to the last in the journals, was written (under date of Nov. 3, 1861) with reference to a minute observation of the effect of a storm upon gravel. It is retained here, out of its context, because of its accidental applicability to the journals as a whole.]

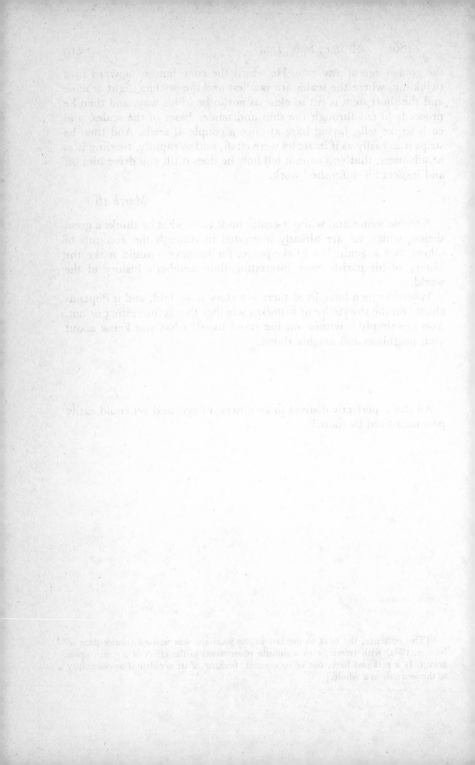

Index

Acorns, edibility of, 62.

Actual, less real than the imagined, 36; invigorating, 98.

Adams, John Quincy, 103.

Age, old, brings no wisdom, 78; earthy, 119; obstinate, 163; happy, 185.

Agriculture, and morality, 26; solidity of, 81.

Alcott, Bronson, Thoreau's delight in, 111; seeks means of livelihood, 118.

America, need for, 41; antiquity of, 75.

Americanisms, defense of, 210.

Apollo, serving Admetus, 51, 59.

Architecture, of Pyramids, 87; based on necessity, 194.

Arrowhead, discovery of, 2; drinking an, 53; found in Concord, 185; longevity of, 207; in Concord, 209.

Art, superficial, 27; likened to a gall, 138.

Assabet, river, 141, 159.

Association for Advancement of Science, letter from, 107.

Authors, two classes of, 26; temptations of, 84.

Battle, preferred to drawing room, 5; never ends, 10; all life a, 108.

Bay-wing, song of, 177.

Beauty, omnipresent, 4, 149.

Bees, method of hunting, 78.

Bells, Sabbath, not pleasing, 7; a peal of, 8; and cowbells, 26; religion in, 103.

Bible, compared with Hindu religious books, 34; miracles reported in, 36.

Bird song, 86, 93, 95; relation of to hearer, 174; does not change with time, 177; of bobolink, 179.

Bittern, green, 159.

Blackbirds, whistle of, 206; flight of, 208.

Bluebird, first, 174, 206; described, 207.

Bobolink, song of, 179.

Body, soul's first proselyte, 14; our duty toward, 18; lives on soul's surplus, 108; Thoreau's all-sentient, 148; thinks, 212.

Books, preservation and destruction of old, 27; good, are wildly natural, 40; inadequate to truth, 127.

Brave man, as a perfect sphere, 11; always in thickest fight, 10; never deserts fortune, 10.

Brooks, Mrs., events at home of, 156.

Brown, Captain John, 211, 216.

Burns, Anthony, returned to slavery, 132.

Business, veils glory of life, 50; necessity of, 164.

Care, form of disease, 31.

Carlyle, Thomas, his writing, 58.

Centrality, of observer, 27, 46.

Chalmers, Dr., life of, 110.

Channing, William Ellery the younger, imitates Thoreau, 64; should write in Latin, 67; invents epithet, 84; suggestion from, 112.

Charity, 120.

Chaucer, Geoffrey, breadth of, 29.

Childhood, dreams of, 23; memories of, 47.

Christ, would be ignored today, 192; a gentleman, 204; foreknowledge of death, 216.

Morality, overestimated, 13; impatience with, 25; absent in best thought, 27; unhealthy, 29; Christianity's exaggeration of, 68.

Music, brings out heroic, 10; an unheard, 16; effects of, 20; reproach and satire, 29; how to hear, 44; in upper air, 50; by moonlight, 51; in youth, 74; of piano, 96; obedient yet free, 127; frozen, 127; of thought, 134; at night, 159; comment on man's life, 170; effects of, 171.

Musketaquid, river, 32; scenery, 55; paddling by night on, 91; Thoreau's farm, 109; town's artery, 213.

Muskrat, heroism, of, 126.

Nations, like insects, 43.

Naturalist, less in the air than poet, 54; danger in life of, 109; studies nature as dead language, 111; Thoreau not ordinary, 129; should have avocation, 159; not so sensitive as formerly, 214.

Nature, true meaning of, 3; in benign mood, 7; never hastens, 9; bears close inspection, 9; does not sympathize with human sorrow, 17; moral aspect of, reflected from man, 27; not fully revealed by poets, 27; prepares one for study of mankind, 43; integrity and health, 46; sympathy with, 54; must be viewed humanly, 92; withdraws us from man, 103; room in, 105; requires human life, 124; soon exhausted, 131; debased by men, 133; incomplete in Concord, 157; nothing compared with men, 166; corresponds to man, 186; has lost no vigor, 191; always encouraging, 194; unobtrusive, 202; uncared for by most men, 217.

News, mere froth and scum, 87; reading, waste of time, 110; helps form literary taste, 165.

Nighthawk, on nest, 115.

Oak, scrub, praised, 166.

Observation, close, not to be long continued, 51; influence of distrusted, 53; disadvantages of, 54; increasing hold of upon Thoreau, 81; carried to excess, 98; dangers of, 109; must be subjective, 129.

Originality, feared by most men, 67.

Ornithology, unhelpful, 11.

Parties, social, unsatisfactory, 66.

Partridge, drumming of, 112.

Past, on trial, 9.

Philanthropy, overpraised, 82; in Concord, 120.

Philosopher, must have known poverty, 145; should have avocation, 159; no sense of great and small, 180.

Pickerel, of Walden, 105.

Pig, pursuit of, 160.

Pine, felling of, 69.

Plowing, noble work, 175.

Poet, should be content with natural, 10; too often tame and civil, 27; equipment, 53; watches moods, 55; must stand aloof, 60; differs from man of science, 80; life, 88; a namer, 118; ripening of, 128; makes paradise of desert, 130; wildness, 130; writes own life, 185; rooted in soil, 189; not to be hired, 195; sees present with halo of distance, 211; good sense, 215.

Poetry, only healthy speech, 28; requires time for germination, 51; its theme the commonplace, 82; made of facts transmuted, 80; little about nature, 183; to compose, requires vigor, 196.

Pout, capture of by mud turtle, 35.

A CATALOGUE OF SELECTED DOVER BOOKS
IN ALL FIELDS OF INTEREST

A CATALOGUE OF SELECTED DOVER BOOKS
IN ALL FIELDS OF INTEREST

AMERICA'S OLD MASTERS, James T. Flexner. Four men emerged unexpectedly from provincial 18th century America to leadership in European art: Benjamin West, J. S. Copley, C. R. Peale, Gilbert Stuart. Brilliant coverage of lives and contributions. Revised, 1967 edition. 69 plates. 365pp. of text.

21806-6 Paperbound $3.00

FIRST FLOWERS OF OUR WILDERNESS: AMERICAN PAINTING, THE COLONIAL PERIOD, James T. Flexner. Painters, and regional painting traditions from earliest Colonial times up to the emergence of Copley, West and Peale Sr., Foster, Gustavus Hesselius, Feke, John Smibert and many anonymous painters in the primitive manner. Engaging presentation, with 162 illustrations. xxii + 368pp.

22180-6 Paperbound $3.50

THE LIGHT OF DISTANT SKIES: AMERICAN PAINTING, 1760-1835, James T. Flexner. The great generation of early American painters goes to Europe to learn and to teach: West, Copley, Gilbert Stuart and others. Allston, Trumbull, Morse; also contemporary American painters—primitives, derivatives, academics—who remained in America. 102 illustrations. xiii + 306pp.

22179-2 Paperbound $3.00

A HISTORY OF THE RISE AND PROGRESS OF THE ARTS OF DESIGN IN THE UNITED STATES, William Dunlap. Much the richest mine of information on early American painters, sculptors, architects, engravers, miniaturists, etc. The only source of information for scores of artists, the major primary source for many others. Unabridged reprint of rare original 1834 edition, with new introduction by James T. Flexner, and 394 new illustrations. Edited by Rita Weiss. 6⅝ x 9⅝.

21695-0, 21696-9, 21697-7 Three volumes, Paperbound $13.50

EPOCHS OF CHINESE AND JAPANESE ART, Ernest F. Fenollosa. From primitive Chinese art to the 20th century, thorough history, explanation of every important art period and form, including Japanese woodcuts; main stress on China and Japan, but Tibet, Korea also included. Still unexcelled for its detailed, rich coverage of cultural background, aesthetic elements, diffusion studies, particularly of the historical period. 2nd, 1913 edition. 242 illustrations. lii + 439pp. of text.

20364-6, 20365-4 Two volumes, Paperbound $6.00

THE GENTLE ART OF MAKING ENEMIES, James A. M. Whistler. Greatest wit of his day deflates Oscar Wilde, Ruskin, Swinburne; strikes back at inane critics, exhibitions, art journalism; aesthetics of impressionist revolution in most striking form. Highly readable classic by great painter. Reproduction of edition designed by Whistler. Introduction by Alfred Werner. xxxvi + 334pp.

21875-9 Paperbound $2.50

ALPHABETS AND ORNAMENTS, Ernst Lehner. Well-known pictorial source for decorative alphabets, script examples, cartouches, frames, decorative title pages, calligraphic initials, borders, similar material. 14th to 19th century, mostly European. Useful in almost any graphic arts designing, varied styles. 750 illustrations. 256pp. 7 x 10.   21905-4 Paperbound $4.00

PAINTING: A CREATIVE APPROACH, Norman Colquhoun. For the beginner simple guide provides an instructive approach to painting: major stumbling blocks for beginner; overcoming them, technical points; paints and pigments; oil painting; watercolor and other media and color. New section on "plastic" paints. Glossary. Formerly *Paint Your Own Pictures.* 221pp.   22000-1 Paperbound $1.75

THE ENJOYMENT AND USE OF COLOR, Walter Sargent. Explanation of the relations between colors themselves and between colors in nature and art, including hundreds of little-known facts about color values, intensities, effects of high and low illumination, complementary colors. Many practical hints for painters, references to great masters. 7 color plates, 29 illustrations. x + 274pp.
20944-X Paperbound $2.50

THE NOTEBOOKS OF LEONARDO DA VINCI, compiled and edited by Jean Paul Richter. 1566 extracts from original manuscripts reveal the full range of Leonardo's versatile genius: all his writings on painting, sculpture, architecture, anatomy, astronomy, geography, topography, physiology, mining, music, etc., in both Italian and English, with 186 plates of manuscript pages and more than 500 additional drawings. Includes studies for the Last Supper, the lost Sforza monument, and other works. Total of xlvii + 866pp. 7⅞ x 10¾.
22572-0, 22573-9 Two volumes, Paperbound $10.00

MONTGOMERY WARD CATALOGUE OF 1895. Tea gowns, yards of flannel and pillow-case lace, stereoscopes, books of gospel hymns, the New Improved Singer Sewing Machine, side saddles, milk skimmers, straight-edged razors, high-button shoes, spittoons, and on and on . . . listing some 25,000 items, practically all illustrated. Essential to the shoppers of the 1890's, it is our truest record of the spirit of the period. Unaltered reprint of Issue No. 57, Spring and Summer 1895. Introduction by Boris Emmet. Innumerable illustrations. xiii + 624pp. 8½ x 11⅝.
22377-9 Paperbound $6.95

THE CRYSTAL PALACE EXHIBITION ILLUSTRATED CATALOGUE (LONDON, 1851). One of the wonders of the modern world—the Crystal Palace Exhibition in which all the nations of the civilized world exhibited their achievements in the arts and sciences—presented in an equally important illustrated catalogue. More than 1700 items pictured with accompanying text—ceramics, textiles, cast-iron work, carpets, pianos, sleds, razors, wall-papers, billiard tables, beehives, silverware and hundreds of other artifacts—represent the focal point of Victorian culture in the Western World. Probably the largest collection of Victorian decorative art ever assembled— indispensable for antiquarians and designers. Unabridged republication of the Art-Journal Catalogue of the Great Exhibition of 1851, with all terminal essays. New introduction by John Gloag, F.S.A. xxxiv + 426pp. 9 x 12.
22503-8 Paperbound $4.50

How to Know the Wild Flowers, Mrs. William Starr Dana. This is the classical book of American wildflowers (of the Eastern and Central United States), used by hundreds of thousands. Covers over 500 species, arranged in extremely easy to use color and season groups. Full descriptions, much plant lore. This Dover edition is the fullest ever compiled, with tables of nomenclature changes. 174 full-page plates by M. Satterlee. xii + 418pp.   20332-8 Paperbound $2.50

Our Plant Friends and Foes, William Atherton DuPuy. History, economic importance, essential botanical information and peculiarities of 25 common forms of plant life are provided in this book in an entertaining and charming style. Covers food plants (potatoes, apples, beans, wheat, almonds, bananas, etc.), flowers (lily, tulip, etc.), trees (pine, oak, elm, etc.), weeds, poisonous mushrooms and vines, gourds, citrus fruits, cotton, the cactus family, and much more. 108 illustrations. xiv + 290pp.   22272-1 Paperbound $2.00

How to Know the Ferns, Frances T. Parsons. Classic survey of Eastern and Central ferns, arranged according to clear, simple identification key. Excellent introduction to greatly neglected nature area. 57 illustrations and 42 plates. xvi + 215pp.   20740-4 Paperbound $1.75

Manual of the Trees of North America, Charles S. Sargent. America's foremost dendrologist provides the definitive coverage of North American trees and tree-like shrubs. 717 species fully described and illustrated: exact distribution, down to township; full botanical description; economic importance; description of subspecies and races; habitat, growth data; similar material. Necessary to every serious student of tree-life. Nomenclature revised to present. Over 100 locating keys. 783 illustrations. lii + 934pp. 20277-1, 20278-X Two volumes, Paperbound $6.00

Our Northern Shrubs, Harriet L. Keeler. Fine non-technical reference work identifying more than 225 important shrubs of Eastern and Central United States and Canada. Full text covering botanical description, habitat, plant lore, is paralleled with 205 full-page photographs of flowering or fruiting plants. Nomenclature revised by Edward G. Voss. One of few works concerned with shrubs. 205 plates, 35 drawings. xxviii + 521pp.   21989-5 Paperbound $3.75

The Mushroom Handbook, Louis C. C. Krieger. Still the best popular handbook: full descriptions of 259 species, cross references to another 200. Extremely thorough text enables you to identify, know all about any mushroom you are likely to meet in eastern and central U. S. A.: habitat, luminescence, poisonous qualities, use, folklore, etc. 32 color plates show over 50 mushrooms, also 126 other illustrations. Finding keys. vii + 560pp.   21861-9 Paperbound $3.95

Handbook of Birds of Eastern North America, Frank M. Chapman. Still much the best single-volume guide to the birds of Eastern and Central United States. Very full coverage of 675 species, with descriptions, life habits, distribution, similar data. All descriptions keyed to two-page color chart. With this single volume the average birdwatcher needs no other books. 1931 revised edition. 195 illustrations. xxxvi + 581pp.   21489-3 Paperbound $3.25

THE ARCHITECTURE OF COUNTRY HOUSES, Andrew J. Downing. Together with Vaux's *Villas and Cottages* this is the basic book for Hudson River Gothic architecture of the middle Victorian period. Full, sound discussions of general aspects of housing, architecture, style, decoration, furnishing, together with scores of detailed house plans, illustrations of specific buildings, accompanied by full text. Perhaps the most influential single American architectural book. 1850 edition. Introduction by J. Stewart Johnson. 321 figures, 34 architectural designs. xvi + 560pp.
22003-6 Paperbound $4.00

LOST EXAMPLES OF COLONIAL ARCHITECTURE, John Mead Howells. Full-page photographs of buildings that have disappeared or been so altered as to be denatured, including many designed by major early American architects. 245 plates. xvii + 248pp. 7⅞ x 10¾. 21143-6 Paperbound $3.00

DOMESTIC ARCHITECTURE OF THE AMERICAN COLONIES AND OF THE EARLY REPUBLIC, Fiske Kimball. Foremost architect and restorer of Williamsburg and Monticello covers nearly 200 homes between 1620-1825. Architectural details, construction, style features, special fixtures, floor plans, etc. Generally considered finest work in its area. 219 illustrations of houses, doorways, windows, capital mantels. xx + 314pp. 7⅞ x 10¾. 21743-4 Paperbound $3.50

EARLY AMERICAN ROOMS: 1650-1858, edited by Russell Hawes Kettell. Tour of 12 rooms, each representative of a different era in American history and each furnished, decorated, designed and occupied in the style of the era. 72 plans and elevations, 8-page color section, etc., show fabrics, wall papers, arrangements, etc. Full descriptive text. xvii + 200pp. of text. 8⅜ x 11¼.
21633-0 Paperbound $5.00

THE FITZWILLIAM VIRGINAL BOOK, edited by J. Fuller Maitland and W. B. Squire. Full modern printing of famous early 17th-century ms. volume of 300 works by Morley, Byrd, Bull, Gibbons, etc. For piano or other modern keyboard instrument; easy to read format. xxxvi + 938pp. 8⅜ x 11.
21068-5, 21069-3 Two volumes, Paperbound $8.00

HARPSICHORD MUSIC, Johann Sebastian Bach. Bach Gesellschaft edition. A rich selection of Bach's masterpieces for the harpsichord: the six English Suites, six French Suites, the six Partitas (Clavierübung part I), the Goldberg Variations (Clavierübung part IV), the fifteen Two-Part Inventions and the fifteen Three-Part Sinfonias. Clearly reproduced on large sheets with ample margins; eminently playable. vi + 312pp. 8⅛ x 11. 22360-4 Paperbound $5.00

THE MUSIC OF BACH: AN INTRODUCTION, Charles Sanford Terry. A fine, nontechnical introduction to Bach's music, both instrumental and vocal. Covers organ music, chamber music, passion music, other types. Analyzes themes, developments, innovations. x + 114pp. 21075-8 Paperbound $1.25

BEETHOVEN AND HIS NINE SYMPHONIES, Sir George Grove. Noted British musicologist provides best history, analysis, commentary on symphonies. Very thorough, rigorously accurate; necessary to both advanced student and amateur music lover. 436 musical passages. vii + 407 pp. 20334-4 Paperbound $2.25

JOHANN SEBASTIAN BACH, Philipp Spitta. One of the great classics of musicology, this definitive analysis of Bach's music (and life) has never been surpassed. Lucid, nontechnical analyses of hundreds of pieces (30 pages devoted to St. Matthew Passion, 26 to B Minor Mass). Also includes major analysis of 18th-century music. 450 musical examples. 40-page musical supplement. Total of xx + 1799pp.

(EUK) 22278-0, 22279-9 Two volumes, Clothbound $15.00

MOZART AND HIS PIANO CONCERTOS, Cuthbert Girdlestone. The only full-length study of an important area of Mozart's creativity. Provides detailed analyses of all 23 concertos, traces inspirational sources. 417 musical examples. Second edition. 509pp. (USO) 21271-8 Paperbound $3.50

THE PERFECT WAGNERITE: A COMMENTARY ON THE NIBLUNG'S RING, George Bernard Shaw. Brilliant and still relevant criticism in remarkable essays on Wagner's Ring cycle, Shaw's ideas on political and social ideology behind the plots, role of Leitmotifs, vocal requisites, etc. Prefaces. xxi + 136pp.

21707-8 Paperbound $1.50

DON GIOVANNI, W. A. Mozart. Complete libretto, modern English translation; biographies of composer and librettist; accounts of early performances and critical reaction. Lavishly illustrated. All the material you need to understand and appreciate this great work. Dover Opera Guide and Libretto Series; translated and introduced by Ellen Bleiler. 92 illustrations. 209pp.

21134-7 Paperbound $1.50

HIGH FIDELITY SYSTEMS: A LAYMAN'S GUIDE, Roy F. Allison. All the basic information you need for setting up your own audio system: high fidelity and stereo record players, tape records, F.M. Connections, adjusting tone arm, cartridge, checking needle alignment, positioning speakers, phasing speakers, adjusting hums, trouble-shooting, maintenance, and similar topics. Enlarged 1965 edition. More than 50 charts, diagrams, photos. iv + 91pp. 21514-8 Paperbound $1.25

REPRODUCTION OF SOUND, Edgar Villchur. Thorough coverage for laymen of high fidelity systems, reproducing systems in general, needles, amplifiers, preamps, loudspeakers, feedback, explaining physical background. "A rare talent for making technicalities vividly comprehensible," R. Darrell, *High Fidelity*. 69 figures. iv + 92pp. 21515-6 Paperbound $1.00

HEAR ME TALKIN' TO YA: THE STORY OF JAZZ AS TOLD BY THE MEN WHO MADE IT, Nat Shapiro and Nat Hentoff. Louis Armstrong, Fats Waller, Jo Jones, Clarence Williams, Billy Holiday, Duke Ellington, Jelly Roll Morton and dozens of other jazz greats tell how it was in Chicago's South Side, New Orleans, depression Harlem and the modern West Coast as jazz was born and grew. xvi + 429pp.

21726-4 Paperbound $2.50

FABLES OF AESOP, translated by Sir Roger L'Estrange. A reproduction of the very rare 1931 Paris edition; a selection of the most interesting fables, together with 50 imaginative drawings by Alexander Calder. v + 128pp. 6½x9¼.

21780-9 Paperbound $1.25

TWO LITTLE SAVAGES; BEING THE ADVENTURES OF TWO BOYS WHO LIVED AS INDIANS AND WHAT THEY LEARNED, Ernest Thompson Seton. Great classic of nature and boyhood provides a vast range of woodlore in most palatable form, a genuinely entertaining story. Two farm boys build a teepee in woods and live in it for a month, working out Indian solutions to living problems, star lore, birds and animals, plants, etc. 293 illustrations. vii + 286pp.

20985-7 Paperbound $1.95

PETER PIPER'S PRACTICAL PRINCIPLES OF PLAIN & PERFECT PRONUNCIATION. Alliterative jingles and tongue-twisters of surprising charm, that made their first appearance in America about 1830. Republished in full with the spirited woodcut illustrations from this earliest American edition. 32pp. 4½ x 6⅜.

22560-7 Paperbound $1.00

SCIENCE EXPERIMENTS AND AMUSEMENTS FOR CHILDREN, Charles Vivian. 73 easy experiments, requiring only materials found at home or easily available, such as candles, coins, steel wool, etc.; illustrate basic phenomena like vacuum, simple chemical reaction, etc. All safe. Modern, well-planned. Formerly *Science Games for Children*. 102 photos, numerous drawings. 96pp. 6⅛ x 9¼.

21856-2 Paperbound $1.25

AN INTRODUCTION TO CHESS MOVES AND TACTICS SIMPLY EXPLAINED, Leonard Barden. Informal intermediate introduction, quite strong in explaining reasons for moves. Covers basic material, tactics, important openings, traps, positional play in middle game, end game. Attempts to isolate patterns and recurrent configurations. Formerly *Chess*. 58 figures. 102pp.   (USO) 21210-6 Paperbound $1.25

LASKER'S MANUAL OF CHESS, Dr. Emanuel Lasker. Lasker was not only one of the five great World Champions, he was also one of the ablest expositors, theorists, and analysts. In many ways, his Manual, permeated with his philosophy of battle, filled with keen insights, is one of the greatest works ever written on chess. Filled with analyzed games by the great players. A single-volume library that will profit almost any chess player, beginner or master. 308 diagrams. xli x 349pp.

20640-8 Paperbound $2.50

THE MASTER BOOK OF MATHEMATICAL RECREATIONS, Fred Schuh. In opinion of many the finest work ever prepared on mathematical puzzles, stunts, recreations; exhaustively thorough explanations of mathematics involved, analysis of effects, citation of puzzles and games. Mathematics involved is elementary. Translated by F. Göbel. 194 figures. xxiv + 430pp.   22134-2 Paperbound $3.00

MATHEMATICS, MAGIC AND MYSTERY, Martin Gardner. Puzzle editor for Scientific American explains mathematics behind various mystifying tricks: card tricks, stage "mind reading," coin and match tricks, counting out games, geometric dissections, etc. Probability sets, theory of numbers clearly explained. Also provides more than 400 tricks, guaranteed to work, that you can do. 135 illustrations. xii + 176pp.

20338-2 Paperbound $1.50

EAST O' THE SUN AND WEST O' THE MOON, George W. Dasent. Considered the best of all translations of these Norwegian folk tales, this collection has been enjoyed by generations of children (and folklorists too). Includes True and Untrue, Why the Sea is Salt, East O' the Sun and West O' the Moon, Why the Bear is Stumpy-Tailed, Boots and the Troll, The Cock and the Hen, Rich Peter the Pedlar, and 52 more. The only edition with all 59 tales. 77 illustrations by Erik Werenskiold and Theodor Kittelsen. xv + 418pp. 22521-6 Paperbound $3.00

GOOPS AND HOW TO BE THEM, Gelett Burgess. Classic of tongue-in-cheek humor, masquerading as etiquette book. 87 verses, twice as many cartoons, show mischievous Goops as they demonstrate to children virtues of table manners, neatness, courtesy, etc. Favorite for generations. viii + 88pp. 6½ x 9¼.
22233-0 Paperbound $1.25

ALICE'S ADVENTURES UNDER GROUND, Lewis Carroll. The first version, quite different from the final Alice in Wonderland, printed out by Carroll himself with his own illustrations. Complete facsimile of the "million dollar" manuscript Carroll gave to Alice Liddell in 1864. Introduction by Martin Gardner. viii + 96pp. Title and dedication pages in color. 21482-6 Paperbound $1.00

THE BROWNIES, THEIR BOOK, Palmer Cox. Small as mice, cunning as foxes, exuberant and full of mischief, the Brownies go to the zoo, toy shop, seashore, circus, etc., in 24 verse adventures and 266 illustrations. Long a favorite, since their first appearance in St. Nicholas Magazine. xi + 144pp. 6⅝ x 9¼.
21265-3 Paperbound $1.50

SONGS OF CHILDHOOD, Walter De La Mare. Published (under the pseudonym Walter Ramal) when De La Mare was only 29, this charming collection has long been a favorite children's book. A facsimile of the first edition in paper, the 47 poems capture the simplicity of the nursery rhyme and the ballad, including such lyrics as I Met Eve, Tartary, The Silver Penny. vii + 106pp. 21972-0 Paperbound $1.25

THE COMPLETE NONSENSE OF EDWARD LEAR, Edward Lear. The finest 19th-century humorist-cartoonist in full: all nonsense limericks, zany alphabets, Owl and Pussycat, songs, nonsense botany, and more than 500 illustrations by Lear himself. Edited by Holbrook Jackson. xxix + 287pp. (USO) 20167-8 Paperbound $1.75

BILLY WHISKERS: THE AUTOBIOGRAPHY OF A GOAT, Frances Trego Montgomery. A favorite of children since the early 20th century, here are the escapades of that rambunctious, irresistible and mischievous goat—Billy Whiskers. Much in the spirit of Peck's Bad Boy, this is a book that children never tire of reading or hearing. All the original familiar illustrations by W. H. Fry are included: 6 color plates, 18 black and white drawings. 159pp. 22345-0 Paperbound $2.00

MOTHER GOOSE MELODIES. Faithful republication of the fabulously rare Munroe and Francis "copyright 1833" Boston edition—the most important Mother Goose collection, usually referred to as the "original." Familiar rhymes plus many rare ones, with wonderful old woodcut illustrations. Edited by E. F. Bleiler. 128pp. 4½ x 6⅜. 22577-1 Paperbound $1.25

LAST AND FIRST MEN AND STAR MAKER, TWO SCIENCE FICTION NOVELS, Olaf Stapledon. Greatest future histories in science fiction. In the first, human intelligence is the "hero," through strange paths of evolution, interplanetary invasions, incredible technologies, near extinctions and reemergences. Star Maker describes the quest of a band of star rovers for intelligence itself, through time and space: weird inhuman civilizations, crustacean minds, symbiotic worlds, etc. Complete, unabridged. v + 438pp. 21962-3 Paperbound $2.00

THREE PROPHETIC NOVELS, H. G. WELLS. Stages of a consistently planned future for mankind. *When the Sleeper Wakes,* and *A Story of the Days to Come,* anticipate *Brave New World* and *1984,* in the 21st Century; *The Time Machine,* only complete version in print, shows farther future and the end of mankind. All show Wells's greatest gifts as storyteller and novelist. Edited by E. F. Bleiler. x + 335pp. (USO) 20605-X Paperbound $2.00

THE DEVIL'S DICTIONARY, Ambrose Bierce. America's own Oscar Wilde—Ambrose Bierce—offers his barbed iconoclastic wisdom in over 1,000 definitions hailed by H. L. Mencken as "some of the most gorgeous witticisms in the English language." 145pp. 20487-1 Paperbound $1.25

MAX AND MORITZ, Wilhelm Busch. Great children's classic, father of comic strip, of two bad boys, Max and Moritz. Also Ker and Plunk (Plisch und Plumm), Cat and Mouse, Deceitful Henry, Ice-Peter, The Boy and the Pipe, and five other pieces. Original German, with English translation. Edited by H. Arthur Klein; translations by various hands and H. Arthur Klein. vi + 216pp. 20181-3 Paperbound $1.50

PIGS IS PIGS AND OTHER FAVORITES, Ellis Parker Butler. The title story is one of the best humor short stories, as Mike Flannery obfuscates biology and English. Also included, That Pup of Murchison's, The Great American Pie Company, and Perkins of Portland. 14 illustrations. v + 109pp. 21532-6 Paperbound $1.00

THE PETERKIN PAPERS, Lucretia P. Hale. It takes genius to be as stupidly mad as the Peterkins, as they decide to become wise, celebrate the "Fourth," keep a cow, and otherwise strain the resources of the Lady from Philadelphia. Basic book of American humor. 153 illustrations. 219pp. 20794-3 Paperbound $1.25

PERRAULT'S FAIRY TALES, translated by A. E. Johnson and S. R. Littlewood, with 34 full-page illustrations by Gustave Doré. All the original Perrault stories—Cinderella, Sleeping Beauty, Bluebeard, Little Red Riding Hood, Puss in Boots, Tom Thumb, etc.—with their witty verse morals and the magnificent illustrations of Doré. One of the five or six great books of European fairy tales. viii + 117pp. 8⅛ x 11. 22311-6 Paperbound $2.00

OLD HUNGARIAN FAIRY TALES, Baroness Orczy. Favorites translated and adapted by author of the *Scarlet Pimpernel*. Eight fairy tales include "The Suitors of Princess Fire-Fly," "The Twin Hunchbacks," "Mr. Cuttlefish's Love Story," and "The Enchanted Cat." This little volume of magic and adventure will captivate children as it has for generations. 90 drawings by Montagu Barstow. 96pp. (USO) 22293-4 Paperbound $1.95

THE RED FAIRY BOOK, Andrew Lang. Lang's color fairy books have long been children's favorites. This volume includes Rapunzel, Jack and the Bean-stalk and 35 other stories, familiar and unfamiliar. 4 plates, 93 illustrations x + 367pp.
21673-X Paperbound $1.95

THE BLUE FAIRY BOOK, Andrew Lang. Lang's tales come from all countries and all times. Here are 37 tales from Grimm, the Arabian Nights, Greek Mythology, and other fascinating sources. 8 plates, 130 illustrations. xi + 390pp.
21437-0 Paperbound $1.95

HOUSEHOLD STORIES BY THE BROTHERS GRIMM. Classic English-language edition of the well-known tales — Rumpelstiltskin, Snow White, Hansel and Gretel, The Twelve Brothers, Faithful John, Rapunzel, Tom Thumb (52 stories in all). Translated into simple, straightforward English by Lucy Crane. Ornamented with headpieces, vignettes, elaborate decorative initials and a dozen full-page illustrations by Walter Crane. x + 269pp.
21080-4 Paperbound $1.75

THE MERRY ADVENTURES OF ROBIN HOOD, Howard Pyle. The finest modern versions of the traditional ballads and tales about the great English outlaw. Howard Pyle's complete prose version, with every word, every illustration of the first edition. Do not confuse this facsimile of the original (1883) with modern editions that change text or illustrations. 23 plates plus many page decorations. xxii + 296pp.
22043-5 Paperbound $2.00

THE STORY OF KING ARTHUR AND HIS KNIGHTS, Howard Pyle. The finest children's version of the life of King Arthur; brilliantly retold by Pyle, with 48 of his most imaginative illustrations. xviii + 313pp. 6⅛ x 9¼.
21445-1 Paperbound $2.00

THE WONDERFUL WIZARD OF OZ, L. Frank Baum. America's finest children's book in facsimile of first edition with all Denslow illustrations in full color. The edition a child should have. Introduction by Martin Gardner. 23 color plates, scores of drawings. iv + 267pp.
20691-2 Paperbound $1.95

THE MARVELOUS LAND OF OZ, L. Frank Baum. The second Oz book, every bit as imaginative as the Wizard. The hero is a boy named Tip, but the Scarecrow and the Tin Woodman are back, as is the Oz magic. 16 color plates, 120 drawings by John R. Neill. 287pp.
20692-0 Paperbound $1.75

THE MAGICAL MONARCH OF MO, L. Frank Baum. Remarkable adventures in a land even stranger than Oz. The best of Baum's books not in the Oz series. 15 color plates and dozens of drawings by Frank Verbeck. xviii + 237pp.
21892-9 Paperbound $2.00

THE BAD CHILD'S BOOK OF BEASTS, MORE BEASTS FOR WORSE CHILDREN, A MORAL ALPHABET, Hilaire Belloc. Three complete humor classics in one volume. Be kind to the frog, and do not call him names . . . and 28 other whimsical animals. Familiar favorites and some not so well known. Illustrated by Basil Blackwell.
156pp.
(USO) 20749-8 Paperbound $1.25

A HISTORY OF COSTUME, Carl Köhler. Definitive history, based on surviving pieces of clothing primarily, and paintings, statues, etc. secondarily. Highly readable text, supplemented by 594 illustrations of costumes of the ancient Mediterranean peoples, Greece and Rome, the Teutonic prehistoric period; costumes of the Middle Ages, Renaissance, Baroque, 18th and 19th centuries. Clear, measured patterns are provided for many clothing articles. Approach is practical throughout. Enlarged by Emma von Sichart. 464pp. 21030-8 Paperbound $3.00

ORIENTAL RUGS, ANTIQUE AND MODERN, Walter A. Hawley. A complete and authoritative treatise on the Oriental rug—where they are made, by whom and how, designs and symbols, characteristics in detail of the six major groups, how to distinguish them and how to buy them. Detailed technical data is provided on periods, weaves, warps, wefts, textures, sides, ends and knots, although no technical background is required for an understanding. 11 color plates, 80 halftones, 4 maps. vi + 320pp. $6\frac{1}{8}$ x $9\frac{1}{8}$. 22366-3 Paperbound $5.00

TEN BOOKS ON ARCHITECTURE, Vitruvius. By any standards the most important book on architecture ever written. Early Roman discussion of aesthetics of building, construction methods, orders, sites, and every other aspect of architecture has inspired, instructed architecture for about 2,000 years. Stands behind Palladio, Michelangelo, Bramante, Wren, countless others. Definitive Morris H. Morgan translation. 68 illustrations. xii + 331pp. 20645-9 Paperbound $2.50

THE FOUR BOOKS OF ARCHITECTURE, Andrea Palladio. Translated into every major Western European language in the two centuries following its publication in 1570, this has been one of the most influential books in the history of architecture. Complete reprint of the 1738 Isaac Ware edition. New introduction by Adolf Placzek, Columbia Univ. 216 plates. xxii + 110pp. of text. $9\frac{1}{2}$ x $12\frac{3}{4}$. 21308-0 Clothbound $10.00

STICKS AND STONES: A STUDY OF AMERICAN ARCHITECTURE AND CIVILIZATION, Lewis Mumford.One of the great classics of American cultural history. American architecture from the medieval-inspired earliest forms to the early 20th century; evolution of structure and style, and reciprocal influences on environment. 21 photographic illustrations. 238pp. 20202-X Paperbound $2.00

THE AMERICAN BUILDER'S COMPANION, Asher Benjamin. The most widely used early 19th century architectural style and source book, for colonial up into Greek Revival periods. Extensive development of geometry of carpentering, construction of sashes, frames, doors, stairs; plans and elevations of domestic and other buildings. Hundreds of thousands of houses were built according to this book, now invaluable to historians, architects, restorers, etc. 1827 edition. 59 plates. 114pp. $7\frac{7}{8}$ x $10\frac{3}{4}$. 22236-5 Paperbound $3.00

DUTCH HOUSES IN THE HUDSON VALLEY BEFORE 1776, Helen Wilkinson Reynolds. The standard survey of the Dutch colonial house and outbuildings, with constructional features, decoration, and local history associated with individual homesteads. Introduction by Franklin D. Roosevelt. Map. 150 illustrations. 469pp. $6\frac{5}{8}$ x $9\frac{1}{4}$. 21469-9 Paperbound $3.50

POEMS OF ANNE BRADSTREET, edited with an introduction by Robert Hutchinson. A new selection of poems by America's first poet and perhaps the first significant woman poet in the English language. 48 poems display her development in works of considerable variety—love poems, domestic poems, religious meditations, formal elegies, "quaternions," etc. Notes, bibliography. viii + 222pp.

22160-1 Paperbound $2.00

THREE GOTHIC NOVELS: THE CASTLE OF OTRANTO BY HORACE WALPOLE; VATHEK BY WILLIAM BECKFORD; THE VAMPYRE BY JOHN POLIDORI, WITH FRAGMENT OF A NOVEL BY LORD BYRON, edited by E. F. Bleiler. The first Gothic novel, by Walpole; the finest Oriental tale in English, by Beckford; powerful Romantic supernatural story in versions by Polidori and Byron. All extremely important in history of literature; all still exciting, packed with supernatural thrills, ghosts, haunted castles, magic, etc. xl + 291pp.

21232-7 Paperbound $2.00

THE BEST TALES OF HOFFMANN, E. T. A. Hoffmann. 10 of Hoffmann's most important stories, in modern re-editings of standard translations: Nutcracker and the King of Mice, Signor Formica, Automata, The Sandman, Rath Krespel, The Golden Flowerpot, Master Martin the Cooper, The Mines of Falun, The King's Betrothed, A New Year's Eve Adventure. 7 illustrations by Hoffmann. Edited by E. F. Bleiler. xxxix + 419pp. 21793-0 Paperbound $2.50

GHOST AND HORROR STORIES OF AMBROSE BIERCE, Ambrose Bierce. 23 strikingly modern stories of the horrors latent in the human mind: The Eyes of the Panther, The Damned Thing, An Occurrence at Owl Creek Bridge, An Inhabitant of Carcosa, etc., plus the dream-essay, Visions of the Night. Edited by E. F. Bleiler. xxii + 199pp. 20767-6 Paperbound $1.50

BEST GHOST STORIES OF J. S. LEFANU, J. Sheridan LeFanu. Finest stories by Victorian master often considered greatest supernatural writer of all. Carmilla, Green Tea, The Haunted Baronet, The Familiar, and 12 others. Most never before available in the U. S. A. Edited by E. F. Bleiler. 8 illustrations from Victorian publications. xvii + 467pp. 20415-4 Paperbound $2.50

THE TIME STREAM, THE GREATEST ADVENTURE, AND THE PURPLE SAPPHIRE— THREE SCIENCE FICTION NOVELS, John Taine (Eric Temple Bell). Great American mathematician was also foremost science fiction novelist of the 1920's. *The Time Stream,* one of all-time classics, uses concepts of circular time; *The Greatest Adventure,* incredibly ancient biological experiments from Antarctica threaten to escape; The *Purple Sapphire,* superscience, lost races in Central Tibet, survivors of the Great Race. 4 illustrations by Frank R. Paul. v + 532pp.

21180-0 Paperbound $3.00

SEVEN SCIENCE FICTION NOVELS, H. G. Wells. The standard collection of the great novels. Complete, unabridged. *First Men in the Moon, Island of Dr. Moreau, War of the Worlds, Food of the Gods, Invisible Man, Time Machine, In the Days of the Comet.* Not only science fiction fans, but every educated person owes it to himself to read these novels. 1015pp. 20264-X Clothbound $5.00

MATHEMATICAL PUZZLES FOR BEGINNERS AND ENTHUSIASTS, Geoffrey Mott-Smith. 189 puzzles from easy to difficult—involving arithmetic, logic, algebra, properties of digits, probability, etc.—for enjoyment and mental stimulus. Explanation of mathematical principles behind the puzzles. 135 illustrations. viii + 248pp.

20198-8 Paperbound $1.25

PAPER FOLDING FOR BEGINNERS, William D. Murray and Francis J. Rigney. Easiest book on the market, clearest instructions on making interesting, beautiful origami. Sail boats, cups, roosters, frogs that move legs, bonbon boxes, standing birds, etc. 40 projects; more than 275 diagrams and photographs. 94pp.

20713-7 Paperbound $1.00

TRICKS AND GAMES ON THE POOL TABLE, Fred Herrmann. 79 tricks and games— some solitaires, some for two or more players, some competitive games—to entertain you between formal games. Mystifying shots and throws, unusual caroms, tricks involving such props as cork, coins, a hat, etc. Formerly *Fun on the Pool Table.* 77 figures. 95pp.

21814-7 Paperbound $1.00

HAND SHADOWS TO BE THROWN UPON THE WALL: A SERIES OF NOVEL AND AMUSING FIGURES FORMED BY THE HAND, Henry Bursill. Delightful picturebook from great-grandfather's day shows how to make 18 different hand shadows: a bird that flies, duck that quacks, dog that wags his tail, camel, goose, deer, boy, turtle, etc. Only book of its sort. vi + 33pp. 6½ x 9¼. 21779-5 Paperbound $1.00

WHITTLING AND WOODCARVING, E. J. Tangerman. 18th printing of best book on market. "If you can cut a potato you can carve" toys and puzzles, chains, chessmen, caricatures, masks, frames, woodcut blocks, surface patterns, much more. Information on tools, woods, techniques. Also goes into serious wood sculpture from Middle Ages to present, East and West. 464 photos, figures. x + 293pp.

20965-2 Paperbound $2.00

HISTORY OF PHILOSOPHY, Julián Marias. Possibly the clearest, most easily followed, best planned, most useful one-volume history of philosophy on the market; neither skimpy nor overfull. Full details on system of every major philosopher and dozens of less important thinkers from pre-Socratics up to Existentialism and later. Strong on many European figures usually omitted. Has gone through dozens of editions in Europe. 1966 edition, translated by Stanley Appelbaum and Clarence Strowbridge. xviii + 505pp. 21739-6 Paperbound $3.00

YOGA: A SCIENTIFIC EVALUATION, Kovoor T. Behanan. Scientific but non-technical study of physiological results of yoga exercises; done under auspices of Yale U. Relations to Indian thought, to psychoanalysis, etc. 16 photos. xxiii + 270pp.

20505-3 Paperbound $2.50